Communications in Computer and Information Science 2644

Rationale
The CCIS series is devoted to the publication of proceedings of computer science conferences. Its aim is to efficiently disseminate original research results in informatics in printed and electronic form. While the focus is on publication of peer-reviewed full papers presenting mature work, inclusion of reviewed short papers reporting on work in progress is welcome, too. Besides globally relevant meetings with internationally representative program committees guaranteeing a strict peer-reviewing and paper selection process, conferences run by societies or of high regional or national relevance are also considered for publication.

Topics
The topical scope of CCIS spans the entire spectrum of informatics ranging from foundational topics in the theory of computing to information and communications science and technology and a broad variety of interdisciplinary application fields.

Information for Volume Editors and Authors
Publication in CCIS is free of charge. No royalties are paid, however, we offer registered conference participants temporary free access to the online version of the conference proceedings on SpringerLink (http://link.springer.com) by means of an http referrer from the conference website and/or a number of complimentary printed copies, as specified in the official acceptance email of the event.

CCIS proceedings can be published in time for distribution at conferences or as post-proceedings, and delivered in the form of printed books and/or electronically as USBs and/or e-content licenses for accessing proceedings at SpringerLink. Furthermore, CCIS proceedings are included in the CCIS electronic book series hosted in the SpringerLink digital library at http://link.springer.com/bookseries/7899. Conferences publishing in CCIS are allowed to use Online Conference Service (OCS) for managing the whole proceedings lifecycle (from submission and reviewing to preparing for publication) free of charge.

Publication process
The language of publication is exclusively English. Authors publishing in CCIS have to sign the Springer CCIS copyright transfer form, however, they are free to use their material published in CCIS for substantially changed, more elaborate subsequent publications elsewhere. For the preparation of the camera-ready papers/files, authors have to strictly adhere to the Springer CCIS Authors' Instructions and are strongly encouraged to use the CCIS LaTeX style files or templates.

Abstracting/Indexing
CCIS is abstracted/indexed in DBLP, Google Scholar, EI-Compendex, Mathematical Reviews, SCImago, Scopus. CCIS volumes are also submitted for the inclusion in ISI Proceedings.

How to start
To start the evaluation of your proposal for inclusion in the CCIS series, please send an e-mail to ccis@springer.com.

Antoine Nongaillard · Anne-Cecile Caron ·
Alfonso González-Briones · Alberto Fernández ·
Dalila Durães · Nada Sharaf
Editors

Highlights in Practical Applications of Agents, Multi-Agent Systems and Computational Social Science

The PAAMS Collection

23rd International Workshops of PAAMS 2025
Lille, France, June 25–27, 2025
Proceedings

Springer

Editors
Antoine Nongaillard
University of Lille
Lille, France

Anne-Cecile Caron
University of Lille
Lille, France

Alfonso González-Briones
University of Salamanca
Salamanca, Salamanca, Spain

Alberto Fernández
Rey Juan Carlos University
Madrid, Spain

Dalila Durães
Universidade do Minho
Braga, Portugal

Nada Sharaf
The German International University
Cairo, Egypt

ISSN 1865-0929 ISSN 1865-0937 (electronic)
Communications in Computer and Information Science
ISBN 978-3-032-05924-6 ISBN 978-3-032-05925-3 (eBook)
https://doi.org/10.1007/978-3-032-05925-3

This Springer imprint is published by the registered company Springer Nature Switzerland AG
The registered company address is: Gewerbestrasse 11, 6330 Cham, Switzerland

Preface

The PAAMS Workshops complemented the regular program with new or emerging trends of particular interest connected to multi-agent systems. PAAMS, the International Conference on Practical Applications of Agents and Multi-Agent Systems, is an international yearly conference for presenting, discussing, and disseminating the latest developments and the most important outcomes related to real-world applications. It provides a unique opportunity to bring multi-disciplinary experts, academics, and practitioners together to exchange their experience in the development of agents and multi-agent systems.

This volume presents the papers that were accepted by the workshops of the 2025 edition of PAAMS: the *Workshop on Adaptive Smart areaS and Intelligent Agents (ASSIA)*, the *Workshop on Deep Learning Applications (DeLA)*, and the *Workshop on Digital Twinning for Training purposes in Industry 4.0 (Twin4Train)*. Each paper submitted to the PAAMS workshops went through a stringent single-blind peer-review process by at least two members of the Program Committee of its workshop. From the 32 submissions received, 17 were selected for presentation at the conference.

This edition of the conference was organized by the SMAC Team of the CRIStAL Lab of the University of Lille (France). We would like to thank all the contributing authors, and the members of the Program Committee for their hard and highly valuable work. Thanks for your help – PAAMS 2025 would not exist without your contribution.

June 2025

Antoine Nongaillard
Anne-Cecile Caron
Alfonso González Briones
Alberto Fernández
Dalila Durães
Nada Sharaf

Organization

General Co-chairs

Philippe Mathieu	University of Lille, France
Fernando De la Prieta	University of Salamanca, Spain

Workshop Chairs

Antoine Nongaillard	University of Lille, France
Anne-Cécile Caron	University of Lille, France
Alfonso González Briones	University of Salamanca, Spain

Advisory Board

Bo An	Nanyang Technological University, Singapore
Paul Davidsson	Malmö University, Sweden
Keith Decker	University of Delaware, USA
Fernando De la Prieta	University of Salamanca, Spain
Yves Demazeau	Centre National de la Recherche Scientifique, France
Frank Dignum	Umeå University, Sweden
Tom Holvoet	KU Leuven, Belgium
Toru Ishida	Kyoto University, Japan
Takayuki Ito	Nagoya Institute of Technology, Japan
Eric Matson	Purdue University, USA
Jörg P. Müller	Clausthal Technical University, Germany
Michal Pěchouček	Czech Technical University in Prague, Czech Republic
Franco Zambonelli	University of Modena and Reggio Emilia, Italy

Organizing Committee

Philippe Mathieu (Chair)	University of Lille, France
Anne-Cécile Caron	University of Lille, France
Antoine Nongaillard	University of Lille, France

Jarod Vanderlynden	University of Lille, France
Jules Bompard	University of Lille, France
Erwan Martin	University of Lille, France

PAAMS'25 Organizers and Sponsors

Organizing Committee

Scientific Organizers

Contents

PAAMS - Workshop on Deep Learning Applications (DeLA)

PAAMS - Workshop on Digital Twinning for Training Purposes in Industry 4.0 (Twin4Train)

PAAMS - Workshop on Adaptive Smart areaS and Intelligent Agents (ASSIA)

Workshop on Adaptive Smart areaS and Intelligent Agents (ASSIA)

In this workshop, we discussed technological solutions for Adaptive Smart Areas, geo-positioned locations with a high need for sensorization, which facilitates their adaptation to significant changes in environmental conditions. Proposed solutions should facilitate decision-making of independent entities fostering collaboration and coordination among them to improve available resources or increase their efficiency in a specific area (cities, buildings, villages, farms, forests, etc...). Adaptive Smart Areas represent a new way of thinking about any kind of space by shaping a model that integrates aspects like energy efficiency, sustainable mobility, protection of the environment, and economic sustainability. These areas provide potentially unlimited settings for intelligent agents to display their ability to react, act proactively, interact among themselves, or otherwise plan, learn, etc., in an intelligent, or somewhat human, manner.

Therefore, this workshop aimed to discuss the use of agent technology for Adaptive Smart Areas to provide intelligence to any of these areas. We welcomed any paper about experiences in the use of agents in Adaptive Smart Areas tackling issues related to smart architectures, simulations, intelligent infrastructure, smart transport, robotics, open data, etc. We also addressed specific methodological and technological issues raised by the real deployment of agents in Adaptive Smart Areas.

Topics that were relevant for the workshop included particularly applications, but also theoretical approaches, based on (but not limited to):

- Smart city modeling
- Smart city simulation
- Precision agriculture
- Smart farming
- Intelligent infrastructures
- Sensors and actuators
- ML-enabled predictive and analytic solutions
- Intelligence applications and crop monitoring
- Smart health and emergency management
- Smart environments
- Smart education
- Smart health
- Smart mobility and transportation
- Intelligent vehicles
- Ethical and legal issues in Adaptive Smart Areas
- Cloud- and edge-assisted applications
- Agricultural robotics
- Data sharing and privacy
- Cost-efficient wireless sensor nodes, network architecture, and implementation
- New environment sensor technologies

Organization

Organizing Committee

Vicente Julián	Universitat Politècnica de València, Spain
Adriana Giret	Universitat Politècnica de València, Spain
Carlos Carrascosa	Universitat Politècnica de València, Spain
Sara Rodríguez	Universidad de Salamanca, Spain
Fernando De la Prieta	Universidad de Salamanca, Spain
Alberto Fernández	Universidad Rey Juan Carlos, Spain
Holger Billhardt	Universidad Rey Juan Carlos, Spain
Marin Lujak	Universidad Rey Juan Carlos, Spain

Program Committee

Alfonso González Briones	University of Salamanca, Spain
Ana Belén Gil González	University of Salamanca, Spain
Gonçalo Marques	Polytechnic Institute of Coimbra, Portugal
Jaume Jordán	Universitat Politècnica de València, Spain
Javier Parra	University of Salamanca, Spain
João Carneiro	ISEP/GECAD, Portugal
José Machado	University of Minho, Portugal
Juan M. Alberola	Universitat Politècnica de València, Spain
Marian Cristian Mihaescu	University of Craiova, Romania
Pasqual Martí	Universitat Politècnica de València, Spain
Radu-Casian Mihailescu	Malmö University, Sweden
Ralf Bruns	Hochschule Hannover, Germany
Ramon Hermoso	University of Zaragoza, Spain
Stella Heras	Universitat Politècnica de València, Spain
Victor Sanchez-Anguix	Universitat Politècnica de València, Spain
Iván Bernabé	Rey Juan Carlos University, Spain
Marcelo Karanik	Rey Juan Carlos University, Spain
Cedric Marco Detchart	Universitat Pública de Navarra, Spain
Jaime Rincón Arango	University of Burgos, Spain

Scalable Hybrid Memory System for Long-Term Conversational Assistants in Healthcare

Carlos Álvarez López[1,2(✉)], Alberto Rodríguez Pérez[2], Sara Rodríguez González[2], Ricardo Alonso-Rincón[1], and Yeray Mezquita[1]

[1] AIR Institute - Deep Tech Lab IoT Digital Innovation Hub, Av. Santiago Madrigal 39, 37003 Salamanca, Castile and León, Spain
{calvarez,ralonso,ymezquita}@air-institute.com

[2] BISITE Research Group, University of Salamanca, Edificio I+D+i, Calle Espejo 2, 37007 Salamanca, Castile and León, Spain
{carlos_alvarez,albertorp,srg}@usal.es

Abstract. Conversational agents in long-term healthcare often lack the ability to retain and recall information across sessions, leading to fragmented and impersonal interactions. This paper presents a scalable hybrid memory system that addresses this limitation by combining short-term memory for real-time dialogue with a persistent long-term memory layer based on MongoDB. The system, developed within the SALUS project, employs a dual-agent architecture: GenAI A handles immediate conversations using a short-term buffer, while GenAI B manages memory consolidation by generating and storing reflections—semantic summaries of past interactions. Inspired by generative agent models, this design enables thematic memory organization, deferred storage, and keyword-based retrieval. Validated through use cases involving elderly patients and routine care scenarios, the architecture improves personalization, minimizes redundancy, and fosters trust in multi-session dialogues. The modular and extensible design supports future enhancements such as semantic search, explainable AI, and integration with socio-sanitary platforms like SALUS.

Keywords: Conversational AI · Hybrid Memory · Long-Term Care · Generative Agents · MongoDB · Personalized Health

1 Introduction

Conversational agents have become a key component in the digital transformation of healthcare, enabling new forms of interaction between patients and AI systems. These systems are particularly promising in long-term care (LTC) environments, where continuous monitoring, personalized support, and effective communication are essential [1]. Recent studies have shown that hybrid AI chatbots in healthcare can reduce patient readmissions and improve engagement [2].

A. Nongaillard et al. (Eds.): PAAMS 2025, CCIS 2644, pp. 5–16, 2025.
https://doi.org/10.1007/978-3-032-05925-3_1

However, despite their potential, current implementations suffer from a critical limitation: the lack of persistent memory.

Most chatbots rely on short-term memory (STM), which restricts their ability to maintain context beyond a single interaction or session [3]. This limitation leads to fragmented communication, reduced personalization, and the constant need for users to repeat information—issues that are especially problematic when dealing with patients in LTC settings who may have chronic conditions or cognitive impairments [2].

Recent research has highlighted the need for long-term memory (LTM) mechanisms in conversational AI systems, enabling them to store and retrieve relevant information across sessions, adapt over time, and build trust with users [4]. This persistent context is not only beneficial for improving natural language understanding and user experience, but it also opens the door to systems that can evolve with the user's behavior and health conditions.

Although the architecture is domain-agnostic and can be applied to other fields, this work focuses on healthcare scenarios due to the critical need for long-term contextual memory in patient care.

In this paper, we present a practical implementation of a hybrid memory system designed to enhance conversational agents in LTC scenarios. Developed as part of the SALUS project, the system integrates a short-term memory for immediate dialogue management and a long-term memory (LTM) based on MongoDB, with supports vector-based search [5], for structured knowledge storage. This architecture supports bidirectional memory flow: retrieving relevant past information when needed, and compressing and storing key conversation elements for future reuse. Inspired by cognitive agent models, the system also implements a memory reorganization mechanism based on reflective processes to ensure efficient storage and semantic categorization of information.

The following sections describe the system's architecture, its memory components, technical implementation details, and a step-by-step use case demonstrating its operation. This work serves as a foundational technical contribution for subsequent developments within SALUS focused on user-centric, explainable, and memory-aware virtual assistants for healthcare.

2 System Overview

To enable context-aware, long-term interactions between users and a conversational assistant, this work implements a hybrid memory architecture designed for scalability and personalization. The system is composed of modular components that separate the responsibilities of real-time conversation handling and long-term memory management. Two collaborating generative agents coordinate to maintain and evolve the assistant's memory throughout its lifecycle. This architecture is developed within the SALUS project, which aims to create explainable and memory-aware virtual assistants for long-term care environments (Fig. 1).

2.1 System Architecture

The architecture follows a layered memory model consisting of:

- **GenAI A Conversation Engine:** Responsible for handling real-time user interactions. It processes user prompts and generates immediate responses based on the contents of the short-term memory buffer.
- **GenAI B Memory Manager:** Oversees memory consolidation. It monitors conversational context, retrieves relevant past information from long-term memory (LTM), and decides when and what to store for future sessions.
- **Short-Term Memory (STM):** A dynamic buffer that stores the recent conversation history, injected into GenAI A's prompt to maintain coherence and continuity in dialogue.
- **Long-Term Memory (LTM):** Implemented using MongoDB, this persistent layer stores compressed reflections, metadata, and user-specific information tagged with searchable keywords.

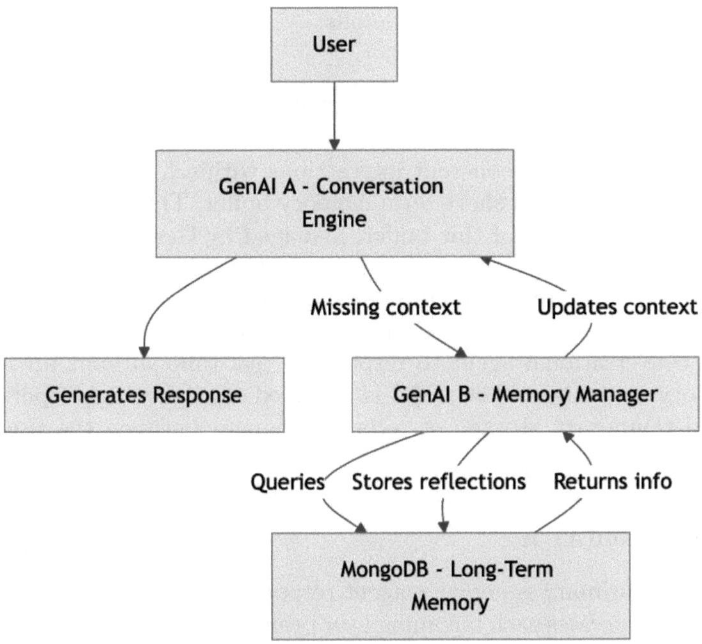

Fig. 1. Modular architecture and interaction flow of the hybrid memory system, highlighting the roles of GenAI A, GenAI B, and the memory layers (STM and LTM).

2.2 Interaction Flow Between Modules

GenAI B is triggered when referential queries (e.g., "What did I say last time?") are detected, or when GenAI A generates low-confidence responses identified by heuristics such as high perplexity, fallback phrases, or entropy thresholds.

The memory system operates through the following steps:

1. The user initiates a conversation with the assistant.
2. GenAI A attempts to generate a response using the contents of the STM.
3. If additional context is needed, GenAI B evaluates the conversation and performs a keyword-based query on the LTM.
4. GenAI B injects the retrieved data into the STM for use by GenAI A.
5. GenAI A generates the final response and delivers it to the user.
6. Once the conversation ends or the STM buffer is full, GenAI B compresses relevant parts into reflections—summarized representations of user-relevant information inspired by generative agent models [1]—and stores them in LTM.

This separation of concerns ensures both responsive dialogue and long-term contextual memory, supporting personalized and coherent multi-session interactions with minimal performance trade-offs.

3 Short-Term Memory Management

To ensure responsive and coherent interactions within a single session, the system maintains a dedicated short-term memory buffer. This section describes the architecture and function of this buffer, managed by GenAI A.

Short-term memory (STM), referred to as MCP (Memoria de Corto Plazo) in this system, plays a central role in preserving dialogue continuity during active conversations. It functions as a high-speed, session-specific memory layer that allows the conversational agent to respond in real time without invoking long-term memory operations. The STM is designed for lightweight operation, fast access, and temporary storage of recent exchanges between the user and the assistant.

3.1 Role of GenAI A

GenAI A is the primary generative agent responsible for handling real-time user interaction. It processes each incoming user prompt and generates an appropriate response based on the conversation history stored in STM. This includes recent turns, assistant replies, user clarifications, and short-term preferences. GenAI A is not aware of the existence of long-term memory; it operates solely based on the current prompt plus the STM buffer provided.

3.2 Structure and Update of STM

The STM is implemented as a dynamic list of message objects. Each object includes a role label (`user` or `assistant`) and the textual content of the message. This structure allows the system to reconstruct the full dialogue context in a structured and chronological manner. After each user prompt, the assistant's response is appended to STM, ensuring an updated and coherent session context.

Example STM structure:

```
[
  {"role": "user", "content": "How is my medication
      schedule today?"},
  {"role": "assistant", "content": "You have two doses:
      one at 9 AM and one at 6 PM."}
]
```

This lightweight memory design is complemented by a persistent long-term memory layer, which is discussed next.

3.3 Token Management and Trimming

To avoid exceeding the token limit of the underlying large language model (LLM), the system includes a token monitoring mechanism. Each time a message is appended, the system recalculates the total token count of the STM. If the limit is surpassed (e.g., 2,000 tokens), the oldest messages are removed in a FIFO (first-in, first-out) fashion. This ensures that the assistant always works within its operational boundaries while maintaining relevant context.

The trimming logic prioritizes retaining:

- The most recent user-assistant pairs
- Messages containing active tasks, temporal expressions, or recent decisions
- System instructions or pre-prompts (if applicable)

This approach balances memory efficiency and contextual richness.

3.4 Real-Time Operation Without LTM Access

As long as STM contains sufficient context to answer the user's query, GenAI A operates independently without querying the long-term memory (LTM). This mode is ideal for most turn-by-turn exchanges, reducing latency and resource usage. For example, reminders, basic questions, and confirmations can be resolved directly within STM.

When the assistant is unable to generate a meaningful response due to lack of historical context (e.g., references to past sessions, long-term preferences, or recurring patterns), GenAI B is triggered to augment the prompt with retrieved memory from LTM.

4 Long-Term Memory Architecture

While short-term memory enables immediate dialogue flow, it cannot support continuity across sessions. To address this, the system integrates a long-term memory layer managed by GenAI B. This section details its structure and use.

The long-term memory layer (LTM) enables the conversational assistant to retain information beyond a single session, providing continuity, personalization, and historical context over time. This component is essential for capturing user-specific data, behavioral patterns, and previous interactions that exceed the capacity or scope of short-term memory.

4.1 Role of GenAI B

GenAI B serves as the system's context-aware memory manager. Unlike GenAI A, which focuses exclusively on real-time interaction, GenAI B supervises the conversational history and evaluates whether external memory retrieval is required to maintain coherence. When the context in STM is insufficient, GenAI B performs a semantic query on the LTM and enriches the prompt passed to GenAI A with the retrieved data. It also decides what portions of a conversation should be retained long-term by compressing them into abstracted reflections for future reference.

4.2 LTM Structure and MongoDB Integration

The LTM is implemented using MongoDB, a NoSQL document-oriented database that offers flexible, scalable storage for semi-structured information. Each stored memory unit (a "reflection") is saved as a document in a dedicated collection. The basic schema includes:

- `timestamp`: The creation date of the memory entry.
- `user_id`: Identifier for the user associated with the memory.
- `summary`: A compressed, human-readable reflection of the original dialogue.
- `keywords`: A list of semantic tags extracted from the conversation.
- `context_type`: Thematic or functional category (e.g., "medication", "appointments").
- `source`: Internal reference to the original conversation (optional).

This structure allows the system to retrieve information efficiently through keyword filtering and context categorization, without requiring full-text search across raw dialogues.

4.3 CRUD Operations and Keyword-Based Retrieval

GenAI B performs full CRUD (Create, Read, Update, Delete) operations on the LTM layer through dedicated service functions. The most frequent operations include:

- **Create:** After each session, selected conversation excerpts are summarized and saved as new memory entries.
- **Read:** When GenAI A lacks context, GenAI B triggers a keyword-based search on LTM to fetch relevant past reflections.
- **Update:** If a topic is revisited or revised, existing memory entries can be updated to reflect the most current user preferences or information.
- **Delete:** Redundant or obsolete entries may be removed periodically to optimize storage and relevance.

Keyword extraction is handled using simple frequency-based heuristics or NLP keyword tagging, depending on the deployment configuration. Retrieved results are ranked based on contextual overlap and relevance to the active session.

Keywords are currently extracted using frequency-based methods such as RAKE or TF-IDF, ensuring lightweight and interpretable tags. More advanced embedding-based keyword extraction is considered for future improvements.

4.4 Memory Storage Criteria

Not every conversational exchange is stored in the LTM. To avoid information overload and preserve relevance, GenAI B applies decision criteria to determine what to store. The current implementation uses the following rules:

- **Relevance:** The message contains useful facts, preferences, or intentions.
- **Novelty:** The content introduces new information not already present in LTM.
- **User-specificity:** The message reflects characteristics or needs unique to the individual.
- **Temporal value:** The information remains useful across sessions (e.g., routines, goals).
- **Summarizability:** The message can be compressed meaningfully into a reflection.

When these conditions are met, GenAI B generates a compact summary ("reflection") and stores it in LTM with associated metadata and tags. This process ensures long-term knowledge accumulation while minimizing noise and duplication.

Relevance and novelty are determined by comparing embeddings of new messages against existing reflections, using cosine similarity thresholds. Named Entity Recognition (NER) is employed to prioritize user-specific information, while message recency and frequency help assess temporal relevance.

To summarize the differences between the short-term and long-term memory components, Table 1 highlights their respective roles, structure, and behavior within the system.

Table 1. Comparison of short-term and long-term memory components

Feature	Short-Term Memory (STM)	Long-Term Memory (LTM)
Purpose	Handle current conversation turns	Retain key knowledge across sessions
Scope	Session-limited	Persistent, multi-session
Format	List of dialogue messages	Reflections with metadata
Storage	In-memory buffer	MongoDB documents
Size Limit	Token-bound (e.g., 2K tokens)	Scalable
Update	Real-time (each turn)	Post-session (summarized)
Retrieval	Injected into prompt	Keyword-based queries
Used by	GenAI A	GenAI B
Retention	Temporary	Long-term
Summarization	Not applied	Generated by LLM

5 Conversation Save Flow and Reorganization

The process of storing information in the long-term memory (LTM) is not continuous but deferred and selective. Rather than storing each message in real time, the system uses a dedicated post-session mechanism that reorganizes and summarizes relevant content. This approach helps maintain a clean, high-value memory layer while avoiding redundancy and unnecessary storage. The conversation save and reorganization process is implemented in the `MemoryReorganizer.py` module.

5.1 Memory Reorganizer Module

The `MemoryReorganizer` class is invoked at the end of each conversation session or when the short-term memory (STM) reaches its token limit. Its role is to process the entire STM buffer and determine which parts are worth preserving. It does so by extracting key messages and generating a structured summary—referred to as a reflection—that captures the semantic essence of the session. These reflections are then stored in the LTM along with metadata and keyword tags for efficient retrieval.

The module supports both synchronous and asynchronous execution, allowing it to run in the background after the user interaction ends. This design prevents delays in the main conversational loop, preserving responsiveness while ensuring long-term knowledge accumulation.

The end of a conversation session is detected either through explicit user cues (e.g., "bye", "that's all") or after a configurable inactivity timeout period.

5.2 Inspiration from Generative Agents

The concept of reflections is inspired by cognitive memory models explored in recent research on generative agents [1]. Rather than storing full conversations, these agents compress experiences into high-level insights that can later inform future behavior. Similarly, the reflections generated by this system aim to capture what was "learned" from the session, focusing on new facts, expressed preferences, user goals, and relevant context.

Reflections typically take the form of natural language summaries, such as:

> "The user usually takes their medication at 9 AM and 6 PM, and prefers reminders in the evening."

This level of abstraction allows the assistant to retrieve semantically rich information while avoiding repetition of raw dialogue.

5.3 Deferred and Categorized Storage

Unlike traditional memory systems that store everything chronologically, this architecture prioritizes thematic and semantic categorization. Reflections are stored along with a `context_type` label (e.g., "medication", "appointments", "routines") and a list of keywords. These labels enable more effective retrieval when GenAI B performs memory queries based on the user's current intent or topic of conversation.

Storage is deferred until one of the following triggers occurs:

- **Conversation End:** When the session is closed or idle for a certain period.
- **Token Threshold:** When the number of tokens in STM exceeds a defined limit.

This deferred design supports efficient post-processing without impacting the responsiveness of the dialogue experience.

5.4 Summary of Process

The complete memory reorganization flow can be summarized as follows:

1. At the end of the session (or when STM is full), the `MemoryReorganizer` is triggered.
2. It analyzes the STM buffer, identifies significant user statements, and filters out operational or low-value messages.
3. It uses a generative model to produce a concise reflection summarizing the session's key points.
4. The reflection is enriched with metadata (user ID, timestamp, keywords, context type).
5. The result is stored in the LTM (MongoDB) for future retrieval by GenAI B.

This mechanism ensures that long-term memory remains concise, structured, and aligned with the user's long-term goals and preferences.

6 Technical Implementation

The proposed hybrid memory system has been fully implemented using Python and MongoDB, structured in modular components that reflect the separation of concerns between short-term and long-term memory management. The key implementation files include:

- `MemoryManager.py`: Coordinates memory retrieval and prompt construction. Interfaces with both the STM buffer and the LTM database.
- `ConversationSaveFlow.py`: Orchestrates the post-conversation storage pipeline, triggering the reorganization process.
- `MemoryReorganizer.py`: Extracts relevant content from STM, generates compressed reflections, assigns context types and keywords, and saves to MongoDB.

Each user message is appended to the STM as a structured object. When context is insufficient, GenAI B performs keyword-based queries on the LTM. Keywords are extracted via basic NLP techniques and used to filter reflections stored with contextual metadata.

The long-term memory (LTM) is backed by MongoDB, using a flexible document schema that supports fields such as user ID, timestamp, summary, keywords, and topic labels. Communication with the database is handled via the `pymongo` driver, using indexes for efficient query performance.

Security and data integrity are ensured through input sanitization, unique session IDs, and optional access control layers for multi-user deployment. The architecture supports both synchronous and deferred execution modes, allowing for background memory operations without blocking user interaction.

7 Use Case: Sample Conversation Flow

To illustrate the system in practice, consider an elderly patient enrolled in the SALUS ecosystem, using a conversational assistant to manage medication and routine care.

Day 1. The patient asks: *"Should I take my blood pressure pills before or after breakfast?"* GenAI A uses the STM to respond: *"You should take them 30 min before eating."* This exchange is stored in the STM buffer.

Post-session. After the conversation ends, GenAI B analyzes the STM and extracts a reflection: *"The user takes blood pressure medication before breakfast."* This summary is stored in the LTM with tags such as `medication`, `routines`, and the user ID.

Day 3. The patient asks: *"What was the advice about my pills in the morning?"* GenAI A cannot resolve the query with STM alone. GenAI B performs a keyword-based query on LTM and retrieves the relevant reflection, which is injected back into the prompt. GenAI A replies: *"You usually take your blood pressure pills before breakfast."*

This flow demonstrates how the assistant retains context over time, enabling continuity in care and reducing user burden. The reflection mechanism supports long-term personalization while minimizing redundant prompts or patient frustration.

8 Discussion and Limitations

The integration of hybrid memory in conversational assistants, as implemented in the SALUS framework, provides significant improvements over traditional stateless systems. By maintaining continuity across sessions, the assistant can offer more personalized, proactive, and coherent support for long-term care (LTC) patients.

Compared to ephemeral memory systems, the proposed architecture reduces repetitive interactions, enables recall of past events, and supports adaptive dialogue. It offloads the cognitive burden from elderly users and aligns with the real needs of chronic care management, such as medication adherence, routine tracking, and long-term goal setting.

However, the current implementation also presents some limitations. The keyword-based retrieval mechanism in LTM, while efficient, may miss semantically relevant entries if keywords are incomplete or ambiguous. This can affect the accuracy of contextual enrichment. Additionally, the reflection-generation process relies on a generative model, which introduces latency during memory reorganization, especially in longer sessions.

Scalability is another challenge: as LTM grows over time, more advanced indexing, ranking, or embedding-based retrieval techniques (e.g., vector similarity search) may be needed to maintain performance. Finally, while privacy is managed via internal IDs and access controls, ethical considerations around memory persistence, consent, and explainability should be addressed in future deployments, particularly in clinical settings.

9 Conclusion and Future Work

This paper presented a hybrid memory architecture for conversational assistants, designed and implemented within the SALUS project to support continuity and personalization in long-term care (LTC) scenarios. The system combines a short-term memory buffer for real-time interaction with a long-term memory layer (LTM) for storing compressed reflections across sessions.

The modular architecture enables GenAI A to handle immediate dialogue while GenAI B manages memory enrichment and persistence. MongoDB provides a scalable backend for structured memory storage, and the reflection mechanism inspired by generative agents allows for semantic compression of relevant information. The system has been validated in practical scenarios involving medication routines and patient preferences, demonstrating its potential to reduce redundancy, enhance recall, and support adaptive care.

Future work will focus on improving the retrieval and summarization mechanisms. Specifically, the current keyword-based search may be extended with semantic search capabilities using Elasticsearch or vector-based retrieval using FAISS [6] or NEO4J Graph embeddings [7]. Integration with Retrieval-Augmented Generation (RAG) [4] could further enhance response quality by grounding the assistant's answers in memory content. Additionally, work is planned to support memory pruning, explainability layers, and memory visualization tools for healthcare professionals.

As part of SALUS, this memory system will serve as a core component for user-facing virtual assistants in LTC environments, supporting both patients and care providers with persistent, intelligent, and human-centered interactions.

Acknowledgments. This publication is part of the project "Personalized long-term care via trustworthy internet of people for senescence (SALUS)" (PLEC2022-009469), funded by MICIU/AEI/10.13039/501100011033 and by the European Union "NextGenerationEU"/PRTR".

Disclosure of Interests. The authors have no competing interests to declare that are relevant to the content of this article.

References

1. Park, J.S., O'Brien, J., Cai, C.J.: Generative agents: interactive simulacra of human behavior. In: Proceedings of the 2023 CHI Conference on Human Factors in Computing Systems, pp. 1–15 (2023). https://arxiv.org/abs/2304.03442
2. Aggarwal, A., et al.: Revolutionizing e-Health: the transformative role of AI-powered hybrid chatbots in healthcare solutions. Front. Public Health **13**, 1530799 (2025). https://doi.org/10.3389/fpubh.2025.1530799
3. Shen, X., et al.: PentestAgent: incorporating LLM Agents to Automated Penetration Testing. arXiv preprint arXiv:2411.05185 (2024)
4. Lewis, P., et al.: Retrieval-augmented generation for knowledge-intensive NLP tasks. In: Advance in Neural Information Processing Systems (NeurIPS), vol. 33, pp. 9459–9474 (2020). https://arxiv.org/abs/2005.11401
5. MongoDB Inc.: Building Generative AI Applications Using MongoDB: Harnessing the Power of Atlas Vector Search and Open Source Models (2023). https://www.mongodb.com/use-cases/generative-ai
6. Johnson, J., Douze, M., Jégou, H.: Billion-scale similarity search with GPUs. IEEE Trans. Big Data **7**(3), 535–547 (2021). https://doi.org/10.1109/TBDATA.2019.2921572
7. Neo4j Developer Blog: Building an LLM-Powered RAG App from PDF Documents (2024). https://neo4j.com/developer-blog/graph-llm-rag-application-pdf-documents

CLIP in the Field: A Study of Plant Disease Detection via Zero-Shot and Fine-Tuning

M. Campos-Mocholí[1(✉)], O. Chacón-Albero[1], and V. Julian[1,2]

[1] Valencian Research Institute for Artificial Intelligence (VRAIN), Universitat Politècnica de València (UPV), Camino de Vera s/n, 46022 Valencia, Spain
{macammoc,odchaalb,vjulian}@upv.es

[2] Valencian Graduate School and Research Network of Artificial Intelligence (VALGRAI), Universitat Politècnica de València (UPV), Camí de Vera s/n, 46022 València, Spain

Abstract. Integrating computer vision into agriculture offers transformative potential for sustainable crop management, particularly in the early detection of plant diseases. Traditional deep learning models, such as Convolutional Neural Networks and Vision Transformers, have shown high accuracy in disease classification but are limited by their dependence on large labeled datasets, lack of generalization, and difficulty adapting to new tasks. This study explores the applicability of CLIP, a multimodal Vision-Language Model, for plant disease detection using zero-shot and fine-tuning strategies. We evaluate CLIP in different experimental setups. Our results highlight the strengths and limitations of CLIP capabilities in the agricultural domain and assess how prompt engineering and domain adaptation can improve performance. The findings contribute to the understanding of how foundation models can be adapted for precision agriculture, potentially reducing the reliance on chemical treatments through early, automated, and scalable disease detection.

Keywords: Computer vision · Zero-shot learning · CLIP · Smart-agriculture

1 Introduction

Computer vision has undergone significant transformations, evolving from simple pattern recognition systems to complex models capable of accurately understanding and interpreting visual data. Advancements in Deep Learning algorithms have fueled this progression, as has the availability of large-scale datasets and increased computational power.

Computer vision has been used to promote sustainable development in agriculture, offering innovative solutions to improve the productivity of farming practices. One of the most significant challenges in agriculture is the incidence of pests and diseases, which directly affects crop yields. To control these threats, farmers resort to plant protection products. In response, the European Green Pact seeks to reduce the use of chemical pesticides by half by 2030, promoting more

A. Nongaillard et al. (Eds.): PAAMS 2025, CCIS 2644, pp. 17–28, 2025.
https://doi.org/10.1007/978-3-032-05925-3_2

sustainable alternatives. Reducing chemical pesticide use increases the risk of undetected pest outbreaks. However, such inspections have limitations, such as reliance on a few individuals to recognize diseases. The integration of computer vision technologies into agriculture has revolutionized the detection and management of plant diseases, offering the potential for increased crop yields and enhanced food security. Traditional methods of disease identification, which rely on manual inspection, are often labor-intensive and time-consuming. In contrast, computer vision systems provide a more efficient and accurate alternative by automating the detection process through advanced image analysis techniques.

Early computer vision models relied heavily on manually crafted features and shallow learning architectures. Techniques such as edge detection, texture analysis, and color histograms were employed to interpret images. While these methods achieved moderate success in constrained environments, they lacked the scalability and adaptability required for diverse and complex visual tasks. The advent of deep learning marked a paradigm shift in computer vision. Convolutional Neural Networks (CNNs) emerged as powerful tools capable of automatically learning hierarchical features from raw pixel data. Architectures like AlexNet, VGGNet, and ResNet demonstrated unprecedented performance on image classification benchmarks, setting new standards in the field.

Convolutional Neural Networks have been widely employed to classify and identify plant diseases from leaf images. For instance, a study [7] demonstrated the application of CNNs in identifying diseases in tomato plants with high precision, utilizing image processing techniques to enhance the detection accuracy.

Beyond CNNs, Vision Transformers (ViTs) have emerged as a promising architecture in computer vision tasks. The PlantXViT [8] model, which integrates ViTs with traditional CNNs, has shown superior performance in identifying a broad range of plant diseases across multiple crops. This model achieved an average accuracy exceeding 93.55% on apple, maize, and rice datasets, highlighting the potential of ViTs in agricultural applications.

Despite their success, traditional models like CNNs and ViTs have notable limitations, including reliance on large labeled datasets, lack of adaptability to new tasks, and vulnerability to distribution shifts. To address these challenges, recent advancements have explored zero-shot and few-shot learning approaches, which enable models to generalize with minimal labeled data. One such approach is OpenAI's CLIP model [6], which leverages image-text pairs to learn a multimodal representation, allowing it to classify and retrieve images without task-specific training. Given its versatility, CLIP presents an exciting opportunity for agricultural applications, particularly in plant disease detection, where annotated data is often scarce.

This study aims to compare different CLIP experimental configurations for plant disease detection. Firstly, a zero-shot classification approach was utilized, simplifying the output to a binary decision: healthy versus diseased plants. Additionally, the model was tested in a zero-shot setting using standard textual prompts that described disease categories and enhanced, contextually enriched prompts designed to align better with the semantic structure of the training data images. Finally, a fine-tuning phase was conducted to determine whether adapting the model specifically for this task could lead to significant improvements compared to the zero-shot baselines. These methods evaluate CLIP's capabilities and limitations when applied to real-world agricultural diagnostics.

2 Methodology

2.1 Dataset

The PlantVillage [5] dataset is a widely used benchmark collection in plant disease detection and classification. It consists of 54,306 high-quality images of plant leaves captured under controlled conditions and annotated across 38 class labels. Each label corresponds to a specific crop-disease pair or a healthy variant of the plant. The dataset includes various crop species, making it suitable for developing and evaluating machine-learning models in agricultural diagnostics. All images are standardized to a resolution of 256 × 256 pixels, facilitating compatibility with modern computer vision architectures.

Given the limitations of CLIP models when dealing with a high number of classes, where performance metrics tend to degrade, we restricted the scope of the dataset in this study. Only three species were retained: tomato, potato, and pepper, along with all their associated disease and healthy classes. The resulting subset comprises 15 distinct classes and a total of 22,698 images. This curated, publicly available dataset[1] serves as the foundation for all experiments presented in this work. The distribution of samples per class is detailed in Table 1.

Table 1. Class-wise distribution of images in the reduced PlantVillage dataset used for experimentation.

Class	Images
`Pepper__bell___Bacterial_spot`	997
`Pepper__bell___healthy`	1,478
`Potato___Early_blight`	1,000
`Potato___Late_blight`	1,000
`Potato___healthy`	152
`Tomato_Bacterial_spot`	2,127
`Tomato_Early_blight`	1,000
`Tomato_Late_blight`	1,909
`Tomato_Leaf_Mold`	952
`Tomato_Septoria_leaf_spot`	1,771
`Tomato_Spider_mites_Two_spotted_spider_mite`	1,676
`Tomato__Target_Spot`	1,404
`Tomato__Tomato_YellowLeaf__Curl_Virus`	3,208
`Tomato__Tomato_mosaic_virus`	373
`Tomato_healthy`	1,591

[1] https://www.kaggle.com/datasets/emmarex/plantdisease.

The dataset has been divided into the three typical subsets of training, validation, and test, with a percentage of 70%, 20%, and 10%, correspondingly, and stratified to preserve the percentage of samples of each class.

2.2 Contrastive Language-Image Pre-training (CLIP)

Despite the success of traditional models like CNNs or ViTs, they also have significant shortcomings: they require extensive labeled datasets for supervised training, which is both costly and time-consuming, and in some domains, annotated data is scarce. Additionally, these models are only capable of performing the specific task for which they were trained, and even small changes (such as adding a new class in image classification) require retraining a new model. Furthermore, they typically lack robustness to distribution shifts, as they are prone to learning spurious correlations [3]. Zero-shot and few-shot learning approaches aim to mitigate these issues by enabling models to generalize to new tasks with little to no labeled data. Building on the success of large-scale pre-trained models on Natural Language Processing [1], OpenAI introduced the Contrastive Language-Image Pre-training (CLIP) [6] model. CLIP leverages a vast corpus of image-text pairs from the internet to learn a multimodal embedding space, enabling zero-shot transfer learning capabilities across various visual tasks.

CLIP architecture consists of an image and a text encoder. Both encoders project their respective inputs into a shared latent space, where the similarity between image and text embeddings is computed. The model is trained using a contrastive objective, encouraging correct image-text pairs to have higher similarity scores than incorrect pairings. This approach allows CLIP to learn visual concepts and their linguistic representations simultaneously. The zero-shot learning capability of CLIP enables it to perform a wide array of tasks without task-specific fine-tuning. For instance, CLIP can classify images into categories specified by arbitrary text prompts and retrieve images based on textual queries. While CLIP achieves strong zero-shot performance on a wide variety of benchmark datasets and robustness to distribution shifts, its generalization ability is still limited by the distribution of its pretraining data [2]. Thus, it struggles with specialized tasks such as satellite image classification or lymph node tumor detection [6]. To adapt the model to such domain-specific tasks, multiple approaches have been proposed, including variations of prompt engineering [13], few-shot adaptation [4,11], and fine-tuning [9]. Different CLIP-based adaptations have shown promising results in specialized domains, such as medical imaging [12] and structural defect detection [10]. However, further research is still necessary to fully harness its potential and understand its limitations. Moreover, a recent study successfully integrated a few-shot CLIP adaption, Vision-Language Model prompts generation and attention mechanisms for crop diseases classification [14], highlighting the promise of CLIP's domain adaption in this field.

2.3 Zero-Shot Learning

Zero-shot learning (ZSL) is a machine learning paradigm that enables a model to classify instances from classes that were not observed during training. By leveraging semantic information, ZSL facilitates the recognition of unseen classes without the necessity for additional data collection and annotation.

Zero-shot can be formalized as follows: Let $\mathcal{S} = \{(x_i, y_i)\}_{i=1}^{n}$ represent the training set, where $x_i \in \mathcal{X}$ denotes the feature representation of the i-th plant leaf image, and $y_i \in \mathcal{Y}^s$ is the corresponding label from the set of seen classes $\mathcal{Y}^s$. The objective is to learn a function $f : \mathcal{X} \rightarrow \mathcal{Y}^u$ that can accurately predict labels for unseen classes $\mathcal{Y}^u$, where $\mathcal{Y}^s \cap \mathcal{Y}^u = \emptyset$.

To bridge the gap between seen and unseen classes, an auxiliary semantic space $\mathcal{A}$ is introduced, wherein each class $y \in \mathcal{Y}^s \cup \mathcal{Y}^u$ is associated with a semantic representation $a(y) \in \mathcal{A}$. These semantic representations can be derived from attributes, textual descriptions, or embeddings from language models. The learning process involves mapping instances $x \in \mathcal{X}$ to the semantic space $\mathcal{A}$, facilitating the transfer of knowledge from seen to unseen classes.

2.4 Prompting

One effective approach to implementing ZSL in plant disease detection is using the CLIP model. These models are trained on vast datasets containing pairs of images and their corresponding textual descriptions, enabling the learning of a joint embedding space where visual and textual information are aligned. In this space, the similarity between an image embedding $v(x)$ and a text embedding $t(a(y))$ can be computed using a similarity measure, such as cosine similarity:

$$\text{sim}(v(x), t(a(y))) = \frac{v(x) \cdot t(a(y))}{\|v(x)\| \|t(a(y))\|}$$

During inference, for an unseen class $y' \in \mathcal{Y}^u$, the model predicts the class label by selecting the class whose semantic representation has the highest similarity with the image embedding:

$$\hat{y} = \arg \max_{y' \in \mathcal{Y}^u} \text{sim}(v(x), t(a(y')))$$

The effectiveness of zero-shot learning depends significantly on the quality and detail of the semantic representations. More precise and distinctive attributes improve the model's ability to differentiate between similar diseases. Additionally, the strength of the visual and textual encoders in capturing relevant features is crucial. Challenges such as domain shift, where the distribution of features in unseen classes differs from that in seen classes, can negatively impact performance. More advanced models must be developed to tackle these challenges, and domain-specific knowledge must be integrated to enhance generalization capabilities.

To thoroughly evaluate the effectiveness of CLIP models in detecting plant diseases, we develop a multi-stage assessment protocol that examines various levels of prompt complexity and model adaptation. Specifically, we conduct experiments using three different zero-shot configurations and a fine-tuning scenario, each employing customized textual prompts to guide the model's predictions.

In the first configuration, we set up a binary classification system where all disease categories were consolidated under a single label, unhealthy leaf. In contrast, healthy specimens were labeled as healthy leaves. This simplified approach enables us to assess whether the model can distinguish between healthy and unhealthy visual patterns without relying on detailed class-level semantics. The prompts used for this configuration are detailed in Table 2.

Table 2. Binary classification prompts: healthy vs. unhealthy leaves.

Label	Plant classes
healthy leaf	`Pepper__bell___healthy`, `Potato___healthy`, `Tomato_healthy`
unhealthy leaf	`Pepper__bell___Bacterial_spot`, `Potato___Early_blight`, `Potato___Late_blight`, `Tomato_Bacterial_spot`, `Tomato_Early_blight`, `Tomato_Late_blight`, `Tomato_Leaf_Mold`, `Tomato_Septoria_leaf_spot`, `Tomato_Spider_mites_Two_spotted_spider_mite`, `Tomato__Target_Spot`, `Tomato__Tomato_YellowLeaf__Curl_Virus`, `Tomato__Tomato_mosaic_virus`

The second configuration expanded the task to a multi-class zero-shot setting, where each image class was linked to a specific textual description. These prompts were concise and clearly stated both the crop and disease types. This setup aims to assess the model's foundational understanding of textual labels directly based on the dataset annotations, as shown in Table 3.

To enhance model guidance, a third configuration introduced refined prompts that incorporated more descriptive and contextually rich language. These prompts emphasized specific visual traits associated with each disease, such as color, shape, and distribution of symptoms. The improved prompts are documented in Table 4.

Finally, to benchmark zero-shot performance against a supervised approach, a fine-tuning phase was carried out. The CLIP model was adapted to the specific task using labeled training data derived from the PlantVillage dataset subset. The prompts used during this phase mirrored the multi-class descriptions in Table 3, ensuring consistency across evaluation modes.

Formally, we have defined the fine-tuning process, considering several mechanisms. For an image x_i and a set of textual prompts $\{t_j\}_{j=1}^{C}$ corresponding to

Table 3. Multi-class classification of each leaf type and their respective prompts.

Class	Prompt
`Pepper__bell___Bacterial_spot`	bell pepper leaf with bacterial spot disease
`Pepper__bell___healthy`	healthy bell pepper leaf
`Potato___Early_blight`	potato leaf with early blight disease
`Potato___Late_blight`	potato leaf with late blight disease
`Potato___healthy`	healthy potato leaf
`Tomato_Bacterial_spot`	tomato leaf with bacterial spot disease
`Tomato_Early_blight`	tomato leaf with early blight disease
`Tomato_Late_blight`	tomato leaf with late blight disease
`Tomato_Leaf_Mold`	tomato leaf with leaf mold disease
`Tomato_Septoria_leaf_spot`	tomato leaf with septoria leaf spot disease
`Tomato_Spider_mites_Two_spotted_spider_mite`	tomato leaf with two-spotted spider mite infestation
`Tomato__Target_Spot`	tomato leaf with target spot disease
`Tomato__Tomato_YellowLeaf__Curl_Virus`	tomato leaf infected by yellow leaf curl virus
`Tomato__Tomato_mosaic_virus`	tomato leaf infected by mosaic virus
`Tomato_healthy`	healthy tomato leaf

Table 4. Multi-class classification of each leaf type and their respective detailed prompts.

Class	Detailed Prompt
`Pepper__bell___Bacterial_spot`	A bell pepper leaf with dark brown bacterial spots
`Pepper__bell___healthy`	A bell pepper leaf with uniform green color and no damage
`Potato___Early_blight`	A potato leaf showing brown spots caused by early blight
`Potato___Late_blight`	A potato leaf with large dark patches indicating late blight
`Potato___healthy`	A fresh and healthy potato leaf with no signs of disease
`Tomato_Bacterial_spot`	A tomato leaf with dark bacterial lesions and yellowing
`Tomato_Early_blight`	A tomato leaf with irregular dark brown early blight lesions
`Tomato_Late_blight`	A tomato leaf covered in irregular patches caused by late blight
`Tomato_Leaf_Mold`	A tomato leaf with fuzzy mold growth typical of leaf mold
`Tomato_Septoria_leaf_spot`	A tomato leaf with grey spots indicating septoria infection
`Tomato_Spider_mites_Two_spotted`	A tomato leaf with visible webbing and small mites from spiders
`Tomato__Target_Spot`	A tomato leaf with circular target-like spots
`Tomato_YellowLeaf__Curl_Virus`	A tomato leaf with yellow curled edges due to yellow leaf virus
`Tomato__Tomato_mosaic_virus`	A tomato leaf showing mosaic patterns caused by mosaic virus
`Tomato_healthy`	A healthy tomato leaf with bright green color and no disease

C classes, the CLIP model computes embeddings via:

$$z_i = f_{\text{img}}(x_i) \in \mathbb{R}^d,$$
$$w_j = f_{\text{text}}(t_j) \in \mathbb{R}^d,$$

where f_{img} and f_{text} denote the image and text encoders, respectively.

The similarity between an image embedding z_i and a text embedding w_j is computed using a dot product scaled by a learnable parameter $\exp(\gamma)$:

$$s_{ij} = \exp(\gamma)\, z_i^\top w_j.$$

Given the true label y_i for image x_i, the cross-entropy loss for that sample is defined as:

$$\mathcal{L}_i = -\log \frac{\exp(s_{i,y_i})}{\sum_{j=1}^{C} \exp(s_{ij})}.$$

The overall loss for a batch of N samples is then:

$$\mathcal{L} = \frac{1}{N} \sum_{i=1}^{N} \mathcal{L}_i.$$

The fine-tuning process uses the AdamW optimizer to update the model parameters θ according to:

$$\theta_{t+1} = \theta_t - \alpha \cdot \frac{\hat{m}_t}{\sqrt{\hat{v}_t} + \epsilon},$$

where α is the learning rate, and $\hat{m}_t$ and $\hat{v}_t$ are the bias-corrected first and second moments, respectively.

To prevent the explosion of gradients, the ℓ_2-norm of the gradients is clipped to a maximum value of 1.0. Formally, if $g = \nabla\mathcal{L}$.

Finally, a learning rate scheduler, the ReduceLROnPlateau, is used to decrease the learning rate when the validation loss plateaus. This adaptive mechanism aids in the convergence of the training process.

3 Experimental Results

In this section, we report and analyze the performance of the CLIP model in both zero-shot and fine-tuning settings. We first evaluate the model under a zero-shot regime using various prompt configurations and then compare these results with those obtained after task-specific fine-tuning.

3.1 Zero-Shot

We begin by assessing the zero-shot capabilities of the CLIP model. In the first configuration, a binary classification approach is employed where all disease categories are grouped as unhealthy leaves while healthy specimens are labeled healthy. The model achieves a high precision of 0.87 and recall of 0.81 for the unhealthy leaf class. However, the performance for healthy leaf is notably lower, with a precision of 0.26 and a recall of 0.37, resulting in a macro-averaged F1-score of 0.57. These results indicate that, in a zero-shot setting, the model is more effective at identifying disease-related patterns than confirming health.

We extended the evaluation to a multi-class scenario to further explore the zero-shot performance. In the second configuration, using a prompt by class, as shown in Table 5, most classes achieve near-zero performance with a macro F1-score of 0.05. This result underscores the difficulty of leveraging brief textual cues to capture the nuanced differences among disease classes.

Table 5. Classification report metrics with Table 3 prompts.

Class	Precision	Recall	F1-score
`bell pepper leaf with bacterial spot disease`	0.14	0.05	0.07
`healthy bell pepper leaf`	0.00	0.00	0.00
`potato leaf with early blight disease`	0.07	0.53	0.13
`healthy potato leaf`	0.00	0.00	0.00
`potato leaf with late blight disease`	0.07	0.07	0.07
`tomato leaf with target spot disease`	0.00	0.00	0.00
`tomato leaf infected by mosaic virus`	0.00	0.00	0.00
`tomato leaf infected by yellow leaf curl virus`	0.67	0.02	0.05
`tomato leaf with bacterial spot disease`	0.00	0.00	0.00
`tomato leaf with early blight disease`	0.03	0.10	0.05
`healthy tomato leaf`	0.00	0.00	0.00
`tomato leaf with late blight disease`	0.22	0.23	0.23
`tomato leaf with leaf mold disease`	0.05	0.32	0.09
`tomato leaf with septoria leaf spot disease`	0.00	0.00	0.00
`tomato leaf with two-spotted spider mite infestation`	0.00	0.00	0.00
Macro avg	0.08	0.09	0.05

A third configuration was designed using more detailed and contextually enriched prompts, as seen in Table 6. This refinement resulted in a slight improvement of macro F1-score of 0.06. For instance, while the prompt "A bell pepper leaf with dark brown bacterial spots" yields a high precision of 0.75, its recall of 0.03 remains very low, indicating that even detailed prompts are insufficient for robust generalization in a zero-shot framework in this context.

3.2 Fine-Tuning

Due to the significant limitations observed in the zero-shot approach, we proceeded with a fine-tuning phase using labeled data from the reduced PlantVillage dataset. The fine-tuning process specifically adapts the CLIP model to the plant disease detection task, enhancing its discriminative ability.

Figure 1 displays the evolution of the evaluation metrics, including macro precision, recall, and F1-score, throughout the fine-tuning process.

The results of Fig. 1 show that, with a single epoch of the fine-tuning process, very high metrics of all metrics are obtained, highlighting the potential of these models that, although their main task is not their use by fine-tuning, can provide very promising results for the task, in this case, the identification of plant

Table 6. Classification report metrics with Table 4 detailed prompts.

Class	Precision	Recall	F1-score
A bell pepper leaf with dark brown bacterial spots	0.75	0.03	0.06
A bell pepper leaf with uniform green color and no visible damage	0.00	0.00	0.00
A potato leaf showing irregular brown spots caused by early blight	0.21	0.22	0.21
A fresh and healthy potato leaf with no signs of disease	0.00	0.00	0.00
A potato leaf with large dark patches indicating late blight	0.08	0.68	0.15
A tomato leaf with circular target-like spots	0.00	0.00	0.00
A tomato leaf showing mosaic patterns caused by mosaic virus	0.11	0.27	0.16
A tomato leaf with yellow curled edges due to yellow leaf virus	0.00	0.00	0.00
A tomato leaf with dark bacterial lesions and yellowing	0.00	0.00	0.00
A tomato leaf with irregular dark brown early blight lesions	0.09	0.35	0.14
A healthy tomato leaf with bright green color and no disease	0.00	0.00	0.00
A tomato leaf covered in irregular patches caused by late blight	0.11	0.30	0.16
A tomato leaf with fuzzy mold growth typical of leaf mold	0.00	0.00	0.00
A tomato leaf with grey spots indicating septoria infection	0.00	0.00	0.00
A tomato leaf with visible webbing and small mites from spiders	0.00	0.00	0.00
Macro avg	0.09	0.12	0.06

diseases. It can also be observed that from epoch 5 onwards, the model's performance stabilizes, thus demonstrating the reduced fine-tuning time necessary to obtain good results. To check for overfitting, the model has been evaluated a posteriori with the test set, obtaining macro precision of 0.9959, recall of 0.9877, and F1-score 0.9915, showing that it has not suffered. Detailed data by class can be found in Table 7.

4 Conclusions

In the present work, we have studied the application of CLIP-type models for plant disease classification, comparing their zero-shot functionality and fine-tuning capabilities. We evaluated the model's performance by simplifying the

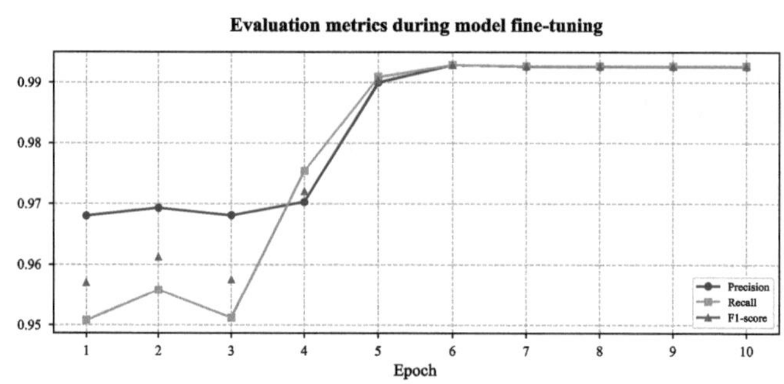

Fig. 1. Evolution of macro precision metrics, recall and F1 during the fine-tuning process.

Table 7. Classification report metrics of the fine-tuned model after 10 epochs.

Class	Precision	Recall	F1-score
`bell pepper leaf with bacterial spot disease`	1.0000	1.0000	1.0000
`healthy bell pepper leaf`	1.0000	1.0000	1.0000
`potato leaf showing early blight symptoms`	1.0000	1.0000	1.0000
`potato leaf affected by late blight`	0.9802	0.9900	0.9851
`healthy potato leaf`	1.0000	0.8667	0.9286
`tomato leaf with bacterial spot disease`	1.0000	0.9953	0.9976
`tomato leaf showing early blight`	1.0000	0.9900	0.9950
`tomato leaf affected by late blight`	0.9948	1.0000	0.9974
`tomato leaf affected by leaf mold disease`	0.9896	1.0000	0.9948
`tomato leaf with septoria leaf spot`	0.9944	1.0000	0.9972
`tomato leaf infested by two-spotted spider mites`	1.0000	0.9881	0.9940
`tomato leaf showing target spot disease`	0.9857	0.9857	0.9857
`tomato leaf infected with yellow leaf curl virus`	0.9938	1.0000	0.9969
`tomato leaf infected with mosaic virus`	1.0000	1.0000	1.0000
`healthy tomato leaf`	1.0000	1.0000	1.0000
Macro avg	0.9959	0.9877	0.9915

problem to a binary classification task, experimenting with basic and refined prompts, and adapting the model through fine-tuning.

As expected, the zero-shot results were poor, likely due to the absence of plant disease-related concepts in CLIP's pretraining data. The complexity of plant disease symptoms, which can vary across species and often resemble each other, further contributes to this challenge. Similarly, when attempting to classify diseases using more complete textual descriptions of each condition, the model also performed poorly, suggesting the need for further research into more effective prompt engineering techniques. However, despite zero-shot limitations, very promising results have been obtained through fine-tuning, achieving a macro precision of 0.9959. This shows that CLIP-based models have the potential to perform classical computer vision tasks traditionally handled by CNNs in the smart agriculture domain.

Building on these results, our next steps will focus on fully harnessing the properties of few-shot vision-language models, minimizing the need for labeled data while improving CLIP's domain adaption in plant disease classification. To achieve this, we plan to compare the performance of different CLIP variants (e.g., SigLIP) and few-shot domain adaptation techniques, as well as to identify the most effective prompts for describing each disease category in a way that aligns with CLIP's representation. Likewise, we aim to assess the model's robustness in more real environments when incorporating new disease categories, using the remaining classes of the PlantVillage dataset and other available open datasets.

Finally, we would like to extend our work to a multi-agent systems framework, integrating CLIP-based models into distributed architectures, enabling collaborative decision-making and real-time distributed processing in agricultural diagnostics.

Acknowledgments. This work is partially supported by grant PID2021-123673 funded by MCIN/AEI/10.13039/501100011033 and by "ERDF A way of making Europe".

References

1. Brown, T., Mann, B., Ryder, N., et al.: Language models are few-shot learners. In: Larochelle, H., Ranzato, M., Hadsell, R., Balcan, M., Lin, H. (eds.) Advances in Neural Information Processing Systems, vol. 33, pp. 1877–1901. Curran Associates, Inc. (2020)
2. Fang, A., et al.: Data determines distributional robustness in contrastive language image pre-training (clip). In: International Conference on Machine Learning (2022)
3. Geirhos, R., et al.: Shortcut learning in deep neural networks. Nat. Mach. Intell. **2**, 665–673 (2020)
4. Gondal, M.W., et al.: Domain aligned clip for few-shot classification. In: 2024 IEEE/CVF Winter Conference on Applications of Computer Vision (WACV), pp. 5709–5718. IEEE Computer Society (2024)
5. Mohanty, S.P., Hughes, D.P., Salathé, M.: Using deep learning for image-based plant disease detection. Front. Plant Sci. **7** (2016)
6. Radford, A., et al.: Learning transferable visual models from natural language supervision. In: International Conference on Machine Learning (2021)
7. Soltani Firouz, M., et al.: Defect detection in fruit and vegetables by using machine vision systems and image processing. Food Eng. Rev. **14**(3), 353–379 (2022)
8. Thakur, P.S., Khanna, P., Sheorey, T., Ojha, A.: Explainable vision transformer enabled convolutional neural network for plant disease identification: Plantxvit (2022), arXiv:2207.07919
9. Wortsman, M., et al.: Robust fine-tuning of zero-shot models, pp. 7949–7961 (2022)
10. Yong, G., Jeon, K., Gil, D., Lee, G.: Prompt engineering for zero-shot and few-shot defect detection and classification using a visual-language pretrained model. Comput.-Aided Civil Infrastruct. Eng. **38** (2022)
11. Zhang, R., et al.: Tip-Adapter: Training-Free Adaption of CLIP for Few-Shot Classification, pp. 493–510 (2022)
12. Zhao, Z., et al.: Clip in medical imaging: a survey. Med. Image Anal. **102**, 103551 (2025)
13. Zhou, K., Yang, J., Loy, C.C., Liu, Z.: Learning to prompt for vision-language models. Inter. J. Comput. Vis. **130** (2022)
14. Zhou, Y., Yan, H., Ding, K., Cai, T., Zhang, Y.: Few-shot image classification of crop diseases based on vision–language models. Sensors **24**(18) (2024)

Agent-Based Social Simulator for Analyzing Well-Being and Resources: An Integrated Approach for Vulnerable Rural Communities

Jairo E. Serrano[1](✉) and Enrique González[2]

[1] Universidad Tecnológica de Bolívar, Cartagena, Colombia
jserrano@utb.edu.co

[2] Pontificia Universidad Javeriana, Bogotá, Colombia
egonzal@javeriana.edu.co

Abstract. This article presents a social simulator based on multi-agent systems designed to analyze the social well-being, health, and resource management of peasant families. Using an emotional BDI (eBDI) architecture, it explicitly integrates emotional factors influencing daily decision-making. Applied to vulnerable rural communities in Montes de María, Colombia, and developed using the Design Science methodology, the simulator integrates local expertise from agriculture, public health, and social domains. Validation through statistical and empirical evaluations confirmed the simulator's accuracy in representing local dynamics. The results emphasize how efficient resource management and emotional well-being substantially enhance quality of life, illustrating its potential to inform public policies for sustainable rural development.

Keywords: Social Simulation · Multi-agent systems · Emotional BDI · Multi-agent simulation

1 Introduction

The application of multi-agent systems offers a powerful approach for developing social simulators that enable a comprehensive analysis of social, emotional, and economic well-being in peasant families. This study applies such a simulator to explore the dynamics of rural life in the Montes de María region of the Colombian Caribbean coast [3], a territory marked by deep-rooted social and economic vulnerabilities. Limited access to land, water, agricultural inputs, and formal credit systems has historically constrained development in the area. Additionally, emotional factors such as uncertainty and stress—stemming from prolonged armed conflict and forced displacement, significantly influence the everyday decision-making processes of people living in these communities [1].

The social simulator, implements an emotional agent architecture [2], and is based on an emotional-BDI model (eBDI), enabling the simulation of complex

A. Nongaillard et al. (Eds.): PAAMS 2025, CCIS 2644, pp. 29–41, 2025.
https://doi.org/10.1007/978-3-032-05925-3_3

dynamics between emotions and productive decision-making in vulnerable rural settings. The Design Science methodology [6], specifically adapted to multi-agent systems, was used is to integrate local knowledge and expert insights from agriculture and social well-being in an iterative manner. The simulator was validated through rigorous statistical analyses and empirical evaluations conducted with experts in rural development and social simulation, who emphasized its ability to accurately represent the conditions observed in the field.

The validation results demonstrate how the effective management of essential resources such as land [13], water, seeds, and agricultural tools, combined with the explicit incorporation of emotional factors [18], significantly enhances agricultural productivity, emotional stability, and overall well-being [17]. These findings suggest that tools like the social simulator are useful for the formulation of more precise and effective public policies, capable of positively impacting life in vulnerable rural contexts such as the region.

In order to further explore the role of emotions in daily life and productivity within these rural communities, the next section presents the theoretical framework on peasant social well-being and the emotional models that serve as the foundation for the eBDI architecture. Section 3 describes the detailed design of the multi-agent system, followed by the validation and results in Sects. 4 and 5, concluding with some final remarks in Section 6.

2 Background and Multi-agent System

The methodology used for the design of the social simulator is based on Design Science [7], specifically adapted for multi-agent-based social simulations (ABSS). This approach is particularly suitable for addressing complex social problems due to its iterative and collaborative structure, which integrates expert knowledge and the specific requirements of peasant communities [6,20]. This ensures that the development of the social simulator appropriately responds to the real needs of the region.

Design Science is characterized by an organization into iterative cycles of relevance, rigor, and design. The relevance cycle connects the simulator to the real social context, ensuring that the specific requirements of peasant communities are considered at every stage. The rigor cycle ensures that the design is supported by solid theories and methods, applying empirical validations to achieve consistency between the model and the rural dynamics to be simulated. Finally, the design cycle represents the phase of creation, testing, and implementation of the social simulator, safeguarding its practical effectiveness and technical consistency [6].

2.1 Social Well-Being and Emotional Models in Peasant Communities

Social well-being in peasant communities is a multidimensional concept that encompasses food security, access to basic services (healthcare, education, potable water), sufficient income, and emotional and social stability [5,15]. In vulnerable rural contexts, particularly in regions affected by army conflicts and structural poverty, these dimensions are interrelated and mutually interdependent [1,3]. Emotional factors such as hope and fear directly influence the perception of quality of life; studies in social psychology show that optimism fosters resilience in economic crises, while insecurity reduces community cooperation [4].

Emotions have a direct influence on daily decision-making [12,14]. Positive states (happiness, hope, optimism) are linked to proactive behaviors, stronger community ties, and more efficient management of agricultural resources. Conversely, negative emotions such as insecurity, fear, or sadness diminish motivation and collaboration, causing suboptimal decisions that hinder resource management and productivity. Emotional insecurity can prompt families to make inefficient choices and limit their economic and social progress.

The results obtained through the social simulator confirm that peasant families with predominantly positive emotional states achieve superior productivity and exhibit higher social well-being, given that optimistic attitudes increase willingness to cooperate and adapt to environmental fluctuations, including adverse climate or economic pressures. These findings underscore the need to integrate emotional factors in public policy formation, as emotional well-being can catalyze improvements in agricultural practices and community resource management, driving sustainable rural development.

Therefore, the following sections detail the design of the multi-agent system and how these emotions are incorporated into the decision-making process of the *PeasantFamily* agent, enabling simulations in which social and emotional variables intertwine with rural challenges.

2.2 Application of Design Science

The social simulator was designed according to a systematic framework derived from Design Science, focusing on a structured definition of the problem, clear objectives, iterative implementation, and the rigorous evaluation of outcomes [20]. This approach ensures that each stage of development remains grounded in real-world conditions, thereby addressing the practical needs of peasant communities while maintaining conceptual rigor and technical coherence. Additionally, the inherent flexibility of this methodology allows for frequent refinements based on stakeholder and expert feedback, reinforcing both the relevance and adaptability of the simulator [6].

These guiding principles were consolidated into eight key elements underpinning the simulator's design and future application: (1) flexibility for navigating complex contexts, (2) adaptability to emergent requirements, (3) a systematic approach for maintaining clarity, (4) methodological rigor supported by robust theoretical foundations, (5) the capability to represent intricate multi-agent systems, (6) comprehensive support for actual implementation, (7) robust formal and empirical validation procedures, and (8) transparent integration of diverse multidisciplinary techniques. By combining these elements, the simulator is now poised to address real-world challenges in rural development, further illustrating how Design Science can be effectively applied to craft meaningful and responsive solutions for vulnerable peasant communities.

2.3 Multi-agent Model

The general architecture of the social simulator Multi-Agent System (see Fig. 1) was designed around nine key types of agents, each fulfilling a distinct role within the simulated context. A primary goal of this architecture is to enable flexible configuration and reconfiguration of agent-specific variables—such as resource thresholds, decision-making parameters, and emotional states—so that diverse scenarios and interventions can be represented. This adaptability ensures that users can tailor each agent type to reflect different farming practices, market dynamics, institutional policies, and behavioral nuances inherent to real-world peasant communities.

- ***PeasantFamily*** acts as the study's main agent, representing rural households engaged in crop cultivation, livestock management, and local commerce. It integrates an emotional BeliefDesireIntention (eBDI) model to capture affective dynamics in everyday decision-making [16,17] and interacts with other agents—namely *AgroEcosystem* and *MarketPlace*—to simulate economic and social exchanges.
- ***AgroEcosystem*** simulates environmental conditions such as climate, vegetation growth, time control [18], and soil conditions, using real data to ensure the accuracy and validity of the simulated agricultural context [13].
- ***CommunityDynamics*** promotes cooperation, mutual support, and shared resource management among peasant families, strengthening community resilience.
- ***CivicAuthority*** simulates governmental functions, particularly those related to land allocation and agricultural regulation.
- ***BankOffice*** manages financial aspects, including essential credit services for the economic development of peasant families.
- ***MarketPlace*** oversees all commercial transactions within the simulator, facilitating the exchange of agricultural products and necessary supplies.
- ***PerturbationGeneration*** introduces disruptive events such as climatic, economic, or biological fluctuations, allowing to incorporate critical situations into the simulation scenarios.
- ***ViewerLens*** provides an interactive visual interface to facilitate the monitoring and analysis of simulation results.
- ***SimulationControl*** manages and controls the overall execution of the simulator, ensuring coherence and technical precision in each interaction and simulated event.

Agents interact dynamically based on activated goals or needs. For instance, when a *PeasantFamily* agent requires water, it queries the *MarketPlace* agent to determine the cost and available quantities. If the resources available to the family are sufficient, the agent proceeds to execute the purchase.

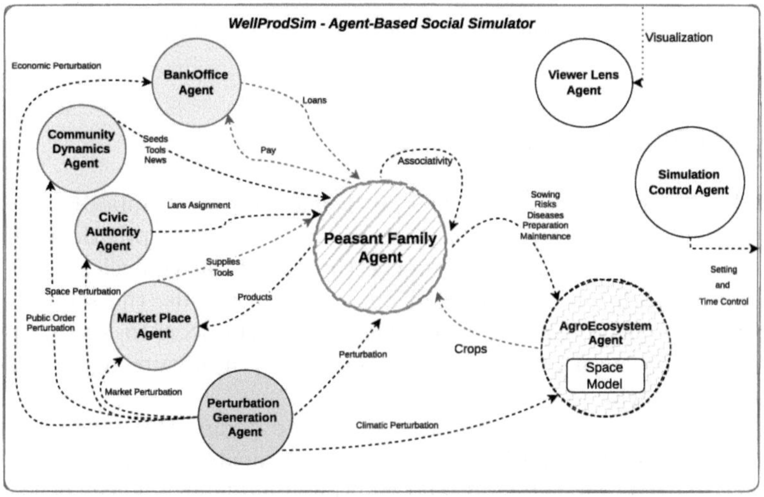

Fig. 1. MultiAgent System for WellProdSim local Desktop.

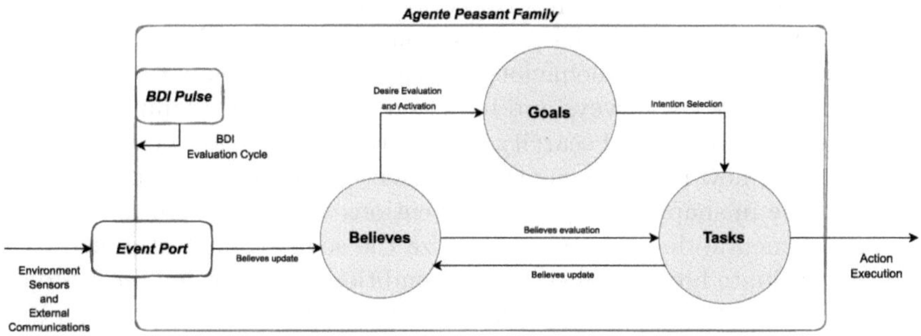

Fig. 2. Conceptual eBDI architecture for the PeasantFamily agent.

To further illustrate the handling of emotional dynamics by the *PeasantFamily* agent, Fig. 2 shows the eBDI conceptual architecture, encompassing beliefs, desires, and intentions, together with an emotion module that modulates agents' goal prioritization and event processing. In this module, shifts in emotional states—such as optimism or fear—can alter the agent's focus, influencing both short-term adaptations and long-term strategies. Through this mechanism, peasant families' economic limitations and social considerations translate into emotionally driven responses, expanding the range of plausible outcomes when simulating real-world challenges.

By integrating these emotional processes into the broader decision-making cycle, the multi-agent design supports a nuanced analysis of how peasant communities react to economic, social, and environmental fluctuations. Moreover, this level of detail strengthens the potential for policy-related experimentation, offering a risk-free setting in which to project various intervention strategies and gauge their likely effects on both agricultural productivity and peasant well-being.

3 Model Validation Strategy

This validation process utilizes a Design Science approach tailored specifically for multi-agent systems and social simulations. It ensures practical relevance, conceptual rigor, and technical coherence through iterative cycles [8,10,19,21]. By integrating both quantitative and qualitative methods, the strategy evaluates the model's effectiveness in replicating real-world decision-making patterns among vulnerable rural populations, supported by literature review and local community feedback.

Aligned with the cycles of relevance, rigor, and design, three main evaluation levels were applied [9,11]. First, factorial experiments analyzed how resource allocations—such as capital, land, and emotional modeling—affect peasant families' well-being, using ANOVA and Taguchi designs to confirm the simulator's internal consistency and predictive power.

Second, statistical validation focused on reproducibility and consistency through ANOVA and orthogonal designs, confirming the eBDI model's robustness for simulating complex behaviors. Lastly, empirical evaluations with rural development experts via surveys and interviews validated the simulator's reflection of hope, uncertainty, and scarcity in vulnerable contexts. Their feedback led to refinements in how negative emotions influence goal prioritization, enhancing the model's role in shaping targeted interventions and public policies.

The experimental design used to analyze the social simulator aimed to systematically evaluate how initial economic conditions, land availability, and emotional states influence agricultural productivity and the well-being of peasant families. This approach helps identify key decision-making factors in rural settings and offers a solid framework to analyze interactions between economic constraints and emotional responses.

Three categories of variables were defined: independent controlled variables (main factors tested), intervening variables (set at fixed values that influence relationships), and dependent measured variables (reflect simulation outcomes). This classification clarifies each variable's role and streamlines the experimental structure (Table 1).

Once the values of the independent variables are defined, the simulation calculates the productivity and well-being indices. The Eq. 1 defines the *Productivity index*, which standardizes the final capital and total production by the number of assigned parcels:

$$\textbf{Productivity Index} = \text{Normalize}\left(\frac{\text{Final Capital} + \text{Total Production}}{\text{Assigned Parcels}}\right) \quad (1)$$

This formula captures how efficiently the resources are utilized under different economic conditions, offering a quantitative benchmark for comparing scenarios within the simulation.

Table 1. Classification of Variables in the Experiment

Category	Variable	Description
Independent Variables	Capital	Financial resources available at the start, reflecting investments.
	Land	Sets the initial land allocation for each *PeasantFamily* agent.
	Emotions	Evaluates the influence of positive, negative, and neutral emotional states on decision-making.
	Resources like tools, seeds and water	Defines the initial resource level in the simulation; options include basic, purchasable, or unlimited.
Controllable Factors	Crops	Rice and yam, chosen for their regional importance.
	Climate Variation	Different climatic conditions throughout the year to reflect real-world variability.
	Simulation Scope	Five years, two parcels per family, 100 families.
	Initial Variance	40% variability introduced to simulate diverse initial conditions and population differences.
Uncontrollable Factors	Data Quality	Data sources include biases and uncertainty from empirical sources and expert knowledge.
	Computational Resources	Cluster with 5 high-performance servers (64GB RAM, 20 cores).
Dependent Variables	Final Capital	The total accumulated money at the end of the simulation, serving as an indicator of financial stability.
	Total Production	The total biomass weight generated throughout the simulation, representing agricultural output.
	Average Health	Dynamic variable that reflects the average of physical condition of the *PeasantFamily* agent over time.
	Average Emotions	Dynamic variable that represents the average of affective state of the *PeasantFamily* agent, positive emotions (eP), negative emotions (eN).

Similarly, Eq. 2 provides the *Well-being Index*, indicating how emotional factors and health collectively shape the quality of life:

$$\textbf{Well-being Index} = \text{Normalize}(\text{eP} - \text{eN} + \text{Average Health}) \qquad (2)$$

By calculating this index, the simulation can quantitatively evaluate the way positive emotions (eP) and negative emotions (eN), coupled with the average health status, drive variations in social and emotional well-being.

The design of this experiment provides a structured and controlled environment to analyze the complex interactions between economic resources, land availability, and emotional factors in peasant decision-making. Furthermore, the ability to compute and compare productivity and well-being indices across scenarios highlights the simulator's potential for evaluating policy impacts, guiding resource allocation, and forecasting the return on social investments in rural communities. By integrating these variables, the social simulator enables the assessment of:

- How different levels of initial capital and land availability influence long-term financial stability.
- The extent to which the emotional component affects decision-making, productivity, and well-being.
- The resilience of peasant families in different climatic and economic scenarios.

The findings from this experiment enhance the understanding of rural development dynamics and provide valuable insights for formulating public policies, developing resource allocation strategies, and designing sustainable intervention models. For instance, if the government invests in areas such as recreation, training, or credit services, the simulator can be used to observe their impact on well-being and productivity. Additionally, it allows for the calculation of the return on investment, aiding more informed decision-making.

4 Results

This section presents and analyzes the simulation outcomes, focusing on how initial resources (financial capital and available land) and agent emotions influence the productivity and social well-being of peasant families. Additionally, Fig. 3 illustrates an alternative user interface designed for laptops, enhancing accessibility for general users. This interface displays a map showing crop distribution and the status of each simulated agent.

A Taguchi L27 experimental design was applied to systematically evaluate how resource allocation influences production and well-being indicators. Specifically, six main factors were analyzed: initial capital, number of lands, emotional states, availability of tools, seeds, and water. The null hypothesis stated that none of these resources, at their various levels, would significantly affect the final results. Table 2 shows the levels assigned to each factor.

Once the Taguchi matrix was configured, each treatment was simulated, and the outcomes for productivity and well-being were compared. Productivity was estimated based on agricultural biomass and accumulated capital, whereas well-being accounted for both health and the influence of positive or negative emotions on decision-making. Subsequently, statistical analysis helped determine the significance of each factor and how their interactions affect the stability and predictability of peasant families' daily activities.Table 3 presents the final data, displaying productivity and well-being indicators, both scaled from the lowest possible value of 0 to a maximum of 1. Interpreting these results reveals several noteworthy insights:

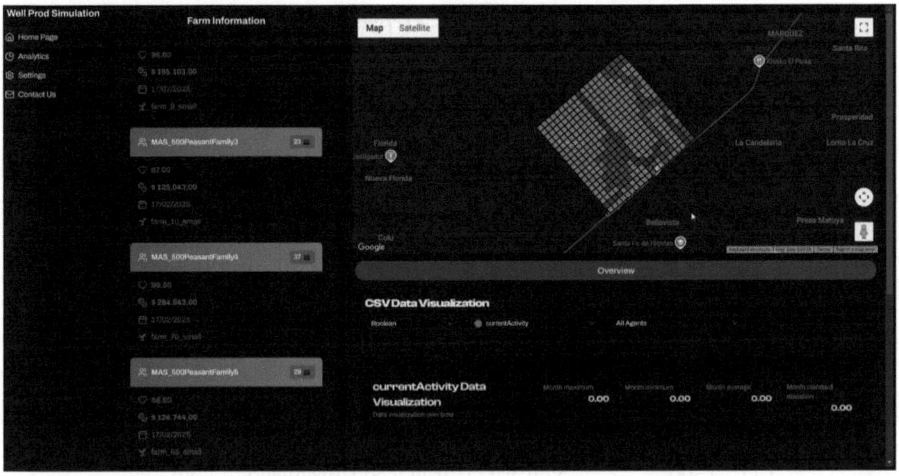

Fig. 3. User interface of WellProdSim local Desktop.

- Higher initial capital fosters early investments, thereby boosting both productivity and well-being. However, allocating more land does not necessarily improve yields, mainly due to labor constraints.
- While having unlimited tools and seeds optimizes performance, acquiring them gradually still proved to be sufficient to maintain acceptable output levels.
- Ensuring a constant water supply stood out as critical for crop growth, underscoring the significance of water security.
- Positive emotional states encouraged more collaborative and productive interactions, whereas emotional instability increased variability in the results.

Overall, these data rejected the null hypothesis and confirmed the influence each factor has on family productivity and well-being. Consequently, the social simulator emerges as a valuable instrument for formulating agricultural policies that address both material needs and emotional dynamics, thereby advancing sustainable development in rural Colombian areas.

5 Conclusions

This study introduced the social simulator, a multi-agent social simulator with an emotional BDI (eBDI) architecture, validated in the vulnerable rural context of the Montes de María region in Colombia. By applying a Design Science methodology adapted to multi-agent systems, the social simulator effectively integrates economic, social, and emotional dimensions, providing a comprehensive representation of peasant family dynamics. The results confirm that emotional factors significantly influence agricultural productivity and social resilience. Positive

Table 2. Summary of Factors and Treatments of the Experiment

ID	Capital	Lands	Emotions	Tools	Seeds	Water
T01	750	2	Positive	Base	Base	No
T02	750	2	Positive	Base	Infinite	Infinite
T03	750	2	Positive	Base	Purchased	Purchased
T04	750	6	Neutral	Infinite	Base	No
T05	750	6	Neutral	Infinite	Infinite	Infinite
T06	750	6	Neutral	Infinite	Purchased	Purchased
T07	750	12	Negative	Purchased	Base	No
T08	750	12	Negative	Purchased	Infinite	Infinite
T09	750	12	Negative	Purchased	Purchased	Purchased
T10	1500	2	Neutral	Purchased	Infinite	Purchased
T11	1500	2	Neutral	Purchased	Purchased	No
T12	1500	6	Negative	Base	Base	Infinite
T13	1500	6	Negative	Base	Infinite	No
T14	1500	6	Negative	Base	Purchased	Purchased
T15	1500	12	Positive	Infinite	Base	Infinite
T16	1500	12	Positive	Infinite	Infinite	Purchased
T17	1500	12	Positive	Infinite	Purchased	No
T18	3000	2	Negative	Infinite	Base	No
T19	3000	2	Negative	Infinite	Infinite	Infinite
T20	3000	2	Negative	Infinite	Purchased	Purchased
T21	3000	6	Positive	Purchased	Base	No
T22	3000	6	Positive	Purchased	Infinite	Infinite
T23	3000	6	Positive	Purchased	Purchased	Purchased
T24	3000	12	Neutral	Base	Base	No
T25	3000	12	Neutral	Base	Infinite	Infinite
T26	3000	12	Neutral	Base	Purchased	Purchased
T27	3000	12	Neutral	Base	Purchased	Infinite

emotions foster collaboration and efficient decision-making, while negative emotions reduce motivation and quality of life, emphasizing the need to consider emotional well-being in the design of public policies for rural development.

The social simulator's capacity to evaluate multiple resource allocation scenarios (land, capital, agricultural inputs) highlights its practical value as a decision-support tool for governmental and non-governmental interventions. The flexibility of the eBDI model and the iterative adaptation of Design Science allows for continuous expert feedback, improving the accuracy and applicability of the simulator's outputs. A key contribution of this research is the explicit integration of emotional variables in the simulation of peasant environments, a

Table 3. Results of experiment, Productivity Index and Well-being Index.

ID	Productivity	Well-being	ID	Productivity	Well-being
T01	0,837	0,847	T14	0,383	0,688
T02	0,692	0,856	T15	0,374	0,704
T03	0,611	0,790	T16	0,137	0,393
T04	0,526	0,759	T17	0,293	0,696
T05	0,158	0,418	T18	0,229	0,737
T06	0,377	0,675	T19	0,494	0,764
T07	0,143	0,363	T20	0,476	0,736
T08	0,143	0,433	T21	0,339	0,739
T09	0,142	0,410	T22	0,424	0,681
T10	0,392	0,754	T23	0,496	0,750
T11	0,473	0,749	T24	0,162	0,528
T12	0,470	0,710	T25	0,219	0,660
T13	0,113	0,411	T26	0,194	0,747
			T27	0,168	0,544

factor often overlooked in traditional models. By incorporating these aspects, the social simulator captures the behavioral patterns that shape technology adoption, resource management, and community organization.

To enhance its effectiveness, several improvements are proposed. Integrating machine learning mechanisms would enable BDI agents to evolve dynamically, adjusting their beliefs and emotional responses based on previous experiences. Additionally, enhancing interactivity by allowing real-time scenario adjustments would improve user engagement and the usability of decision-making applications based on the simulator. Expanding the modeling of external factors, such as migration patterns and extreme climate events, would further increase the realism and applicability of the simulator, enabling a more comprehensive assessment of rural development challenges.

Finally, extending the social simulator to different rural regions and cultures would facilitate comparative analyses, refining global intervention strategies in rural development. By incorporating machine learning, interactive scenario adjustments, and broader environmental and cultural modeling, the social simulator can evolve into a powerful policy-oriented tool, strengthening the connection between computational social simulation and real-world rural planning.

Acknowledgements. The author Jairo Enrique Serrano Castañeda thanks MINCIENCIAS, the Pontificia Universidad Javeriana and the Universidad Tecnológica de Bolívar for the support received to pursue a doctoral degree within the programme "Becas de la Excelencia Doctoral del Bicentenario (corte 1)".

References

1. Abitbol, P.: En busca de la permanencia digna en el territorio. Economía & Región **11**(2), 339–359 (2017)
2. Adam, C., Gaudou, B.: BDI agents in social simulations: a survey. Knowl. Eng. Rev. **31**(3), 207–238 (2016). https://doi.org/10.1017/S0269888916000096
3. Aguilera Diaz, M.: Montes de María: Una subregión de economía campesina y empresarial. Banco de la Republica, p. 93 (2013)
4. Bourgais, M., Taillandier, P., Vercouter, L., Adam, C.: Emotion modeling in social simulation: a survey. JASSS **21**(2) (2018). https://doi.org/10.18564/jasss.3681
5. DANE: Pobreza monetaria (2021). https://www.dane.gov.co/index.php/estadisticas-por-tema/pobreza-y-condiciones-de-vida/pobreza-monetaria
6. Hevner, A.: A three cycle view of design science research. Scandinavian J. Inform. Syst. **19**(2) (1 2007)
7. Hevner, A.R., March, S.T., Park, J., Ram, S.: Design science in information systems research 1. Design Sci. IS Res. MIS Q. **28**(1), 75 (2004)
8. Junges, R., Klugl, F.: Behavior abstraction robustness in agent modeling. In: 2012 IEEE/WIC/ACM International Conferences on Web Intelligence and Intelligent Agent Technology, WI-IAT 2012, pp. 228–235. IEEE, Washington, DC, USA (Dec 2012). https://doi.org/10.1109/WI-IAT.2012.157
9. Melo, O.O., Luis, M., López, A., Sandra, P., Melo, E.: Diseño de Experimentos Métodos y Aplicaciones. Tech. rep
10. Mohajeri Parizi, M., Sileno, G., van Engers, T., Klous, S.: Run, agent, run! architecture and benchmarking of actor-based agents. In: Proceedings of the 10th ACM SIGPLAN International Workshop on Programming Based on Actors, Agents, and Decentralized Control., vol. 10, pp. 11–20. ACM, New York (Nov 2020). https://doi.org/10.1145/3427760.3428339
11. Naranjo-Palacios, F., Rios-Lira, A.J., Pantoja-Pacheco, Y.V., Tapia-Esquivias, M.: Diseños ortogonales de Taguchi fraccionados. Ingeniería, investigación y tecnología **21**(2), 1–12 (2020). https://doi.org/10.22201/FI.25940732E.2020.21N2.011
12. Ortony, A., Clore, G.L., Collins, A.: The Cognitive Structure of Emotions. Cambridge University Press (July 1988). https://doi.org/10.1017/CBO9780511571299
13. Rivera, M.A., Serrano, J.E., González, E.: World Model for the WellProdSim Agent-Based Social Simulator. CCIS, vol. 177, pp. 150–163 (2023). https://doi.org/10.1007/978-3-031-36357-3_12
14. Sánchez, Y., Coma, T., Aguelo, A., Cerezo, E.: ABC-EBDI: an affective framework for BDI agents. Cogn. Syst. Res. **58**, 195–216 (2019). https://doi.org/10.1016/J.COGSYS.2019.07.002
15. Secretaria Distrital de Desarrollo Económico: Economía campesina , soberanía y seguridad alimentarias . La experiencia de Mercados Campesinos en Bogotá y la región central de Colombia, pp. 1–271 (2011)
16. Serrano, J.E., González, E.: BDI Peasants Model for the WellProdSim Agent-Based Social Simulator, pp. 367–379 (2024). https://doi.org/10.1007/978-3-031-47372-2_29
17. Serrano, J.E., González, E.: Emotional BDI model (eBDI) of the peasants families WellProdSim social simulator. CCIS, vol. 2208, pp. 99–114 (2024). https://doi.org/10.1007/978-3-031-75233-9_8
18. Serrano, J.E., Rivera, M.A., González, E.: Time model for the WellProdSim agent-based social simulator. CCIS, vol. 1775, pp. 136–149 (2023). https://doi.org/10.1007/978-3-031-36357-3_11

19. Taillandier, P., Al, E.: Participatory modeling and simulation with the GAMA platform. J. Artif. Soc. Soc. Simul. **22**(2), 1–3 (2019)
20. Wieringa, R.J.: Statistical Difference-Making Experiments. In: Design Science Methodology for Information Systems and Software Engineering, pp. 295–317. Springer, Heidelberg (2014). https://doi.org/10.1007/978-3-662-43839-8_20
21. Zatelli, M.R., Ricci, A., Hübner, J.F.: Evaluating different concurrency configurations for executing multi-agent systems. In: Baldoni, M., Baresi, L., Dastani, M. (eds.) EMAS 2015. LNCS (LNAI), vol. 9318, pp. 212–230. Springer, Cham (2015). https://doi.org/10.1007/978-3-319-26184-3_12

Digital Twins and Virtual Assistants for Proactive Long-Term Care: The SALUS Architecture

Carlos Álvarez López[1,2(✉)], Alberto Rodríguez Pérez[2], Ricardo Alonso-Rincón[1], Albano Carrera[1], and Sara Rodríguez González[2]

[1] AIR Institute - Deep tech lab IoT Digital Innovation Hub, Av. Santiago Madrigal 39, Salamanca 37003, Castile and León, Spain
{calvarez,ralonso,acarrera}@air-institute.com
[2] BISITE Research Group, University of Salamanca, Edificio I+D+i, Calle Espejo 2, Salamanca 37007, Castile and León, Spain
{carlos_alvarez,albertorp,srg}@usal.es

Abstract. To address the growing need for intelligent long-term care (LTC) solutions, we introduce *SALUS*, a modular framework that integrates digital twin technology, conversational AI, and wearable IoT devices. The system maintains a dual digital twin architecture: a *physical twin* updated in real time with physiological data from non-intrusive smartwatches, and a *psychological twin* constructed through structured interactions with a Large Language Model (LLM)-based virtual assistant. These models are continuously synchronized to provide a holistic, longitudinal view of the patient's physical and cognitive-emotional health status.

SALUS enables the delivery of validated psychological assessments through natural, multimodal conversations adapted to the cognitive needs of elderly users, while concurrently monitoring biometric trends such as sleep quality, heart rate variability, and physical activity. Predictive analytics and explainable AI components support the early detection of health deterioration and allow caregivers to make timely, evidence-based decisions. The system adheres to ethical AI principles, supports HL7 FHIR-based interoperability, and includes dynamic form management for clinical adaptability.

Real-world scenarios demonstrate the framework's versatility across home care, cognitive rehabilitation, and institutional settings. SALUS contributes to the shift toward data-driven, user-centered LTC models capable of anticipating and responding to individual health trajectories.

Keywords: Digital Twin · Long-Term Care · Conversational AI · Elderly Monitoring · IoT Healthcare · Explainable Artificial Intelligence

A. Nongaillard et al. (Eds.): PAAMS 2025, CCIS 2644, pp. 42–53, 2025.
https://doi.org/10.1007/978-3-032-05925-3_4

1 Introduction

The global demographic shift towards aging populations presents an urgent challenge for health systems worldwide. As the need for long-term support increases, existing care models—based on intermittent check-ins and human-dependent monitoring—struggle to capture changes in a patient's physical and mental health as they occur. Long-Term Care (LTC) services are essential for individuals with chronic illnesses, disabilities, or age-related conditions requiring sustained assistance with activities of daily living. As global life expectancy continues to rise, the number of people requiring LTC is projected to increase significantly, placing growing pressure on health systems, caregivers, and families. In this context, LTC extends beyond purely medical care and encompasses physical, emotional, cognitive, and social support in both institutional and home settings.

The complexity and cost associated with LTC have prompted the exploration of new models of care that are proactive, continuous, and scalable. Technology-assisted approaches—particularly those involving remote monitoring and AI—are emerging as crucial enablers of personalized, efficient care delivery for older populations and individuals with progressive functional decline.

Despite advances in healthcare technology, several critical challenges persist in the domain of LTC. Physical health monitoring remains fragmented, often reliant on periodic in-person assessments, which fail to capture dynamic health fluctuations. Additionally, current systems are poorly equipped to detect subtle deteriorations or early warning signs—especially in decentralized, non-clinical environments. Mental health monitoring presents even greater limitations. Cognitive decline, depressive symptoms, and emotional distress are often underdiagnosed in LTC populations due to the lack of continuous, non-intrusive evaluation mechanisms. Traditional assessments rely on sporadic interviews or paper-based tools, which may not be well-suited for aging individuals, particularly those with mild cognitive impairment or communication barriers. Furthermore, existing solutions are rarely designed with user-centered adaptability, multimodal interaction, or data-driven personalization in mind. The integration of mental and physical health data remains minimal, hindering holistic understanding and proactive intervention.

To address these challenges, we present *SALUS*, a modular framework that enhances LTC through the convergence of Digital Twin (DT) technology, AI-powered Virtual Assistants, wearable Internet of Things (IoT) devices, and ethical artificial intelligence. The system is designed to construct a real-time, dynamic digital representation of both the physical and psychological state of the patient. In healthcare, a digital twin refers to a virtual model of a patient that is continuously updated with real-time data. Unlike static records, it integrates physiological signals, behavioral patterns, and historical clinical data into a dynamic representation. This model enables early detection of health deterioration, predictive simulation, and tailored intervention planning [5–7].

SALUS introduces a dual digital twin architecture—comprising a *physical twin* updated in real time with physiological data from non-intrusive smartwatches, and a *psychological twin* constructed through structured interactions with a Large Language Model (LLM)-based virtual assistant. These models are continuously synchronized to provide a holistic, longitudinal view of the patient's physical and cognitive-emotional health status [7,8].

To support psychological modeling, SALUS employs a conversational agent powered by an LLM. This assistant engages with patients in natural dialogue, administers validated psychological assessments, and adapts to cognitive and linguistic needs [2]. Unlike rule-based chatbots, LLMs offer semantic comprehension, contextual memory, and the flexibility to interact empathetically with users, particularly older adults. The system delivers clinically validated forms through multimodal conversations, ensuring inclusivity and accessibility for elderly users.

Additionally, SALUS leverages the Internet of People (IoP) paradigm by using smartwatches and ambient sensors to passively collect physiological data such as heart rate, sleep patterns, and activity levels [1,4]. These devices are non-intrusive and designed for daily use, making them ideal for long-term adherence in aging populations. The combination of ambient and wearable sensing allows SALUS to monitor physical health without requiring manual input, thereby reducing user burden and preserving autonomy.

The architecture is designed with interoperability as a core principle, ensuring compatibility with standard electronic health record (EHR) systems through HL7 FHIR, and incorporates explainable AI (XAI) components to guarantee transparency and trustworthiness in its predictive analytics [3]. This integration of semantic analysis, ethical AI design, and interoperability facilitates the creation of proactive, data-driven LTC models capable of anticipating and responding to individual health trajectories.

The main contributions of this work are: (i) the design of a bifocal digital twin architecture for synchronized physical and psychological health monitoring; (ii) the development of an LLM-based conversational assistant capable of delivering validated psychological assessments through natural dialogue adapted to elderly users; (iii) the implementation of interoperable, ethical AI modules for early risk detection and caregiver support; and (iv) the demonstration of SALUS's applicability across home care, cognitive rehabilitation, and institutional LTC settings through realistic use-case scenarios.

2 SALUS System Architecture

2.1 Overview of Methods and Technologies

The development of the SALUS architecture relies on the systematic integration of multiple advanced technologies, each contributing to the overall objective of proactive long-term care. The key technological components include:

- **Digital Twin Models**: Virtual representations of patients' physical and psychological states, updated in real time using multimodal data sources.
- **Large Language Model (LLM)-based Conversational AI**: A virtual assistant that administers validated psychological assessments and engages users in adaptive, empathetic dialogues.

- **Wearable IoT Devices**: Non-intrusive smartwatches that continuously capture physiological data such as heart rate, sleep quality, and activity levels.
- **Synchronization Engine**: A mechanism that aligns and integrates data from the physical and psychological twins, providing a unified health profile.
- **Explainable AI (XAI) Modules**: Predictive analytics components designed to detect early signs of health deterioration, with transparent and interpretable outputs.
- **Interoperability Layer**: RESTful APIs and HL7 FHIR-based standards ensuring seamless integration with electronic health records (EHR) and external systems.

The following subsections describe the architecture's structural layers and synchronization mechanisms in detail.

2.2 Overall Structure: IoP + AI + Interfaces + Digital Twin

The SALUS system is designed as a modular, scalable framework that integrates multiple technologies to enable intelligent, human-centered long-term care. Its architecture combines four main layers: (i) non-invasive data acquisition via Internet of People (IoP) devices, (ii) artificial intelligence modules for semantic understanding and prediction, (iii) adaptive user interfaces for conversational interaction, and (iv) real-time digital twin modeling.

At the foundation of the system lies the physical sensing layer, which uses smartwatches and ambient IoT sensors to capture vital signs and environmental data continuously. These data streams are sent to the SALUS backend through secure communication protocols, where AI modules process the inputs to update the patient's digital twin.

The intelligent interface layer consists of a virtual assistant powered by a Large Language Model (LLM). It facilitates naturalistic, multimodal communication with the user, enabling the delivery and interpretation of psychological assessments and general interaction. This component is responsible for generating structured and unstructured data for the psychological twin, while maintaining engagement and trust with elderly users.

Finally, a synchronization engine unifies both the physical and psychological dimensions of the digital twin into a coherent longitudinal representation. This multi-perspective model forms the basis for analytics, recommendations, and alerts, allowing caregivers to monitor patients holistically and proactively.

2.3 Synchronization Between Physical and Psychological Twins

The twin synchronization mechanism ensures that data collected from different modalities are temporally aligned and semantically harmonized. The physical twin continuously ingests biometric signals such as heart rate, blood oxygen saturation, sleep quality, and physical activity. In parallel, the psychological twin is constructed through regular interactions with the conversational assistant, which administers validated clinical instruments (e.g., GDS, GAD-7) and collects contextual feedback.

Both data streams are timestamped and stored in a common health event timeline. A set of synchronization rules—defined by domain experts and adaptable to patient profiles—determines how updates to one twin influence the other. For instance, a sudden increase in heart rate variability coupled with signs of anxiety in questionnaire responses may trigger a priority flag for caregiver review.

This integration allows SALUS to move beyond siloed monitoring systems and toward a unified model of the patient's evolving health status, in line with emerging digital twin frameworks in healthcare [8].

2.4 Interoperability, APIs, and Form Management

SALUS is designed with interoperability as a core principle, ensuring compatibility with standard electronic health record (EHR) systems and third-party services. The system implements RESTful APIs to facilitate secure data exchange, and follows widely adopted health information standards (e.g., HL7 FHIR) for structured data representation.

The psychological twin relies heavily on dynamic form management. Forms are not hardcoded but are defined through a flexible metadata schema that allows clinicians to deploy new assessments or modify existing ones without developer intervention. The LLM-based assistant interprets these form schemas to conduct structured dialogues, collect patient input, and store the results in a queryable database.

Furthermore, the API layer provides access points for caregiver dashboards, mobile health applications, and research analytics modules. This openness enables the integration of SALUS into broader care ecosystems, supporting real-world clinical decision-making and patient-centered innovation.

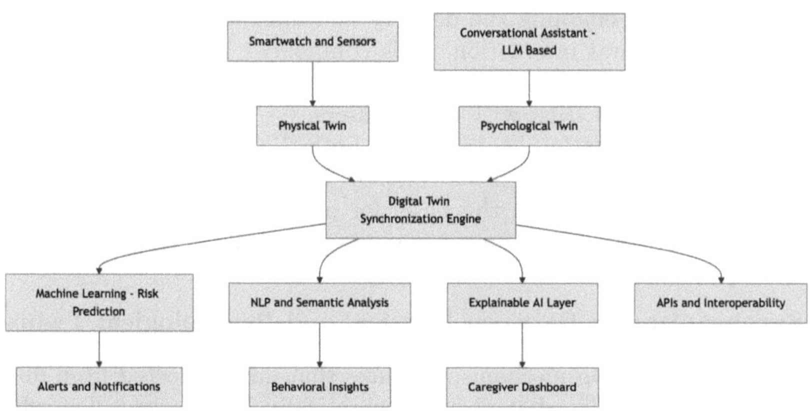

Fig. 1. SALUS system architecture integrating smart sensing, conversational AI, digital twin synchronization, and explainable predictive analytics.

3 Psychological Evaluation via Conversational AI

3.1 LLM-Based Chatbot Design

At the core of the psychological twin lies a virtual assistant powered by a Large Language Model (LLM), designed to interact naturally and empathetically with elderly users. Unlike conventional chatbots limited to rule-based responses, the LLM-based assistant in SALUS exhibits contextual awareness, semantic comprehension, and adaptability to individual cognitive capabilities.

The chatbot is deployed through a multimodal interface (text and voice) and tailored to accommodate sensory and cognitive limitations, ensuring inclusive and barrier-free communication. Through daily or weekly interactions, the assistant guides users in completing psychological assessments, tracks mood and engagement, and prompts self-reflection without clinical pressure.

To maintain clinical reliability, the assistant is constrained by a safety layer that ensures the preservation of medical intent, correct form delivery, and the detection of anomalous input. Additionally, it can escalate concerns to caregivers when certain behavioral or emotional thresholds are exceeded, thus serving as a proactive gatekeeper in long-term monitoring.

3.2 Administered Questionnaires (GDS, GAD-7, Pfeiffer)

SALUS incorporates validated and widely recognized psychological instruments into its conversational routines. Among these, the following tools are central to assessing mental well-being:

- **Geriatric Depression Scale (GDS)**: Evaluates depressive symptoms with age-appropriate phrasing and scoring.
- **Generalized Anxiety Disorder 7-item (GAD-7)**: Detects levels of anxiety through seven targeted items.
- **Pfeiffer Short Portable Mental Status Questionnaire (SPMSQ)**: Screens cognitive function and identifies potential impairment.

These assessments are delivered conversationally, with the LLM interpreting user responses in real time. The system handles both direct responses and nuanced expressions, adjusting the pacing, tone, and clarification prompts to match user behavior. This makes the evaluation process more comfortable and more representative of the patient's actual condition, especially for those who may struggle with traditional test administration formats.

3.3 NLP and Semantic Analysis of Responses

Once the user provides input—either through free-form language or selected responses—the system processes the data using Natural Language Processing (NLP) pipelines that extract semantic and affective features. Sentiment analysis, emotional tone detection, and entity recognition are applied to generate a rich feature vector for each interaction.

These vectors are then mapped onto the psychological digital twin model to create a dynamic profile of the user's mental and emotional state over time. Importantly, the NLP layer is tuned to minimize biases and misinterpretations, particularly in the context of aging-related linguistic variation and cultural diversity.

In accordance with guidelines for trustworthy AI in healthcare, all NLP decisions are logged and traceable for validation and clinician oversight [3].

3.4 Adaptive Multimodal Interaction

Recognizing the heterogeneity in LTC patient populations, SALUS offers adaptive interaction modes that account for sensory, cognitive, and emotional preferences. The assistant automatically adjusts its speech rate, complexity, and interactivity based on prior user behavior and real-time engagement signals.

Visual aids, simplified interfaces, and alternative input modalities (e.g., touch or voice selection) are also supported to ensure accessibility. These features not only improve the quality and completeness of the psychological data collected but also foster long-term user adherence and trust in the system [9].

The integration of these adaptive mechanisms into the conversational loop represents a significant innovation in human-AI collaboration in geriatric care, bridging the gap between clinical assessment and day-to-day patient experience.

4 Physical Monitoring via IoT Devices and the Physical Twin

4.1 Collected Parameters and Physiological Data Streams

The SALUS framework continuously monitors a range of physiological parameters using non-intrusive wearable devices, primarily smartwatches. These devices are equipped with sensors capable of capturing health-related metrics such as heart rate (HR), blood oxygen saturation (SpO_2), step count, sleep quality, and physical activity intensity.

Unlike traditional point-in-time assessments, SALUS ensures a high temporal resolution of data acquisition, which allows for the detection of subtle trends and transient anomalies. Data are streamed securely in real time, encoded with metadata for contextualization (e.g., time of day, motion state), and stored in a time-series database to support longitudinal analysis and twin modeling.

This continuous feed forms the foundation of the physical digital twin, which evolves dynamically and serves as the input for higher-level predictive models.

4.2 Wearable Device Integration and User Adherence

Smartwatches were selected based on their accessibility, user familiarity, and ability to balance precision with comfort. Their non-invasive nature is particularly beneficial for elderly users, who may be reluctant or unable to interact with more obtrusive or clinical-grade devices [4].

The system includes modules to ensure data integrity and user adherence. For instance, feedback loops monitor signal quality and device usage patterns, prompting the user via the conversational assistant if data collection is interrupted. Battery level monitoring and device connectivity checks are also integrated into the backend, minimizing gaps in physiological monitoring.

The data pipeline includes preprocessing steps such as artifact filtering, normalization, and segmentation, which enhance the reliability of downstream analytics and synchronization with psychological data.

4.3 Correlations Between Physical and Mental Health

One of the distinguishing features of SALUS is its ability to identify correlations between physiological indicators and psychological assessments. For example, poor sleep quality, reduced physical activity, or elevated resting heart rate may correlate with depressive or anxious states, and their co-occurrence can serve as early indicators of health deterioration.

By aligning time-stamped sensor data with the results of LLM-administered psychological forms, the system can generate hypotheses about cause-effect relationships or latent health states. This multimodal integration enables the derivation of complex behavioral health trajectories and supports timely clinical interventions.

These cross-domain associations are visualized within the caregiver interface, offering insights into patient conditions that may not be immediately evident through unidimensional data views. This reflects a broader trend in healthcare towards holistic, data-driven care strategies facilitated by intelligent systems [8].

5 Predictive Modeling and Explainability

5.1 Machine Learning Models for Risk Detection

A core functionality of the SALUS system is its ability to detect early signs of health deterioration through predictive modeling. Data collected from the physical and psychological digital twins are transformed into structured feature sets, which are fed into supervised machine learning models trained to identify deviations from individual health baselines.

Models implemented include decision trees, gradient boosting machines, and temporal convolutional networks for time-series analysis. These algorithms are trained using historical labeled data and continuously updated as new data from the patient stream in. The prediction targets include events such as cognitive decline, onset of depressive symptoms, acute physiological instability, or significant changes in behavior patterns.

The personalization of these models is achieved through adaptive thresholds and patient-specific baselining. Rather than relying on population-wide norms, the system emphasizes intra-individual trends, which improves both sensitivity and specificity of alerts.

5.2 Trustworthy and Transparent Inference

To ensure clinical reliability and acceptance, SALUS incorporates explainable AI (XAI) mechanisms that provide transparency into how decisions and predictions are generated. The system uses techniques such as SHAP (Shapley Additive Explanations) and LIME (Local Interpretable Model-agnostic Explanations) to identify which input features most significantly influenced a given prediction.

The system presents visual and textual summaries to both clinicians and caregivers, facilitating interpretability. This supports informed decision-making, improves accountability, and builds trust in AI-assisted care pathways.

The transparency layer is not limited to clinicians; simplified explanations are also provided to patients and families to promote understanding and engagement with the system's recommendations.

5.3 Ethical and Regulatory Considerations

The use of AI in healthcare—particularly with vulnerable populations such as elderly individuals—demands strict adherence to ethical and legal frameworks. SALUS is developed in alignment with the principles of Trustworthy AI as defined by the European Commission: human agency, technical robustness, privacy and data governance, transparency, non-discrimination, and accountability.

Data collected from wearables and conversations are stored and processed in compliance with GDPR, and all user-facing components include explicit consent mechanisms. Risk prediction models are audited periodically to detect potential biases or unintended discrimination, particularly with respect to age, gender, or cognitive ability.

SALUS also provides mechanisms for human-in-the-loop validation, enabling clinicians to override or annotate AI-generated insights when clinical judgment deems it necessary. This approach ensures that AI acts as an augmentative tool—supporting, not replacing—expert human care.

Additionally, one limitation of the current version is the reliance on continuous connectivity and device wearability, which may affect data completeness in real-world deployments.

Despite their promise, digital twins face technical and organizational challenges in healthcare, including data integration, standardization, and scalability [10], which SALUS addresses through modular design and interoperability with HL7 FHIR.

6 Use Cases and Impact

SALUS provides tangible benefits across multiple dimensions of long-term care. By combining real-time physiological monitoring with conversational psychological assessment, it enables early detection of health deterioration that might otherwise go unnoticed. Its dual digital twin architecture supports both reactive and proactive interventions, allowing for timely, personalized responses tailored to the patient's evolving condition.

The system also enhances care coordination by offering caregivers a comprehensive, continuously updated model of the patient's status. Context-aware prompts, behavioral trend analysis, and predictive alerts facilitate more accurate decisions and reduce the burden on both formal and informal care teams. This improves resource allocation, strengthens preventive care, and promotes greater autonomy for elderly users. These capabilities align with current advances in AI-supported health monitoring and demonstrate the potential of digital twins to transform long-term care delivery.

The following use cases demonstrate SALUS's practical applications across distinct long-term care environments:

- **Scenario 1: Home Monitoring.** An elderly patient lives alone and is monitored via a smartwatch and conversational assistant. After a drop in sleep quality and a rise in anxiety-related dialogue cues, the system detects a pattern consistent with early depressive symptoms and notifies the assigned caregiver.
- **Scenario 2: Cognitive Rehabilitation.** A patient in cognitive rehabilitation interacts with the assistant daily. Changes in reaction time and form responses over several weeks reveal a decline in attention consistency. The clinician uses this information to adjust therapeutic goals.
- **Scenario 3: Facility-Level Monitoring.** A long-term care facility deploys SALUS across multiple residents. The aggregated data helps staff identify environmental patterns affecting sleep quality and mobility, prompting an adjustment in activity scheduling.

These use cases illustrate how SALUS can increase responsiveness, enable early interventions, and deliver measurable improvements in care quality across diverse LTC scenarios.

7 Conclusions

This paper has presented SALUS, an integrated architecture that combines digital twin modeling, LLM-based virtual assistants, and wearable IoT devices to enable proactive and personalized long-term care. The system integrates real-time data streams from physical and psychological sources, maintaining synchronized digital twins that evolve alongside the patient's condition.

By leveraging conversational AI, SALUS facilitates continuous and accessible mental health assessments, while wearable devices ensure unobtrusive physical monitoring. Predictive analytics and explainable AI modules transform this data into actionable insights, supporting timely and informed decision-making by caregivers. The modular design ensures interoperability, patient-centered adaptability, and compliance with ethical principles in data governance.

The analyzed use-case scenarios demonstrate SALUS's capacity to detect early signs of health deterioration, personalize interventions, and enhance care coordination in both home and institutional long-term care settings.

Nevertheless, the system faces certain limitations that must be addressed. The psychological twin currently relies on structured assessments, which may limit its sensitivity to subtle or spontaneous cognitive and emotional changes. Additionally, integration with heterogeneous electronic health record (EHR) systems and acceptance by clinical staff pose further challenges that need to be considered for large-scale adoption.

7.1 Future Work

Future development efforts will focus on validating SALUS through clinical trials and real-world deployments in diverse long-term care environments, assessing its impact on health outcomes, caregiver workload, and patient engagement over extended periods.

To mitigate current limitations, future work will expand the psychological twin by incorporating naturalistic interaction analysis, emotional reasoning, and advanced natural language processing techniques to better capture subtle behavioral and emotional changes. The adoption of federated learning strategies is also planned to enhance model generalization while preserving data privacy.

Interoperability with existing healthcare infrastructures will be addressed through improved compatibility with standards such as HL7 FHIR and by engaging healthcare professionals in co-design processes. Additionally, the development of tailored explainability tools will ensure that AI-generated insights are interpretable and actionable for caregivers with varying levels of technical expertise.

These efforts aim to ensure the effective integration of SALUS into routine care workflows, fostering its adoption as a valuable tool for patient-centered long-term care.

Acknowledgments. This publication is part of the project "Personalized long-term care via trustworthy internet of people for senescence (SALUS)" (PLEC2022-009469), funded by MICIU/AEI/10.13039/501100011033 and by the European Union "NextGenerationEU"/PRTR".

Disclosure of Interests. The authors have no competing interests to declare that are relevant to the content of this article.

References

1. Hossain, M.S., Muhammad, G., Hossain, M.A., Muhammad, F.: IoT-based smart healthcare for monitoring elderly people at home. IEEE Access **7**, 135139–135152 (2019)
2. Enam, M.A., Murmu, C., Dixon, E.: Artificial intelligence - carrying us into the future: a study of older adults' perceptions of LLM-based chatbots. Int. J. Hum.-Comput. Interact. **22**, 1–24 (2025). https://doi.org/10.1080/10447318.2025.2476710

3. Aziz, N.A., Manzoor, A., Qureshi, M.D.M., Qureshi, M.A., Rashwan, W.: Unveiling Explainable AI in Healthcare: Current Trends, Challenges, and Future Directions. medRxiv (2024). https://doi.org/10.1101/2024.08.10.24311735
4. Alam, M.R., Reaz, M.B.I., Ali, M.A.M.: A review of smart homes—past, present, and future. IEEE Trans. Syst. Man Cybern. C Appl. Rev. **42**(6), 1190–1203 (2012). https://doi.org/10.1109/TSMCC.2012.2189204
5. El-Warrak, L., de Farias, C.M.: The state of the art of digital twins in health–a quick review of the literature. Computers **13**(9), 228 (2024). https://doi.org/10.3390/computers13090228
6. Garanin, A.A., Aydumova, O.Y., Kiselev, A.R.: Digital twins in healthcare administration: a systematic review on novel approaches to management and planning. Russian Open Med. J. **14**, e0104 (2025)
7. Mikołajewska, E., Masiak, J., Mikołajewski, D.: Applications of artificial intelligence-based patient digital twins in decision support in rehabilitation and physical therapy. Electronics **13**(24), 4994 (2024). https://doi.org/10.3390/electronics13244994
8. Nadeem, M., Kostic, S., Dornhöfer, M., Weber, C., Fathi, M.: A comprehensive review of digital twin in healthcare in the scope of simulative health-monitoring. Digit. Health **11**, 20552076241304080 (2025)
9. Miner, A.S., Milstein, A., Schueller, S.M., Thakur, N., Lattie, E.G., Mohr, D.C.: Objective measurement of patient engagement with mental health apps: systematic review and meta-analysis. J. Med. Internet Res. **22**(5), e17698 (2020)
10. Quazi, F., Raju, N., Viradia, V., Bhat, A.: Digital twin technology in healthcare: applications, challenges, and future insights. Int. J. Glob. Innov. Solut. (IJGIS) (2024). https://doi.org/10.21428/e90189c8.bdb0264f

Development of a Method for Calculating the Parameters of an Agricultural Crop for a Digital Twin of Plants

Petr Skobelev[1(✉)], Aleksey Tabachinskiy[2], Elena Simonova[3], Aleksey Galuzin[3], and Mihail Tabachinskiy[3]

[1] Samara Federal Research Scientific Center RAS, 3a Studencheskiy Lane, 443001 Samara, Russia
petr.skobelev@gmail.com
[2] Samara State Technical University, 244, Molodogvardeyskaya Street, 443100 Samara, Russia
tabachinski.as@samgtu.ru
[3] Samara National Research University, 34 Moskovskoye Shosse, 443086 Samara, Russia
simonova.elena.v@gmail.com

Abstract. The article proposes a new robust method for calculating the parameters of an agricultural crop in a digital twin of plants, depending on weather conditions and resource constraints. The method will enable the use of decision-making rules from a knowledge base in a multi-agent planning tool for adaptive recalculation of plant growth and development stages based on an ontological model of the crop variety and environmental factors. The method's effectiveness is confirmed by an example of the implementation of a digital twin prototype for winter wheat culture.

Keywords: precision agriculture · smart farming · digital twin of plants · crop variety model · multi-agent technology · knowledge base · ontology

1 Introduction

Currently, traditional farming practices are becoming increasingly ineffective due to the following reasons: global climate changes leading to moisture shortages, soil erosion, insect migration, etc.; outdated knowledge, as crop varieties change more rapidly and new machinery and technologies emerge; a decrease in the land area suitable for crop production; a reduction in labor resources available for agriculture; and growing demands for environmentally friendly products.

In the era of Agriculture 4.0, agriculture is transitioning to intelligent farming systems [1]. The monograph [2] analyzes a wide range of crop production technologies, including precision farming, decision support systems, digital twins, and more, as well as their application prospects covering the entire agricultural production and supply chain.

The main goal of developing a digital twin of plants (DTP) is to create a tool for agronomists and crop production farms to simulate and forecast crop development at

A. Nongaillard et al. (Eds.): PAAMS 2025, CCIS 2644, pp. 54–65, 2025.
https://doi.org/10.1007/978-3-032-05925-3_5

all stages of their life cycle. This approach considers the plant simulation as a complex adaptive system based on the formalization of domain knowledge. Its behavior is determined by the interaction between its "integrity" and relatively autonomous "elements" that can perceive environmental conditions, make independent decisions, and coordinate these decisions with each other, taking into account existing preferences and constraints based on environmental factors and agronomic characteristics of the crops.

The article has the following structure. The introduction defines the goal of developing DTP. Section 2 provides a brief overview of publications on plant growth simulation methods. Section 3 describes the agent-based concept of the DTP. Section 4 discusses the method for calculating plant parameters using an ontological variety model of the crop. Section 5 presents experimental validation of the DTP prototype's functionality. Section 6 summarizes the results of the current developments and outlines directions for further advancement of the DTP.

2 State of the Art

In recent years, the use of digital twins has become common practice in agricultural farms for managing greenhouse infrastructure [3], water and soil resources [4, 5], field landscape modeling [6], and agricultural supply chain management [7].

In the field of plant growth and development simulation two dominant approaches have traditionally been used: process-based (physical) models and data-driven statistical methodologies [8]. Process-based models consist of mathematical equations that predict plant behavior, morphology, and growth as functions of environmental conditions, genetics, and management practices.

The AGROTOOL system describes the main processes within the "soil-plant-atmosphere" system from sowing to full maturity [9]. The plant is considered a self-regulating system in which the distribution of growth resources among various vegetative and generative organs depends on the balance of key limiting nutrients. The core algorithm of the model, based on a system of finite-difference equations, allows for the recursive computation of the vector of values that define the characteristics of the agroecosystem at the next calculation step, given the known state of this vector at the previous step.

There are well-known systems for simulating biophysical processes based on functional dynamic simulation modeling of agro-biosystem processes within the process-based approach. These include WOFOST – World Food Studies Simulation Model (Netherlands) [10], DSSAT – Decision Support System for Agrotechnology Transfer and CSM – DSSAT Cropping System Model (Austria), the IBSNAT project – International Benchmark Sites Network for Agrotechnology Transfer (USA), and APSIM –Agricultural Production Systems SIMulator (Australia) [11]. The listed models are semi-empirical, have a similar structure and differ in the nomenclature and details of the description of individual blocks.

Data-driven models incorporate computational algorithms that process large volumes of historical and operational real-time data using statistical methods, machine learning, pattern recognition, or data mining techniques. The models are designed to analyze the characteristics of collected data to provide general insights into trends and development patterns [12].

M. Stock et al. note that models often operate at a single point in the time-space domain, limiting their applicability beyond the initial conceptualization [8]. Therefore, promising developments lie at the intersection of the paradigms of physical plant growth simulation and machine learning [13].

Agent-based modeling (ABM) has become a widely accepted methodology in many areas of biology, ranging from the cellular level to ecological populations and communities [14]. ABMs are bottom–up models that can reproduce at the macro level the processes resulting from interactions at the micro level. Therefore, ABMs are naturally suitable for modeling various scale phenomena in crop production, including plant growth, resource allocation, reproduction, and more.

The analysis of plant growth and development models has shown that process-based models are complex to apply and adjust to the individual characteristics of crops in farms. Their expansion, modification, and development by agronomists require significant computational resources. Data-driven models require large volumes of training data and provide approximate results. By combining physical process modeling with real-world data using machine learning methods in DTP, more accurate predictions and agro-technological decisions can be achieved.

The development of ontologically adaptable agent-based methods for planning growth stages in DTP facilitates the scaling of DTP applications by creating knowledge bases and variety models for different crops.

3 Description of the Concept of the Digital Twin of Plants

A digital twin of a plant is a virtual representation of a real crop, enabling the prediction and simulation of its state and behavior in a computer environment. In the authors' research, concepts and approaches were developed for planning the production process of plant as a sequence of stages and a set of parameters characterizing each stage [15, 16].

Agents were identified to meet the requirements and business processes of a farm while accounting for the specific features of the plant production process. These include agents for the field, crop, entire plant, resources and plant parts, growth and development stages, environment, and agronomist.

Agent negotiations are conducted according to a modified Contract-Net protocol, which regulates the interaction between task (order) agents and resource agents based on the compensation method [17]. Conflict resolution among agents for resources is carried out through a series of modifications to individual agent plans until a solution is reached that satisfies all agents (in terms of the system's overall objective function) and no possible rearrangement can further improve the solution. A fragment of the agents' negotiation protocol is shown in Fig. 1.

The digital twin operates based on a discrete-event principle [18], where the agent dispatcher sequentially allocates a time quantum to each agent for processing its state, and then the agent returns control to the dispatcher.

The algorithm of the DTP functioning is presented below, according to which an adaptive plan for the growth and development of culture is formed:

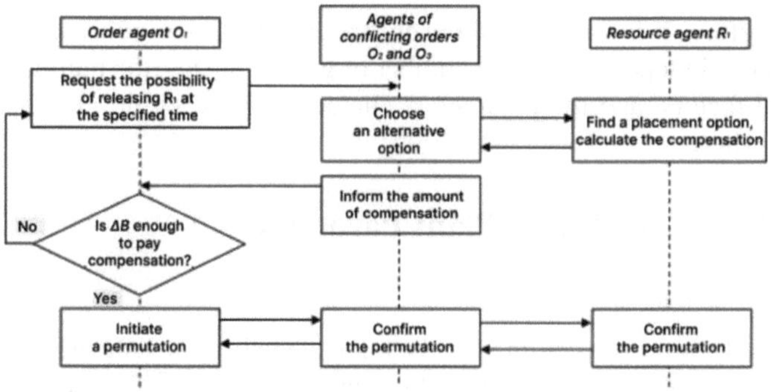

Fig. 1. A fragment of the agents' negotiation protocol.

1. An agent is created for each field, taking into account its agronomic conditions—terrain relief, previous crops, soil condition, and fertilization history.
2. Agents for plants and growth stages are created for each crop in every field based on the description of growth stages specified in the knowledge base. A nominal plant development plan (averaged for the crop) is formed by simulating the timing of stage transitions, during which agro-technological operations, field sensor readings, or agronomist field visits are expected to take place.
3. The set of agents within the overall multi-agent environment creates a multi-agent scene of the agricultural farm.
4. At each time step, each DTP agent reads the step-by-step event log observed in the scene, evaluates input data related to a specific event, executes rules describing the transition process to the next stage, and outputs the calculation results back into the scene, returning control to the dispatcher.
5. Crop agents set critical monitoring dates and schedule agro-technical operations for the crops.
6. The agent of each field determines the difference between the nominal (stored in the knowledge base) and actual plant development plans based on events. Upon receiving data updates on soil or weather conditions, the field agent activates the corresponding crop agent to recalculate its state at each associated growth stage. After recalculating, it sends a message with adjustments to the schedule of agro-technical operations.
7. The agent of each crop compares its input parameters with actual data, and when they reach a critical level, it signals the multi-agent planner about the need for additional resources, such as fertilizers and protective measures, and initiates the corresponding operations.
8. The results of DTP simulation are stored in a database and are available for users to view at any time. Thus, the proposed approach simulates the interaction between the plant as a whole and its growth stages, where stage agents collaboratively coordinate growth plans based on synchronization with real plants to achieve maximum yield.

The creation of DTP involves solving a complex multifactorial problem that must account for environmental conditions and the internal state of the plant, which is characterized by nonlinear growth dynamics. The broad taxonomy of agricultural crops leads to significant physiological and morphological differences between various crops and varieties. Therefore, it is essential to develop a universal method for calculating plant parameters that is independent of the number of growth stages, the number and types of environmental factors, and the parameters characterizing each development stage and the plant as a whole.

4 Method for Calculating Plant Parameters

4.1 Method Description

For each stage of the crop, as defined in the knowledge base, a dedicated software agent is created, responsible for determining the plant parameters. The ontological variety model includes growth stages, their input and output parameters, whose values serve as input parameters for the multi-agent stage planning model. Input parameters refer to environmental factors that directly affect plants at a specific growth stage, as well as sowing parameters such as sowing technology, seed quality characteristics, variety, crop type, etc.

For a given agricultural crop variety, the development process is defined as a sequence of stages $Process = \{stage_i\}, i = \overline{1, L}$, where L – the number of growth stages. For each stage, a list of input and output parameters is defined. For each input and output parameter, a set of discrete values is specified over the entire modeling interval: $X_i = \{x_{ij}\}, j = \overline{1, K}$, K – the number of influencing parameters for the i-th growth stage of the crop; $Y_i = \{y_{ik}\}, k = \overline{1, M}$, M – the number of output parameters for the i-th growth stage of the crop. The output parameters of one stage can serve as input parameters for the next stage: $X_{i+1} \subset Y_i$.

For each plant variety, an ontological model is created based on the ontology of plant cultivation, which includes a semantic network of input and output parameters of plant stages. The ontological model of variety is specified in the developed system by uploading a JSON-file.

The calculation of the stage agent is based on the assessment of environmental factors, or in other words, the agent's satisfaction with each factor and the evaluation of their combined impact. To calculate the agent's satisfaction, actual (or forecasted, if the calculation is for a future date) factor values are used, as well as growth rules of the crop, which define the plant's sensitivity and response to each factor. The set of unique growth rules and responses is contained in the ontological variety model, which allows for evaluating the satisfaction of a sowing parameter with a specific factor and defining the development dynamics if the output parameter of the current stage depends on the value of the same parameter received as an input from the previous stage. A fragment of the variety model for winter wheat of the "Basis" variety is presented in Table 1.

The variety model uses a parameter tube that defines the range of variation for each parameter influencing plant development. This includes an optimal value, representing the best possible growth, as well as an arbitrary number of other points that determine different plant behavior within the intervals defined by these points. It also includes critical values, beyond which normal plant development becomes impossible. An example of the parameter tube is shown in Fig. 2.

For each output parameter, tubes are specified that define the rules of influence of the input parameter on the output: $tube^l_{ik} = \left\{tubeItem^{lq}_{ik}\right\}, l = \overline{1, L}, q = \overline{1, Q}$, where L

Table 1. A fragment of the variety model for winter wheat of the "Basis" variety.

Stage	Input parameter	Interval	Subject to change	
			Stem length, cm	Yield, t/ha
Tillering	Air temperature, °C	30	13	68
		14	14	71
		3	11	66
	Humidity, %	90	13	68
		65	14	71
		15	11	66
	Stem length, cm	15	17	70
		10	14	71
		7	11	66

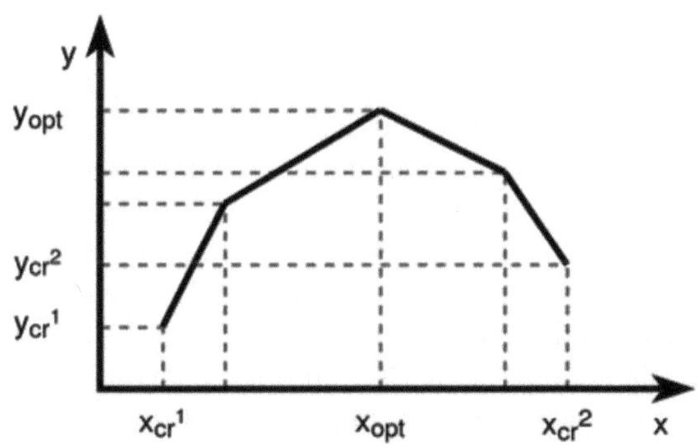

Fig. 2. Plant parameter tube in the variety model.

– the number of input parameters affecting the k-th output parameter of the i-th stage, and Q – the number of intervals in the tube. The interval of the parameter tube is defined as follows:

$tubeItem_{ik}^{lq} = \{tubeBorder_{ik}^{lq}, tubeBorder_{ik}^{l(q+1)}, deltaOutValue_{ik}^{lq}\}$,

$deltaOutValue_{ik}^{lq} = \left\{deltaOutValue_{ik}^{lqp}\right\}, p = \overline{1, P}$, P – the number of intervals for the duration of the input parameter's influence on the output parameter within one tube interval.

The change in the output parameter within a single parameter tube interval is calculated as $\Delta y_{ip} = \frac{deltaOutValue_{ik}^{lq}}{stageDuration_i} * intervalDuration_{ip}$. The final change in the output parameter value is the sum of its changes over the intervals of continuous inclusion in the parameter tube $\Delta Y_i = \sum \Delta y_{ip}$. The output parameter value of the stage $Y_i = Y_i + \Delta Y_i$.

Plant development deviations are accounted for using penalties B. The penalty-based multi-agent model is built on calculating the stage agent's satisfaction with each output parameter, with rules defined in the variety model for each stage, each input parameter, and each factor. The maximum satisfaction of the agent corresponds to the optimal value of the output parameter, i.e., the optimal trajectory of plant development at the stage represented by the agent. The predicted value of the output parameter, returned by the agent, is necessary to determine the agent's satisfaction with this parameter, which is equal to the ratio of the predicted value Y to the optimal value *Yopt*. Satisfaction S can be understood as a value logically inverse to the penalty B: $S = 1 - |B|$, where the penalty value is taken in absolute terms to account for the decrease in satisfaction in cases of both exceeding and not reaching the output parameter value. A negative penalty means an increase in the parameter due to the influence of the factor.

$$B = \frac{Y_{opt} - Y}{Y_{opt}} \cdot 100\%.$$

The duration of the stage based on the sum of active temperatures (SAT) is calculated using the formula:

$$\sum_{i=0}^{n} T_i < T_{SAT} < \sum_{i=0}^{n+1} T_i,$$

where T – the set of daily temperature output values, i – the day index.

The stage duration based on SAT is determined by the first index at which the cumulative temperature exceeds the value specified in the KB as T_{CAT}.

The duration increment ("delta") is an additional parameter of the crop, which, depending on the influence of factors, either increases or decreases the duration of the stage calculated based on the primary rule for SAT specified in the variety model. For example, the agent's satisfaction with air temperature depends non-linearly on air humidity. When calculating the "delta," this allows accounting for the plant's resource needs, as high temperature and high humidity create optimal growth conditions for the plant. In such conditions, the stage is extended to increase the vegetative mass. The intervals of the dependency of the stage duration on temperature and air humidity are described in the variety model as follows:

$$\Delta_i = \frac{x_i}{x_{opt}}; x \in \left(-\infty; x_{opt}\right],$$

$$\Delta_i = \frac{2x_i}{x_{\max crit}}; x \in \left(x_{opt}; +\infty\right],$$

where x – the humidity tube values from the variety model

For each factor, a daily assessment of the violation intervals is performed, after which the resulting "delta" for the violation is determined as the product of the violation duration coefficient ($k_{duration}$) to the arithmetic mean of the daily "delta" value:

$$\Delta_{res} = k_{duration} \cdot \mu(\Delta_i) = \frac{i}{n_{stage}} \cdot \mu(\Delta_i),$$

where the duration coefficient is equal to the ratio of the number of violation days to the duration of the stage calculated in the previous iteration (for $i = 1$, the base stage duration is assumed).

Next, the impact of the combination of factors on the stage duration is determined. Stages may end upon the occurrence of events defined in the KB, such as the "non-growing period start" for winter cultures. During the non-growing period, development stops: daily penalties are not considered, planting parameters remain unchanged, and a new growth stage does not begin. If the non-growing is not started for the crop, vegetation does not stop under any conditions.

To implement the continuous process of plant growth and development, the rules in the KB that drive the multi-agent model estimates correlation between the output parameter values at the current stage and the values of the same parameters received from agents of previous stage. This represents the rate of change in the specified parameter during the stage duration, i.e. the plant's potential for growth. The potential is equal to the difference between the parameter value at the previous stage and the target value at the end of the current stage. Table 2 shows the rule for the dependence of the stem length at the "Leaf development" stage on the stem length in the previous "Seedling emergence" stage, for the winter wheat variety "Basis", as defined in the variety model.

Table 2. The potential of the "Stem length" parameter, as defined in the variety model.

Parameter	Value	"Seedling Emergence"	"Leaf development"
Stem length, cm	Critical max	15	16
	Optimal	6	11
	Critical min	4	8

If other influences on the plant (input and output parameters) are optimal, then when the plant reaches a stem length of 6 cm at the "Seedling" stage, it will grow to 11 cm at the "Leaf development" stage, which is considered normal. If the plant has overdeveloped and reached a stem length of 15 cm by the end of the "Seedling" stage, then its growth during the next stage will be minimal, reaching only 16 cm. Thus, based on this parametric dependency, the potential of the plant is determined. This is achieved over the duration of the entire stage, provided that the agent's satisfaction with all factors during the stage equals one. When the actual value of the parameter, calculated in the previous stage, lies within a given interval, the potential of the parameter for the next stage is determined using linear interpolation.

4.2 Algorithm for Calculating Plant Development Parameters

Algorithm 1 presents pseudocode for calculating crop output parameters in a stage agent. The calculation of parameters is performed after calculating the duration of all stages (with increments), inactive days of the production process and penalties by the environmental input parameters.

```
Algorithm 1: Algorithm for calculating plant parameters by
the stage agent
Input: stages - a list of the culture-specific stages, in-
put_value_list - a table of values for input parameters
Output: output_parameters_set - a list of stage-specific out-
put parameters
1:  previous_stage_value = 0
2:  output_parameters_set = []
3:  plant_alive = true
4:  for stage in stages do
5:    output_parameters = phase.output_parameters
6:    output_parameters_list = []
7:    for output_parameter in output_parameters do
8:      input_parameters = output_parameter.input_parameters
9:      stage_deltas = []
10:     for input_parameter in input_parameters do
11:       critical_range = get_critical_range(input_parameter,
12:       input_value_list[phase])
13:       if input_parameter < critical_range.min OR
14:       input_parameter > critical_range.max then
15:         plant_alive = false
16:         break
17:       end if
18:       delta = calculate_delta(input_parameter,
19:       input_value_list[phase])
20:       phase_deltas add delta
21:     end for
22:     if not plant_alive then
23:       print "The plant died"
24:       break
25:     end if
26:     average_delta = calculate_average(phase_deltas)
27:     output_value = average_delta + previous_stage_value
28:     output_parameters_list add output_value
29:     previous_stage_value = output_value
30:   end for
31:   output_parameters_set add output_parameters_list
32: end for
33: return output_parameters_set
```

The algorithm starts with entering the values of the input parameters for all stages according to their duration. At each phase (4), for each output parameter (7), the entered value is compared with the corresponding tube of this input parameter (13–14): if the value goes beyond the critical values of the tube, the plant dies (15); if not, the output parameter delta is calculated (18). Then, the average value of the output parameter delta is calculated for all input parameters (26). The final value of the output parameter is calculated as the sum of the average value of the output parameter and the value from the previous stage (27). As a result, the obtained values of the plant output parameters for each phase are added to the list (31).

5 Experimental Studies

The functionality of the agricultural crop parameter calculation method was experimentally tested using the software prototype of the DTP (Fig. 3), which implements the following features:

1. Maintaining a list of fields on the agricultural farm and the crops planted on them;
2. Managing the list of crops: defining crops, varieties, sowing dates, and technological maps for crops;
3. Managing the list of connected weather stations for collecting environmental data;
4. Viewing the simulation results of crop parameters;
5. Entering actual data obtained from crop scouting for synchronizing virtual crops;
6. Creating hypothetical crop growth scenarios to test "what-if" scenarios.

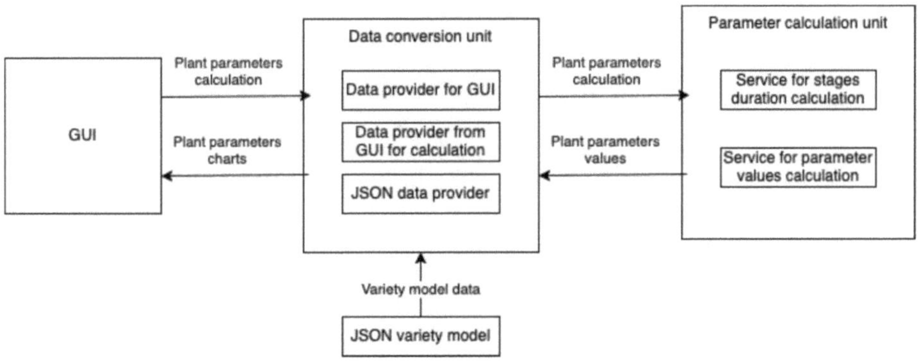

Fig. 3. Dataflow of the system.

For simulation, input parameter tubes for the winter wheat variety "Basis" were used, which were entered into the DTP KB. Observations of crops were conducted on experimental plots of the Samara Research Institute of Agriculture in 2023–2024. The graph of the boundary values of the "Air temperature" factor tube and the input value of the factor at each stage is shown in Fig. 4.

Figure 5 shows the results of experiments with different scenarios: (1) optimal cultivation conditions; (2) nutrient excess – more than optimal moisture in the soil is simulated in the early stages of plant growth; (3) drought conditions – low moisture is simulated in the early stages of plant growth; (4) nutrient lack – nitrogen deficiency in the soil is simulated in the early stages of plant development.

The conducted researches have shown, that the developed model adequately reacts to external events, and corresponds with field experiments. This proves the model can be applied by agronomists and can be further developed.

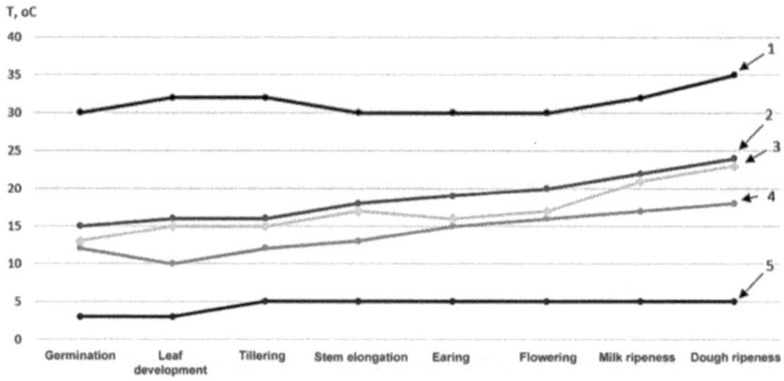

Fig. 4. Chart of air temperature: 1 – critical maximum, 2 – recommended maximum, 3 – the input value of the factor, 4 – recommended minimum, 5 – critical minimum.

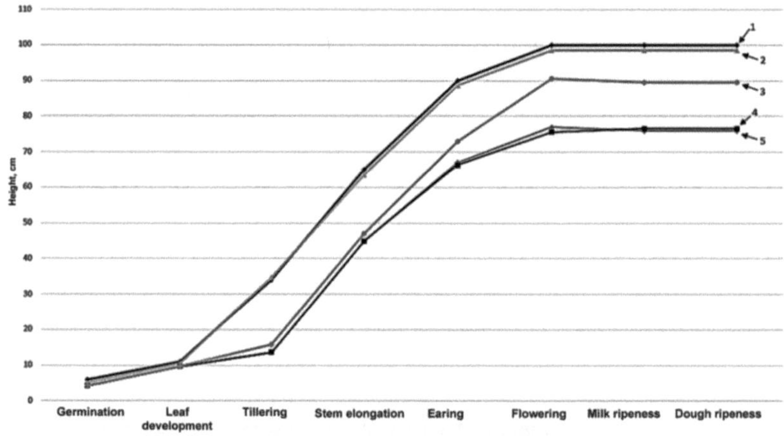

Fig. 5. The height of plant chart chart: 1 – normal height, 2 – optimal conditions, 3 – nutrient excess, 4 – drought, 5 – nutrient lack.

6 Conclusion

The authors have developed methods for calculating the duration of plant development stages based on the satisfaction of the crop agent with environmental parameters according to the rules described in the ontological variety model stored in the KB, and penalties for deviations of the plant from the normal growth trajectory. Active and inactive periods of plant vegetation are also taken into account, as well as changes in the plant's development rate depending on environmental parameters, and the increase in the plant's quantitative parameters per stage and per unit of time. Schemes of algorithms for adaptive planning of plant growth and development stages are presented. The results of experimental studies of the developed DTP prototype demonstrate the practical applicability of the presented methods for calculating plant parameters based on weather conditions and resource constraints. The method is universal due to the ontological configuration of parameters, which allows for its scalability to different cultures.

Acknowledgments. This study was funded by the Ministry of Science and Higher Education of the Russian Federation.

References

1. Liu, J., Zhou, Y., Li, Y., et al.: Exploring the integration of digital twin and generative AI in agriculture. In: Proceedings of IHMSC 2015, pp. 223–228. IEEE (2023)
2. Kalaiselvy, K., Anand, A.J., Tanwar, P., Raza, H. (eds.): Advanced Technologies in Smart Agriculture. River Publishers, NY (2024)
3. Kantaros, A., Piromalis, D.: Setting up a digital twin assisted greenhouse architecture. Am. J. Eng. Appl. Sci. **15**(4), 230–238 (2022)
4. Tsakiridis, N.L., Samarinas, N., Kalopesa, E., Zalidis, G.C.: Cognitive soil digital twin for monitoring the soil ecosystem: a conceptual framework. Soil Syst. **7**(4), 88 (2023)
5. Alves, R.G., Maia, R.F., Lima, F.: Development of a digital twin for smart farming: irrigation management system for water saving. J. Clean. Prod. **388**, 135920 (2023)
6. Machl, T., Donaubauer, A., Kolbe, T.H.: Planning agricultural core road networks based on a digital twin of the cultivated landscape. J. Digit. Landsc. Archit **4**, 316–327 (2019)
7. Lezoche, M., Hernandez, J.E., Alemany, M., et al.: Agri-food 4.0: a survey of the supply chains and technologies for the future agriculture. Comput. Indust. **117**, 103187 (2020)
8. Stock, M., Pieters, O., De Swaef, T., Wyffels, F.: Plant science in the age of simulation intelligence. Front. Plant Sci. **14**, 1299208 (2024)
9. Topaj, A., Mirschel, W.: Abnormal shapes of production function: model interpretations. Comput. Electron. Agric. **145**, 199–207 (2018)
10. World Food Studies Simulation Model (WOFOST): Food & Agriculture Organization of the United Nations. https://www.fao.org/land-water/land/land-governance/land-resources-planning-toolbox/category/details/en/c/1236431/. Accessed 12 Feb 2025
11. Keating, B.A.: Modelling crops and cropping systems – evolving purpose, practice and prospects. Eur. J. Agron. **100**, 163–176 (2018)
12. De Meyer, S., Cruz, D.F., De Swaef, T., et al.: Predicting yield of individual field-grown rapeseed plants from rosette-stage leaf gene expression. PloS Comput. Biol **19**, e1011161 (2023)
13. Eirini Pantazi, X., Moshou, D., Bochtis, D. (eds.): Chapter 2 – Artificial intelligence in agriculture. In: Intelligent Data Mining and Fusion Systems in Agriculture, pp. 1–15. Academic Press (2020)
14. Zhang, B., DeAngelis, D.L.: An overview of agent-based models in plant biology and ecology. Ann. Bot. **126**, 539–557 (2020)
15. Skobelev, P., Tabachinskiy, A., Simonova, E., et al.: Developing digital twin of plant based on emergent intelligence concept, ontology and multi-agent technology. In: Borangiu, T., Trentesaux, D., Leitão, P., Berrah, L., Jimenez, J.F. (eds.) SOHOMA 2023, SCI, vol. 1136, pp. 430–441. Springer, Cham (2024)
16. Skobelev, P., Tabachinskiy, A., Simonova, E., et al.: Multiparametric variety models in digital twin of plant for winter wheat. In: Proceedings of ITNT 2024, pp. 1–9. IEEE (2024)
17. Vittikh, V., Skobelev, P.: Method of coupled interactions for real-time management of resource allocation. Avtometriya **2**, 78–87 (2009)
18. Kelton, W.D., Low, A.M.: Simulation Modelling and Analysis. 3rd ed. McGraw Hill (2004)

Redefining Transportation Simulation: Multi-agent Models Powered by LLMs

Christian Calderón[1(✉)], Pasqual Martí[1], Jaume Jordán[1], Javier Palanca[1], and Vicente Julian[1,2]

[1] Valencian Research Institute for Artificial Intelligence (VRAIN), Universitat Politècnica de València, Camí de Vera s/n, 46022 Valencia, Spain
ccalderon@upv.es, pasmargi@vrain.upv.es, {jjordan,jpalanca,vinglada}@dsic.upv.es

[2] Valencian Graduate School and Research Network for Artificial Intelligence, Universitat Politècnica de València, Camí de Vera s/n, 46022 Valencia, Spain

Abstract. Urban mobility systems are increasingly strained by dynamic societal demands, environmental pressures, and infrastructural limitations. Traditional simulation approaches—rooted in fixed rules and simplified behavioural assumptions—struggle to capture the complexity and variability of human travel decisions. This paper presents a novel framework that integrates Large Language Models (LLMs) into multi-agent mobility simulations to enable context-aware, adaptive, and intelligent decision-making in urban transport planning. Our approach leverages real-world survey data to generate diverse traveller profiles, embedding demographic, behavioural, and contextual factors into SimFleet, a cutting-edge mobility simulation platform. Unlike traditional rule-based models, our framework allows agents to learn, adapt, and refine their travel choices through iterative interactions with simulated urban environments. The framework, built on the SimFleet platform, is evaluated using diverse user profiles and varying levels of contextual information. Results show that LLM-driven agents can achieve high decision quality, behavioural consistency, and realistic adaptation over time. This work highlights the potential of combining LLM reasoning with multi-agent systems to support more intelligent, interpretable, and flexible simulation tools for urban mobility.

Keywords: Multi-agent System · Large Language Models · Multi-agent Simulations · Intelligent Transportation Systems

1 Introduction

The rapid growth of cities and the increasing demand for mobility have created critical challenges in urban transport planning and management. Traffic congestion, environmental pollution, and inefficient resource distribution affect quality of life and exacerbate socioeconomic inequalities [10]. These problems have been further intensified by converging crises—climate change, economic instability,

A. Nongaillard et al. (Eds.): PAAMS 2025, CCIS 2644, pp. 66–78, 2025.
https://doi.org/10.1007/978-3-032-05925-3_6

and structural inequality—that weaken the resilience of mobility systems and limit equitable access to job opportunities and essential services [3,10].

The interdependence of urban systems and the rigidity of traditional infrastructures increase cities' vulnerability to unexpected crises. In this context, the need for flexible and intelligent planning models is more urgent than ever. Agent-Based Modelling (ABM) has emerged as a tool for analysing urban mobility patterns, assessing transport policies, and strengthening cities' ability to respond to changing socioeconomic dynamics [3]. Recent studies have highlighted the role of ABM in modelling human behaviour in urban environments, enabling the simulation of different scenarios and the optimisation of public policies [3].

In recent years, the integration of Large Language Models has emerged as an innovative strategy for enhancing the decision-making and reasoning capabilities of agents within simulation environments [4,12]. LLMs offer the ability to generate decisions flexibly and contextually, without relying exclusively on predefined rules or large volumes of data [4]. This allows agents not only to choose a mode of transport but also to adjust their decisions based on past experiences and dynamic real-time conditions [12]. LLMs can simulate urban residents by generating realistic activity trajectories based on personal habits and motivations, offering enhanced semantic fidelity in urban mobility modelling [7].

The application of LLMs in urban mobility has also shown advancements in predicting demand patterns and public events. Recent studies have explored how these models can improve mobility forecasting under large-scale events, using textual data to enhance the accuracy of traditional models [7]. Recent work demonstrates that LLMs can simulate realistic urban mobility behaviours by reasoning over individuals' daily routines, preferences, and contextual constraints [11]. In this regard, the convergence between ABM and LLMs represents an opportunity to develop more dynamic, intelligent, and adaptive virtual urban transport models. However, it also presents challenges in terms of computational scalability, operational costs, and model explainability [4,11,12].

To address these challenges, we propose a framework that combines the multi-agent simulator SimFleet with LLMs to generate realistic and adaptive travel decisions. Agents reason based on socio-demographic traits, preferences, and contextual constraints, using LLMs to plan their trips in natural language. Simulation outcomes are then used to update agent memory, closing the decision-feedback loop—that is, a process where decisions influence the environment, which in turn shapes future choices. This approach contributes a novel integration of LLM-based reasoning in mobility simulations and enables dynamic, behaviourally rich simulation load.

The rest of the paper is structured as follows: Sect. 2 reviews existing approaches to decision-making in urban mobility and recent advances in the use of LLMs and agent-based models. Section 3 introduces the proposed framework, describing the agent architecture, memory system, and simulation workflow. Section 4 presents experimental results comparing different LLMs in terms of decision quality, behavioural stability, and preference alignment. Finally,

Sect. 5 summarises the main contributions and outlines directions for future research.

2 State of the Art

Large Language Models offer a flexible and context-aware alternative to traditional mobility modeling approaches. This section explores their role in decision-making, adaptive multi-agent simulation, and the integration of key behavioural variables.

2.1 Dynamic Decision-Making Based on LLMs

Decision-making in mobility models has traditionally been approached through methods such as discrete choice models and heuristic rules, which require rigid assumptions about traveller behaviour [1,3,12]. However, these methods struggle to capture the inherent variability of human decisions, particularly in dynamic urban contexts.

LLMs offer a learning and inference-based alternative. Through natural language processing and few-shot learning techniques, LLMs can generate detailed explanations and reasoning about mobility decisions, providing a level of justification and transparency unavailable in traditional models [1]. Additionally, their adaptability allows for the exploration of optimal strategies based on historical data and emerging events [4].

Recent approaches demonstrate that LLMs can generate realistic travel survey data by leveraging encoded mobility knowledge and contextual reasoning across diverse urban settings [1]. In this sense, the combination of supervised and reinforcement learning enables LLMs to evaluate multiple mobility options and select the most efficient one based on context.

Transparency in decision-making is another key aspect that distinguishes LLMs from traditional models. Unlike rule-based approaches with opaque processes, LLMs can generate natural language explanations about why a specific transport option was chosen, facilitating the interpretation of their recommendations [9]. This is particularly useful in mobility policy evaluation, where interpretability of decisions is crucial for acceptance and implementation.

2.2 Adaptive Multi-agent Simulation with LLMs

Agent-based mobility simulation has been widely used in urban studies to evaluate transport strategies, analyse mobility patterns, and design smart infrastructures [3]. However, most of these models rely on static approaches that require extensive calibration and do not consider the evolution of user behaviour over time. The incorporation of LLMs in ABM enables agents to develop advanced decision-making capabilities, allowing them to learn from previous iterations and dynamically adjust their mobility choices [1,12]. An LLM-driven agent can process information about environmental conditions, travel history, costs, and past experiences to select the best transport option for the following day [4]. This adaptive approach enhances simulation realism and provides a more robust tool for assessing the impact of transport policies in evolving urban scenarios.

Moreover, recent research on reasoning in LLMs has revealed that these models, while capable of processing information in a sophisticated manner, exhibit cognitive limitations similar to those of humans, particularly in heuristic decision-making [9]. These observations highlight the importance of designing mechanisms to improve planning and adaptation capabilities of agents within urban simulation environments.

2.3 Key Variables in Urban Mobility Modeling

To simulate realistic and adaptive behaviour in urban mobility systems, agent-based models increasingly rely on user-level variables that reflect the diversity of individual choices and constraints. Traditional models often simplify or aggregate behavioural aspects, whereas recent studies emphasise the importance of incorporating socio-demographic characteristics, behavioural preferences, and contextual constraints [5,6,14]. This work structures agent profiles using three main dimensions:

1) Socio-demographic Factors. Mobility behaviour varies significantly by age, gender, education, occupation, and income. For example, younger adults are more likely to use emerging modes (e.g., e-scooters), while older individuals tend to prefer private cars [6]. Gender differences affect safety perceptions [14], and income level influences budget sensitivity and mode accessibility [5].

2) Preferences in Modal Choice. Subjective traits such as time sensitivity, comfort, environmental awareness, budget, and reliability play a key role in transport decisions. Users valuing speed tend to choose private modes; those with budget constraints prefer low-cost options; individuals with strong environmental values may lean toward active or shared mobility; and those prioritising comfort or reliability avoid shared or unpredictable options [13,14].

3) Environmental Constraints. Contextual variables, such as available modes, infrastructure, and required arrival times, further condition mobility decisions. For instance, a strict arrival deadline or limited access to certain modes directly narrows the set of feasible options [5].

By combining these dimensions with LLM-based reasoning, our framework enables agents to make context-aware decisions that evolve with experience, enhancing behavioural realism in multi-agent simulations.

3 System Overview

This section outlines the proposed architecture of the simulation framework, which combines cognitively inspired agents with LLM-based decision-making. We describe the agent model, the reasoning loop, and the integration with the SimFleet environment for realistic urban mobility simulation.

3.1 Simulation Environment: SimFleet

SimFleet [8] is employed as the core simulation engine. It is an event-driven, multi-agent platform capable of simulating diverse urban mobility scenarios with mixed transport modes and agent strategies [2].

Agents in SimFleet are categorized as *Customer agents*, who issue trip requests, and *Transport agents*, who fulfill them. Each simulation is defined through a JSON file encoding spatial data, global parameters, and agent configurations. The system operates in discrete time steps and generates detailed event logs (e.g., pickup, arrival, rejection). In our framework, SimFleet acts as both an executor of decisions and a feedback provider. LLM-generated plans are transformed into simulation inputs; after execution, events are parsed to compute key performance indicators (e.g., cost, duration), which are transformed into memory updates for each agent.

SimFleet's modularity and support for agent interactions (e.g., competition) make it suitable for evaluating behaviour under realistic constraints [2]. However, its agents follow fixed strategies and lack native learning, requiring our external engine module to orchestrate adaptive, multi-day behaviour. Despite this limitation, SimFleet offers the necessary granularity and flexibility to validate LLM-driven travel decisions in complex urban settings.

3.2 Agent Model and Decision Loop

At the heart of the proposed framework is a cognitively inspired agent model—designed to emulate human-like traits such as memory, learning from experience, and adaptive decision-making—within an iterative loop. Each agent represents an individual traveller, whose behaviour is shaped by a structured identity, a dynamic memory, and an interaction loop with a LLM for autonomous planning and reasoning. Figure 1 illustrates the internal architecture and its interaction with the simulation environment.

Each agent's **identity** encapsulates key user-level variables grounded in urban mobility literature, including socio-demographic factors (e.g., age, income), individual preferences (e.g., reliability, comfort), and environmental constraints (e.g., infrastructure). These traits are encoded in natural language and persist throughout the simulation, guiding reasoning and trade-offs.

In parallel, the agent maintains a two-tiered **memory system**. Short-term memory tracks recent trip outcomes (e.g., travel time, cost), while long-term memory stores aggregated reflections across iterations. This design mimics human decision-making, allowing agents to adapt based on both immediate feedback and accumulated experience. At each simulation step, the agent engages in a **decision loop**. A prompt is constructed from the agent's identity and memory and submitted to a LLM via API.

The model returns a travel plan—including selected transport mode, departure time, and justification in natural language. If the LLM fails to return a valid or structured output (e.g., malformed JSON), the agent resorts to the

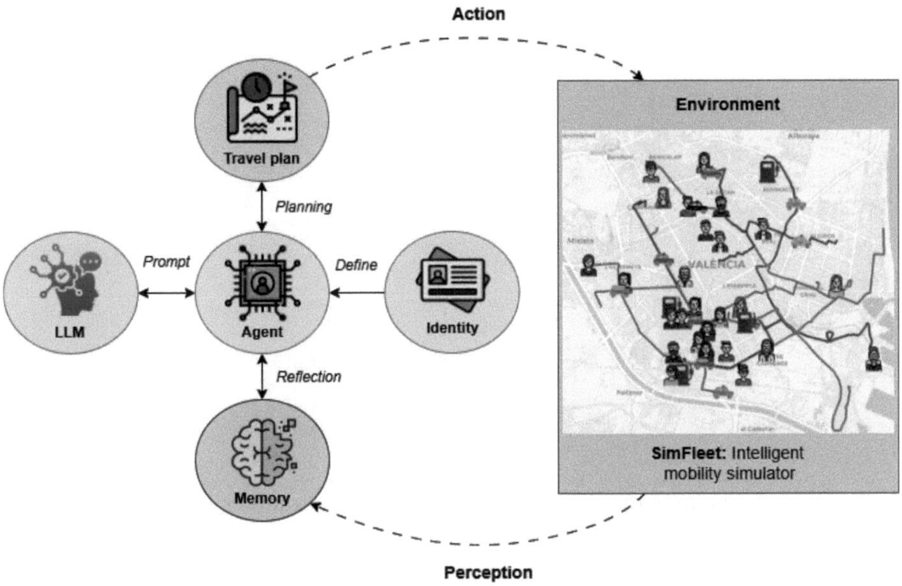

Fig. 1. Internal Agent Processes and Feedback Loop in SimFleet

decision made on the previous day. This fallback mechanism ensures robustness and simulation continuity, as further quantified in Sect. 4.

The resulting plan is translated into simulation parameters. After the trip is executed in SimFleet, relevant events are parsed and used to update the agent's memory, closing the perceptionaction loop. This architecture enables agents to learn and adapt over time, expressing realistic behavioural evolution in response to emerging travel patterns and system dynamics.

3.3 Framework Architecture and Workflow

The framework integrates cognitive agent modelling with a modular simulation pipeline to reproduce daily travel decisions in dynamic urban settings. As shown in Fig. 2, it comprises two main modules: an **engine module** for agent reasoning and coordination, and a **simulation module** based on SimFleet, which executes the agents' decisions within a high-fidelity mobility environment.

Each simulation day begins with three JSON input files: (i) a general configuration with global parameters, (ii) an environment context detailing transport modes (e.g., taxis) in Simfleet format, and (iii) customer profiles specifying agent attributes and available actions (e.g., taxi, bike, car, walk).

The engine runs a four-step loop:

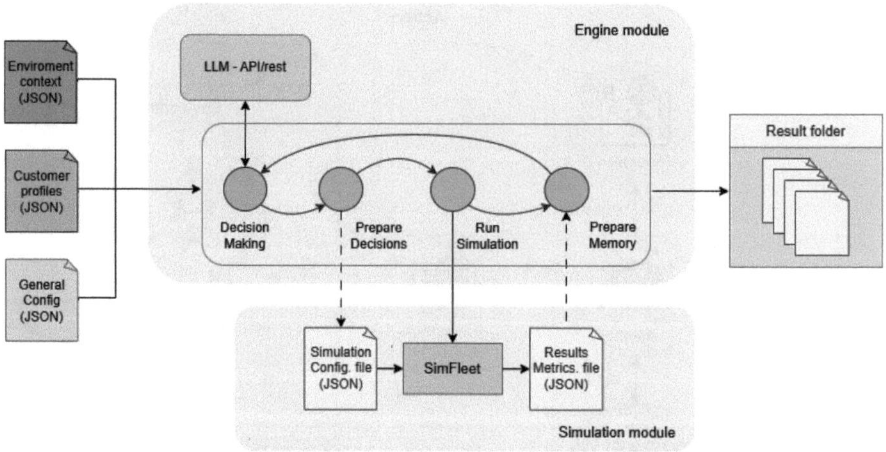

Fig. 2. Overall system workflow. The engine module coordinates LLM-based decision-making and memory updates. SimFleet executes travel simulations and outputs agent-level results.

1. **Decision Making**: For each agent, a tailored prompt is sent to the LLM, which returns a travel plan and explanation[1].
2. **Prepare Decisions**: Valid responses are parsed, validated against a schema[2], and consolidated into a simulation configuration file.
3. **Run Simulation**: SimFleet executes the scenario, capturing events like travel time, delays, and costs.
4. **Prepare Memory**: Outputs are parsed and converted into natural language summaries to update the agent's memory.

Fallbacks to previous decisions are used when LLM outputs are invalid, ensuring simulation continuity. All decisions, events, and memories are stored for post-hoc analysis. The modular design separates reasoning from execution and supports extensibility via prompt templates and parsing logic, enabling the exploration of diverse mobility policies and behavioural hypotheses.

4 Experimental Results

4.1 Experimental Setup

To evaluate the reliability and behavioural performance of LLM-driven agents in transport decision-making, we conducted a series of simulations using the SimFleet platform, as outlined in Sect. 3.

[1] Prompts follow a predefined structure that includes: (a) agent identity, (b) short- and long-term memory summaries, and (c) explicit travel goals for the day.

[2] The LLM is instructed to output a structured JSON containing fields such as `mode`, `departure_time`, and `justification`. For each agent, the action (*Simfleet behaviour*) and departure time (*Simfleet delay*) are added to the configuration file.

We define three representative user profile groups, each comprising 20 agents: *EcoFemaleUser* (Eco), prioritising environmental impact; *TimeMaleUser* (Time), focusing on time efficiency; and *ComRelFemaleUser* (ComRel), emphasising comfort and reliability. Profiles include demographic traits, stated preferences, fixed departure windows, and daily trip purposes. In addition, seven LLMs with diverse architectures were evaluated: `gemma2-9b`, `phi4-14b`, `mistral-nemo`, `llama70b`, `qwen2.5`, `nemotron-mini`, and `llava7b`. Each model was evaluated under three context levels:

- **Low context (1A):** Profile and task instruction only.
- **Medium context (1B):** Profile, short-term memory, and instruction.
- **High context (1C):** Profile, full memory, reflections and instruction.

Each iteration represents one simulated day. Agents are prompted to select a transport mode and departure time, generating a plan with natural language justification. Plans are parsed, validated, and executed in SimFleet. Simulation outcomes (e.g., duration, delays, cost) are used to update the agent's memory before the next decision. If a model fails to produce a valid JSON response, the fallback mechanism described in Sect. 3 is triggered, reusing the previous day's decision to preserve simulation continuity.

4.2 Core LLM Evaluation

The performance of each LLM was evaluated across all three context levels using four core metrics:

- **Speed:** Mean generation time across all prompts and contexts (in seconds).
- **Valid JSON:** Proportion of responses with syntactically correct JSON.
- **Robustness:** Ratio of logically coherent and contextually grounded justifications to total LLM outputs.
- **Stability**[3]: Normalised measure of the variance of agent's modal choice over time, where 1 indicates strong behavioural consistency and 0 reflects high exploration.

Table 1 shows detailed results per context level, followed by a total average row for each model. Among the tested models, `gemma2-9b`, `phi4-14b`, and `mistral-nemo` demonstrated near-perfect performance across all dimensions, combining structural validity, reasoning coherence, and consistent behavioural patterns. While `mistral-nemo` offers a particularly attractive balance with low latency, `phi4-14b` and `gemma2-9b` may be better suited for long-term stable deployments. `qwen2.5` is the fastest model, but its lower stability under high-context scenarios may introduce undesirable exploratory variance. In contrast, `llama70b` offers strong outputs but suffers from excessive latency, limiting its applicability in large-scale simulations. Finally, `nemotron-mini` and especially `llava7b` underperform in robustness and validity, requiring frequent fallback interventions. These results highlight the importance of output validation and fallback mechanisms when integrating LLMs into critical decision-making loops.

[3] The score is computed per agent and then normalised with respect to the average intra-group and inter-group variance for each model.

Table 1. Performance of LLMs across all context levels.

Model	Context	Speed (s)	Valid JSON (%)	Robustness (%)	Stability (%)
`gemma2-9b`	1A	3.46	100.00	100.00	85.00
	1B	3.51	100.00	100.00	81.67
	1C	8.45	100.00	100.00	80.00
Total		**5.14**	**100.00**	**100.00**	**82.22**
`phi4-14b`	1A	5.20	100.00	100.00	80.33
	1B	6.91	100.00	100.00	83.00
	1C	8.21	100.00	100.00	81.11
Total		**6.78**	**100.00**	**100.00**	**81.11**
`mistral-nemo`	1A	3.06	100.00	100.00	82.33
	1B	3.81	100.00	100.00	82.00
	1C	5.15	99.90	99.90	78.00
Total		**4.01**	**99.97**	**99.97**	**80.11**
`qwen2.5`	1A	2.21	100.00	100.00	83.67
	1B	2.07	100.00	100.00	79.67
	1C	3.74	100.00	92.87	72.67
Total		**2.67**	**100.00**	**97.62**	**78.67**
`llama70b`	1A	14.09	99.90	96.35	81.67
	1B	13.40	100.00	95.90	80.67
	1C	22.77	99.90	93.61	80.00
Total		**16.75**	**99.97**	**96.45**	**80.78**
`nemotron-mini`	1A	2.34	100.00	100.00	85.00
	1B	2.62	99.90	99.90	73.33
	1C	3.85	15.48	15.48	84.67
Total		**2.94**	**71.80**	**71.80**	**81.00**
`llava7b`	1A	2.93	100.00	100.00	85.00
	1B	2.45	5.26	5.23	98.90
	1C	5.71	0.10	0.10	100.00
Total		**4.70**	**35.13**	**35.11**	**94.50**

4.3 Stability Over Time

Beyond assessing average model performance, we examine the evolution of agents' behavioural stability over time. Each agent retains a fixed origindestination pair and travel purpose, while departure time and transport mode are re-evaluated daily by the LLM using memory and contextual inputs. This design enables the analysis of behavioural convergence under stable task conditions, revealing whether agents tend toward habitual choices or sustained exploration. Table 2 presents the weekly evolution of stability scores for each model and user profile. Models such as `phi4-14b` and `gemma2-9b` exhibit rapid convergence and high behavioural consistency from the second week onward, indicating strong internal coherence and a tendency toward habit formation. `mistral-nemo` and `llama70b` follow a similar trajectory, with a brief exploratory phase in the first week and swift stabilisation thereafter—suggesting efficient use of early feedback. By contrast, `qwen2.5` maintains greater behavioural variability in the first half of the simulation, particularly for the *TimeMaleUser* profile, before gradually converging—making it better suited to contexts favouring exploration.

Table 2. Results by group and week for various LLMs with high context level.

	W1	W2	W3	W4
ComRel	0.15	0.94	0.95	0.97
Eco	0.12	0.98	1.00	1.00
Time	0.06	0.87	0.96	0.98
Total	0.11	0.93	0.97	0.98

(a) qwen2.5

	W1	W2	W3	W4
ComRel	0.09	1.00	1.00	1.00
Eco	0.05	0.99	1.00	1.00
Time	0.07	1.00	1.00	1.00
Total	0.07	1.00	1.00	1.00

(b) qwen2.5

	W1	W2	W3	W4
ComRel	0.18	0.85	1.00	0.99
Eco	0.24	1.00	1.00	1.00
Time	0.20	0.83	1.00	1.00
Total	0.21	0.89	1.00	1.00

(c) nemotron-mini

	W1	W2	W3	W4
ComRel	0.08	0.98	0.99	0.98
Eco	0.09	1.00	0.99	1.00
Time	0.04	0.99	1.00	1.00
Total	0.07	0.99	0.99	0.99

(d) mistral-nemo

	W1	W2	W3	W4
ComRel	0.13	0.98	0.98	0.98
Eco	0.11	0.96	0.98	0.98
Time	0.08	1.00	1.00	1.00
Total	0.11	0.98	0.99	0.99

(e) llama70b

	W1	W2	W3	W4
ComRel	0.09	1.00	1.00	1.00
Eco	0.17	1.00	1.00	1.00
Time	0.09	1.00	1.00	1.00
Total	0.12	1.00	1.00	1.00

(f) gemma2-9b

`nemotron-mini` exhibits erratic, profile-dependent behaviour, limiting its reliability for stable decision-making. By contrast, all top-performing models converge by the final week. `phi4-14b` and `gemma2-9b` stabilise rapidly from week two, while `mistral-nemo` and `llama70b` follow a slightly more gradual, yet comparably consistent, trajectory. This suggests that all four models support effective habit formation under memory-informed conditions. `qwen2.5`, meanwhile, maintains higher variability, reflecting a more exploratory behavioural pattern. The sharp rise in stability from the first to the second week reflects an intentional system design. Agents are prompted to explore different transport modes when memory is unavailable. As experience accumulates, decisions increasingly draw on structured memory and preference-based reasoning, leading to rapid behavioural consolidation. This shift from exploration to exploitation is expected and reflects a transition towards habit formation once meaningful context is available.

4.4 Modal Preferences Under High Context

We now analyse the aggregate transport mode choices produced by each model under the high-context condition (1C), focusing on how user preferences interact with model behaviour to shape mode selection. Table 3 shows the distribution of modal decisions across agent profiles for each LLM.

Table 3. Transport mode use preferences by model and type of user.

	bike	car	taxi	walk
ComRel	0.31	0.45	0.19	0.05
Eco	0.85	0.05	0.05	0.05
Time	0.36	0.28	0.19	0.17

a) qwen2.5

	bike	car	taxi	walk
ComRel	0.05	0.85	0.05	0.05
Eco	0.85	0.05	0.05	0.05
Time	0.05	0.85	0.05	0.05

b) phi4-14b

	bike	car	taxi	walk
ComRel	0.05	0.76	0.09	0.10
Eco	0.05	0.85	0.05	0.05
Time	0.05	0.78	0.05	0.12

c) nemotron-mini

	bike	car	taxi	walk
ComRel	0.17	0.73	0.05	0.05
Eco	0.18	0.61	0.16	0.05
Time	0.23	0.67	0.05	0.05

d) mistral-nemo

	bike	car	taxi	walk
ComRel	0.08	0.82	0.05	0.05
Eco	0.65	0.21	0.05	0.09
Time	0.08	0.82	0.05	0.05

e) gemma2-9b

	bike	car	taxi	walk
ComRel	0.09	0.75	0.10	0.06
Eco	0.30	0.20	0.05	0.45
Time	0.17	0.65	0.13	0.05

f) llama70b

Models such as `phi4-14b`, `gemma2-9b`, and `llama70b` demonstrate high alignment with stated user preferences: *EcoFemaleUser* agents heavily favour bikes, while *TimeMaleUser* agents consistently opt for cars or faster options. These models appear to internalise preference context effectively, maintaining low variance within groups. `mistral-nemo` follows a similar pattern but allows slightly more flexibility, particularly for the *Time* and *ComRel* profiles, suggesting adaptive trade-offs between time and comfort. In contrast, `qwen2.5` shows higher diversity in mode use, particularly for the *ComRel* group, with a notable mix of cars and bikes, indicating more exploration even under high-context conditions.

Finally, `nemotron-mini` exhibits skewed behaviour, overselecting cars across all profiles regardless of preference, reflecting limited sensitivity to contextual signals. The most preference-consistent models are `phi4-14b`, `gemma2-9b`, and `llama70b`, while `mistral-nemo` provides a more adaptive compromise. `qwen2.5` encourages diversity but at the cost of alignment, and `nemotron-mini` fails to personalise decisions reliably.

5 Conclusion

This study introduces a novel framework combining LLMs with agent-based simulation to model realistic and adaptive urban mobility decisions. By embedding socio-demographic profiles, user preferences, and environmental constraints within a cognitively inspired agent architecture, the proposed system enables dynamic, context-driven decision-making that evolves over time.

Our results demonstrate that LLMs can effectively simulate human-like reasoning in transport choices, with top-performing models such as `phi4-14b`, `gemma2-9b`, `mistral-nemo` achieving high levels of structural validity, behavioural stability, and alignment with user preferences. The framework's fallback mechanisms ensure robustness even under imperfect LLM outputs, preserving simulation continuity. Furthermore, the inclusion of memory and identity in the prompting process proves essential for sustaining long-term consistency and reflecting habit formation. From a methodological standpoint, this approach enhances the realism of multi-agent mobility simulations without requiring extensive behavioural calibration or handcrafted rules. It also provides a flexible basis for testing mobility policies, transport innovations, and user-centric scenarios, offering public decision-makers a tool to simulate equitable, inclusive, and context-sensitive strategies that promote individual well-being. In doing so, the framework supports the development of socially responsible transport systems aligned with the United Nations' Sustainable Development Goal 11 for sustainable and inclusive cities.

Nevertheless, challenges remain in terms of computational efficiency and the need for further refinement in model interpretability and context management. Future work will explore hybrid architectures combining symbolic reasoning and LLM outputs to improve scalability and planning robustness. In sum, the convergence between LLMs and ABM opens promising avenues for developing intelligent, adaptive, and human-centered urban transport systems.

Acknowledgements. This work is partially supported by grant TSI-100930-2023-9 funded by "Ministerio para la Transformación Digital y Función Pública", by grant PID2021-123673 funded by MCIN/AEI/10.13039/501100011033 and by "ERDF A way of making Europe".

References

1. Bhandari, P., Anastasopoulos, A., Pfoser, D.: Urban mobility assessment using LLMs. In: Proceedings of the 32nd ACM International Conference on Advances in Geographic Information Systems, pp. 67–79. SIGSPATIAL '24, New York, NY, USA. Association for Computing Machinery (2024). https://doi.org/10.1145/3678717.3691221
2. Calderón, C., Martí, P., Jordán, J., Palanca, J., Julian, V.: Redefining transportation modelling with advanced agent-based simulations. In: Novais, P., et al. (eds.) International Symposium on Ambient Intelligence, pp. 251–262. Springer, Cham (2024). https://doi.org/10.1007/978-3-031-83117-1_24
3. Divasson-J., A., Macarulla, A.M., Garcia, J.I., Borges, C.E.: Agent-based modeling in urban human mobility: a systematic review. Cities **158**, 105697 (2025). https://doi.org/10.1016/j.cities.2024.105697
4. Gao, C., et al.: Large language models empowered agent-based modeling and simulation: a survey and perspectives. Hum. Soc. Sci. Commun. **11**(1), 1–24 (2024). https://doi.org/10.1057/s41599-024-03611-3
5. Huang, E., Yin, Z., Broaddus, A., Yan, X.: Shared e-scooters as a last-mile transit solution? Travel behavior insights from Los Angeles and Washington D.C. Travel Behav. Soc. **34**, 100663 (2024). https://doi.org/10.1016/j.tbs.2023.100663
6. Jafarzadehfadaki, M., Sisiopiku, V.P.: Embracing urban micromobility: a comparative study of e-scooter adoption in Washington, D.C., Miami, and Los Angeles. Urban Sci. **8**(71) (2024). https://doi.org/10.3390/urbansci8020071
7. Liang, Y., Liu, Y., Wang, X., Zhao, Z.: Exploring large language models for human mobility prediction under public events. Comput. Environ. Urban Syst. **112**, 102153 (2024). https://doi.org/10.1016/j.compenvurbsys.2024.102153
8. Palanca, J., Terrasa, A., Carrascosa, C., Julián, V.: SimFleet: a new transport fleet simulator based on MAS. In: De La Prieta, F., et al. (eds.) PAAMS 2019. CCIS, vol. 1047, pp. 257–264. Springer, Cham (2019). https://doi.org/10.1007/978-3-030-24299-2_22
9. Palminteri, S., Nicolas Yax, H.A.: Studying and improving reasoning in humans and machines. École Normale Supérieure - INSERM (2023). https://doi.org/10.21203/rs.3.rs-3124634/v1
10. United Nations, Department of Economic and Social Affairs: World social report 2024 (2024). https://www.un.org/development/desa/dpad/publication/world-social-report-2024/
11. Wang, J., et al.: Large language models as urban residents: an LLM agent framework for personal mobility generation. In: Advances in Neural Information Processing Systems. vol. 37, pp. 124547–124574. Curran Associates, Inc. (2024)
12. Wang, L., et al.: A survey on large language model based autonomous agents. Front. Comput. Sci. **18**(6), 186345 (2024). https://doi.org/10.1007/s11704-024-40231-1
13. Yan, X.J., Jin, X.: Mobility-on-demand transit for smart and sustainable cities. Technical Report, University of Florida (2023)
14. Yang, W., et al.: Shared e-scooter user characteristics and usage patterns across four us cities. Transp. Res. Rec. **2678**(6), 196–207 (2024). https://doi.org/10.1177/03611981231194626

Towards a Decentralized Digital Twin for Waste Collection Fleets

Marin Lujak(✉), Alberto Fernández, and Miguel Ángel García Martínez

CETINIA, University Rey Juan Carlos, Madrid, Spain
{marin.lujak,alberto.fernandez}@urjc.es, ma.garciam.2021@alumnos.urjc.es

Abstract. This paper introduces a decentralized framework for the dynamic management and optimization of waste collection fleets. Combining distributed multi-agent coordination, dynamic optimization, and digital twin technologies, this framework not only promises significant reductions in operational costs and environmental impact but also enhances real-time responsiveness to disruptions. We detail the architecture and functionality of the proposed system, which includes real-time monitoring, simulation of truck movements, and the distributed and adaptive coordination of routes based on real-time data. Our preliminary simulation results show promise of monitoring and controlling routes of large fleets in daily waste container collections, decreasing operational expenses, thereby advancing the state of urban waste management.

Keywords: Route optimization · fleet management · digital twin · multi-agent simulation · multi-agent coordination · waste collection

1 Introduction

Urban waste management is a critical component of sustainable city planning, influencing both environmental impact and quality of urban life. Efficient waste collection not only contributes to cleaner living environments but also reduces the overall carbon footprint of cities. The complexity of dynamically routing a fleet of waste collection vehicles in real-time poses significant challenges, particularly in response to daily fluctuations in traffic, weather conditions, and varying waste bin fill levels. Traditional methods often fall short in addressing these challenges dynamically and in real-time. Optimizing truck routes and operational efficiency not only cuts costs but also contributes to environmental sustainability.

The advent of digital twin technology [9], which involves creating digital replicas of physical entities and processes, offers a promising solution to these challenges. A digital twin allows for the simulation, analysis, and real-time monitoring of systems, which can be particularly beneficial in managing complex logistics operations such as waste collection. By integrating digital twin technology with advanced computational techniques such as distributed multi-agent

A. Nongaillard et al. (Eds.): PAAMS 2025, CCIS 2644, pp. 79–90, 2025.
https://doi.org/10.1007/978-3-032-05925-3_7

coordination, complex event processing, and dynamic optimization, it is possible to significantly enhance the efficiency and adaptability of waste management systems. This paper introduces a novel approach to managing waste collection fleets (WCF) through a distributed digital twin framework. Our system utilizes real-time data for route optimization and incorporates distributed optimization along with multi-agent coordination to enhance decision-making processes. These technologies allow the system to dynamically respond to changes in the urban environment, thus enhancing operational efficiency and reducing environmental impacts. This approach leverages distributed multi-agent coordination, significantly improving the management of waste collection services. Additionally, we present preliminary results demonstrating the development and implementation of a simulation environment for monitoring and optimization of fleet routes.

The remainder of this paper is organized as follows: Sect. 2 reviews the current literature on simulations of waste management fleets and digital twin technologies. Section 3 describes the modular, layered architecture of our proposed system, including detailed functionalities of each module. Section 5 provides a use-case scenario demonstrating the application of our simulator in an urban setting, supported by preliminary results that showcase the system's effectiveness. In Sect. 6, we conclude the paper with a summary of our findings and a discussion of potential areas for future research.

2 State of the Art

Efficient routing and decentralized coordination for cooperative vehicle fleets are critical for reducing costs, improving service quality, and enhancing sustainability [14]. These fleets rely on real-time, autonomous decision-making without centralized control, aligning with multi-agent system principles [15]. However, achieving fair and efficient task distribution remains challenging due to unpredictable factors like traffic, breakdowns, and fluctuating service demand.

Digital Twin (DT) technology offers a potential solution by integrating real-world data into dynamic, self-adaptive models that reflect the current state of physical systems [9]. DT adoption has expanded over the past decade [11,12], offering potential for wide-ranging applications across diverse spatial and temporal scales. Their use in developing cost-effective, self-adaptive systems driven by real-world data is demonstrated in [6,7]. A key challenge is the high resource demand and complexity involved in developing accurate physical twins [19].

Smart waste collection strategies have evolved from conventional fixed routes to dynamic systems that adapt to real-time bin fill-levels. [1] evaluated a GIS-based smart collection system (SCS) against traditional methods, focusing on time, pollution, and cost efficiencies. The study tested various scenarios in a local residential area, utilizing data from a field survey across diverse households. It featured a knowledge-based decision-making algorithm for bin selection based on historical fill data, assessing both standard and reduced waste generation scenarios. This work not only proposes an integrated SCS architecture but also addresses key considerations for implementing smart waste management systems. Additionally, [16] used simulation to: (i) evaluate the current planning methodology, which is still based on static cyclic schedules for container emptyings; (ii) explore various dynamic planning possibilities; (iii) quantify the benefits of transitioning to a dynamic collection process; and (iv) assess the advantages of investing in fill-level sensors. After simulating all scenarios, they concluded that significant improvements can be achieved in terms of both logistical costs and customer satisfaction. Waste levels cannot be estimated with complete certainty as they are only revealed at collection. Furthermore, in large cities and clustered urban areas, multiple depots from which collection routes originate are common, although cooperation among vehicles from different depots is rarely considered. [10] analyses a rich version of the waste collection problem with multiple depots and stochastic demands by proposing a hybrid algorithm combining metaheuristics with simulation. Their approach allows for studying the effects of cooperation among different depots, thus quantifying the potential savings this cooperation could provide to city governments and waste collection companies.

The main objective of [8] is to evaluate the cost efficiency of a Product-service system for waste collection enabling dynamic scheduling, comparing it to the performance of more common schemes (e.g. fixed routing and scheduling service and call-based service). Hybrid simulation modelling – based on system dynamics, discrete events and agent based modelling- has been applied to test the transition from a fixed to a "pay-as-you-throw" fee in waste from electrical and electronic equipment. A test case regarding an Italian municipality has been proposed to assess quantitative results based on a simulation model.

Advanced waste management systems using digital twins and dynamic scheduling depend on robust architectures tailored to urban complexities, ensuring seamless integration with existing infrastructure and adaptability to evolving demands (e.g., [5,18]). A central aspect of these architectures is their scalable data processing for managing large data volumes from urban waste activities, ensuring efficiency and adaptability for real-time dynamics (e.g., [2]). Dynamic optimization algorithms at the core of the architecture continuously adapt to changes like traffic and bin capacities, optimizing routes in real-time to minimize delays and cut costs (e.g., [17]). Such an architecture should include multi-agent systems for coordination among autonomous entities like sensor-equipped vehicles and bins, enhancing decentralized decision-making and efficiency in complex environments (e.g., [13]). It requires high interoperability to integrate with urban infrastructures, facilitating information and resource sharing to improve operational efficiency (e.g., [4]). Additionally, robust security protocols are crucial to protect data integrity and ensure privacy, supporting public trust and regulatory compliance (e.g., [3]).

3 Proposed Architecture

Next, we present our proposed architecture for efficient, distributed WCF management, evolving from a centralized to a decentralized digital twin approach.

3.1 Centralized Physical vs Digital Twin

Figure 1a shows a typical architecture supporting the operation of a WCF. The WCF consist of a set of trucks in charge of running (usually pre-established) routes for the collection of garbage containers. A Fleet Management Fleet (FMS) receives information about the location and status of each truck (e.g. available capacity) and incidents (e.g. breakdowns). The FMS processes the data and may propose actions to improve the operation or overcome the contingencies detected. A user interface (UI) provides visual information to fleet operators, including physical trucks, pending containers, etc. FMS supports the operators in their decision-making or, if adequately configured, autonomously triggers actions.

FMSs include algorithms for the planning of optimal routes, processing online information from the operation, monitoring the status and proposing corrective actions if needed (for example, dynamic adaptation of routes). For the design and assessment of fleet operation managing strategies, it is convenient to count on the support of simulation environments (Fig. 1b) before the actions are applied in the real world.

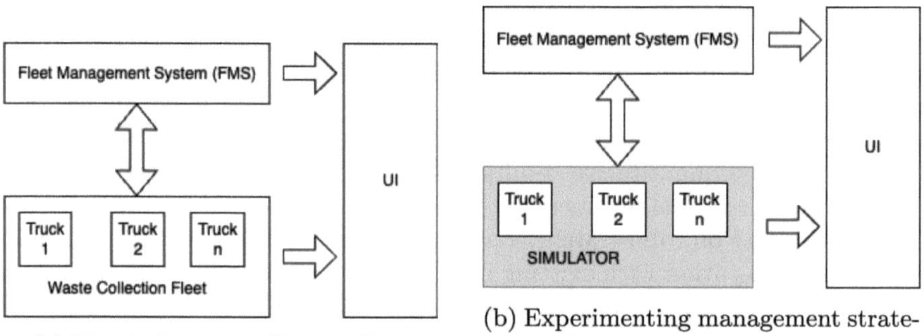

(a) Physical waste collection fleet

(b) Experimenting management strategies with simulator

Fig. 1. Context: Physical waste collection fleet vs simulator

The concept of digital twin allows the combination of the operation of the physical WCF with the digital versions of the main components (trucks) in a virtual environment that includes simulation capabilities. This idea is reflected in Fig. 2. Each truck in the WCF has a digital twin that reflects its behavior. Movements and actions carried out by trucks in the real world are updated in their digital twins. The FMS uses the digital versions to make decisions, probably using simulations, that are applied in the physical fleet.

3.2 Distributed Digital Twin

A distributed digital twin is a type of digital twin where the computational tasks are spread across multiple networked computers or processors. This approach is

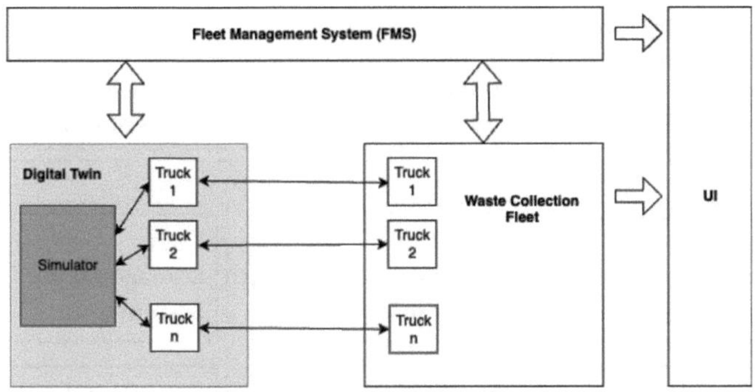

Fig. 2. Digital Twin approach

particularly useful for large-scale applications that require substantial computational resources or for applications that involve multiple interacting components that can be naturally partitioned.

The distributed digital twin aims to efficiently simulate, visualize, and control the movement of garbage collection trucks by breaking down the digital twin model into smaller, manageable sub-models for simpler computation and enhanced problem-solving. This division can be based on geographical, functional, or other logical segments. Unlike centralized models that rely on a single control point, the distributed approach uses networked agents (fleet trucks and waste bin sensors). Each agent is linked to a processor that collects data and makes decisions locally, but can also communicate and coordinate with other agents, leveraging parallel processing to accelerate the simulation and enhance system resilience. This multi-agent setup allows for more robust and flexible decision-making, as each part of the system can adapt to changes in its immediate environment while still aligning with the broader operational goals.

The system integrates real-time data from various sources, including GPS tracking data from trucks, sensor data from waste bins, and traffic updates. This data is used to simulate scenarios, forecast outcomes, and recalibrate operations dynamically. The distributed digital twin can learn in a distributed way from past data and adapt to new situations. It uses historical performance data and ongoing input to optimize routes and operations continuously, ensuring that the system becomes more efficient over time.

3.3 Decentralized Digital Twin

In large-scale urban areas, multiple waste management companies often operate concurrently, which can lead to overlapping routes and redundant operations. In the distributed digital twin, the overall model of the whole system is decomposed among a number of collaborative agents while keeping all the relevant information available to all of them. On the other hand, in the decentralized digital twin, which is more appropriate for competitive environments, each agent has available

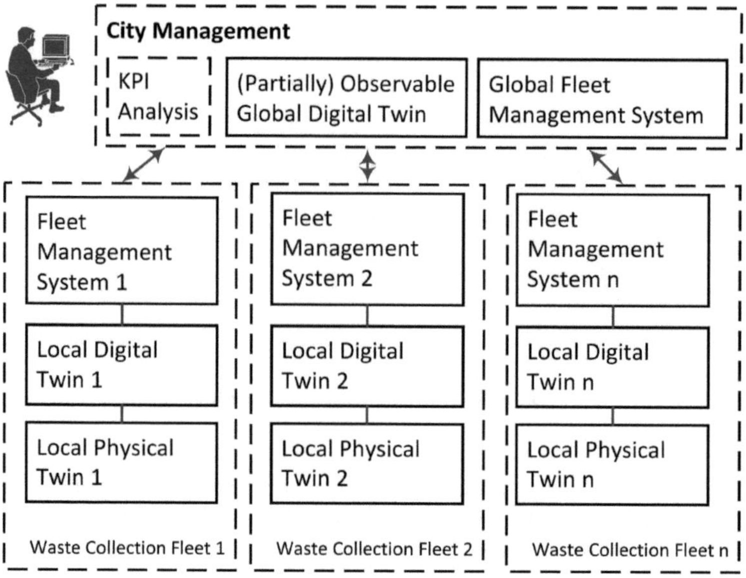

Fig. 3. Decentralized digital twin approach for multiple waste collection fleets

local private information and only discloses the non-sensitive information with the rest of the agents. We call this information global public information.

A decentralized digital twin framework for WCFs in urban environments is proposed in Fig. 3, focusing on competitive scenarios where multiple companies operate simultaneously. The goal is to enable these companies to share minimal yet crucial information to predict probable alternative scenarios in waste collection management, enhancing overall system efficiency without compromising competitive advantage. Each company maintains its own digital twin, simulating its fleet operations. These digital twins are interconnected through a secure, shared platform that allows for the exchange of minimal operational data, such as traffic conditions, route completions, and bin statuses, without revealing sensitive competitive data. Thus, the global view of the digital twin in the city management layer in Fig. 3 is partially observable from the city management point of view. The core of the proposed system is a carefully designed data-sharing protocol that ensures each participant receives only the necessary information to improve their operational decisions. Companies share anonymized data about traffic delays observed by their fleets. Completed route notifications are shared to prevent overlapping services in the same areas, optimizing route planning across companies. Information about bin fill levels from shared sensors aids in preventing multiple companies from servicing half-full bins unnecessarily.

Benefits of this system include reduced operational redundancy and optimized routes, which decrease fuel usage and time spent on collections. Additionally, lower operational costs result from shared insights into route and bin status efficiencies, and decreased carbon emissions are achieved through streamlined operations and reduced fleet idle times. The system ensures that all shared data is anonymized and limited to what is strictly necessary for operational efficiency. Robust cybersecurity measures protect against unauthorized data access, maintaining the integrity and confidentiality of each company's sensitive information.

4 Simulator

In the following, we focus on the first step in the realization of the distributed and decentralized digital twins, which is a simulator for the WCFs. The proposed Simulator framework for WCFs should not only optimize operational processes but also enhance adaptability and efficiency, paving the way for more sustainable urban environments.

The functionalities of the WCF simulator include (i) reading the location and characteristics (e.g., capacity) of the containers and trucks from a file or database (DB), (ii) loading the fill state of the containers from a file or DB to inform routing decisions, (iii) obtaining optimal routes to be taken by each truck based on the aforementioned data, (iv) displaying on a map the locations of the containers and the routes defined for each truck, (v) simulating the movement of trucks along these routes, and (vi) collecting and analyzing performance metrics, such as average, minimum, and maximum time per truck, and the quantity of waste collected per truck.

These functionalities aim to streamline operations, enhance efficiency, and reduce operational costs through optimized route planning and real-time tracking of fleet movements.

4.1 Simulator Architecture

Figure 4 shows the architecture of the WCF simulator.

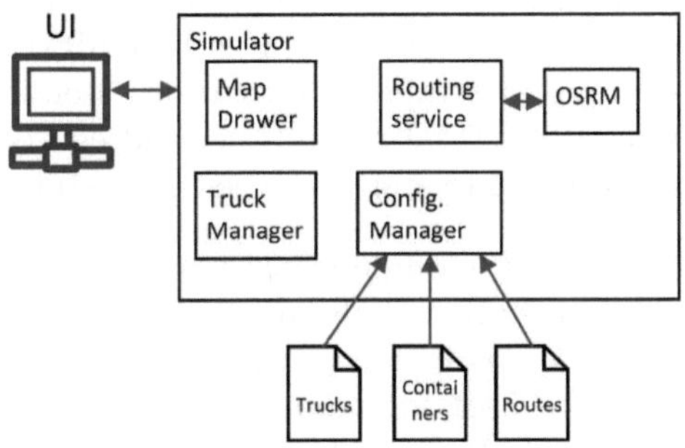

Fig. 4. Simulator architecture

In the figure, three different elements can be seen, namely a User Interface (UI), several configuration files and the core simulation engine.

The *User Interface (UI)* shows the simulation environment, allowing users to interact and receive real-time updates on truck positions. The main part UI is a map, which displays the various moving trucks, existing containers, and planned routes (showing the part already covered). Moreover, the simulator generates several metrics for the analysis of the fleet performance, such as time spent for each truck and route, uncompleted routes, etc.

Simulation experiments can be configured by specifying different parameters, which are specified in different files. In particular, three different (.csv formatted) files are used, including the following information:

- *Containers.* Information about existing containers, including a container ID, neighborhood, address, and location longitude and latitude. It also includes the initial garbage load that, in a real physical scenario, would be obtained from smart containers or estimated from historical data.
- *Trucks.* It contains the track ID, capacity (volume of trash it can collect), and the initial location of each track in the fleet.
- *Routes.* Each route is specified as a sequence of containers. The planned routs are provided to the simulator, no matter how they have been designed.

4.2 Main Modules

The core *simulator* consists of four main modules: the configuration manager, the routing service, the truck manager and the map drawer.

Configuration Manager. Its responsibilities include reading information about the municipality's containers and truck routes from csv files stored in the data folder. This process uses the Pandas library.

Routing Service. The main function of the Routing Service is to calculate the optimal detailed paths between containers and provide the necessary data for their representation on the map. For this purpose, OSRM[1] (Open Source Routing Machine) is used, which generates optimized routes given geographical points, in this case, the containers. The route generated by OSRM not only defines the optimal path but also provides detailed information essential for the simulator, including: total route distance, total route time, and coordinates of route sub-points, which are the intermediate steps between each stop.

Map Drawer. The `Map Drawer` module generates the map displaying the various routes using the Folium library. Folium is a high-level tool that facilitates the creation of interactive maps in Python and is based on Leaflet, a powerful JavaScript library widely used for map visualization on the web. The map generated by Folium is in HTML format. JavaScript has been used to achieve interaction with the trucks in real-time. In particular, to connect the map to the simulator via a WebSocket connection, allowing the truck icon to move as it sends its position data. Also, to highlight the path to the next container for each truck by increasing its thickness compared to the rest of the route.

[1] https://project-osrm.org/.

Truck Manager. This module is responsible for managing the trucks and their movement through the established routes. It preprocesses the routes using the Routing Service, and starts a subprocess for each truck, which will send the position of the truck each time a relevant movement is made. It also acts as the orchestrator of the program, processing the information received from the trucks and transmitting it to the user interface using the Map Drawer.

4.3 System Flow

The operational workflow of the application is intricately designed to facilitate seamless interactions among the user interface, and the modules that compose the simulator, ensuring efficient real-time management of WCF operations.

The process unfolds as follows. Initially, the simulation is activated through the user interface, either by an operator or an automated system. This initiation triggers a command to the simulator to start the route optimization process. The simulator, upon receiving this command, calculates the most efficient paths for the waste collection trucks. These calculations consider various dynamic factors such as current traffic conditions, road work, and the status of waste bins.

Once the optimal routes are determined, the truck manager begins a detailed emulation of the trucks' movements along these prescribed routes. This phase includes managing potential real-time disruptions such as traffic delays or unexpected route blockages. Throughout this simulation, the trucks' processes continually update the server with the trucks' positions and any notable events or deviations from the initial route plan. Concurrently, the map drawer processes the data received from the simulator and updates the user interface to reflect the real-time conditions of the fleet. This includes visualizing the trucks' movements on a digital map and displaying key performance metrics. These updates are crucial for operational oversight, allowing users to monitor and, if necessary, intervene to adjust routes to optimize daily operations. This dynamic and integrated system flow ensures that the fleet is managed efficiently, with minimal need for manual intervention. The continuous feedback loop between the simulator and the server, supported by real-time data processing, significantly enhances the system's capability to respond to on-the-ground challenges.

4.4 Communication Between Modules

Since the agents often need to interact (e.g., exchanging data or events), there must be a mechanism for their mutual communication. This is typically achieved through networking protocols and message passing interfaces like MPI (Message Passing Interface) or through service-oriented architectures using APIs.

Two different strategies were evaluated for managing communications between the various modules: push and pull. In the push strategy, the truck actively sends its new position to the simulator when it moves. In the pull (or polling) strategy, the truck starts its journey, and the simulator repeatedly requests the truck's position, waiting for a time interval between each request. The push strategy was chosen for its real-time tracking benefits and efficiency, as it ensures all messages sent are relevant to the system. Additionally, an algorithm has been implemented to check whether the truck's movement is truly relevant. A movement is considered relevant if it exceeds three seconds or if the truck moves to a container. If a movement is deemed not relevant, its duration is added to the next one, rechecking its relevance.

The Truck Manager and each truck communicate via HTTP requests. Each truck runs in a separate subprocess. It communicates with the manager by sending an asynchronous HTTP message with the truck's new position and, if necessary, additional information such as available space, the number of containers collected so far, or if it is collecting a container.

The Simulator and the User Interface communicate via a WebSocket connection. This allows the simulator to send updates to the interface as soon as they are received. This connection is advantageous because it is local, and the number of concurrent connections remains consistent, ensuring stability and real-time responsiveness. To ensure the simulation's accuracy and consistency, synchronization between the different parts of the digital twin is crucial. This can be challenging, especially in real-time simulations, as it involves coordinating the simulation clock across all nodes to ensure that all sub-models are in sync. Techniques like conservative or optimistic synchronization can be used.

5 Simulation Use-Case

In this section, we explore specific simulations to demonstrate how our simulator operates. The simulation shown in Fig. 5 of this section presents an urban setting with a fleet of five trucks. For the simulation experiments, a set of tasks is defined within the space, representing locations to visit. The trucks are expected to collaboratively assist the container recollection tasks.

Preliminary results indicate that the system's implementation has led to an initial reduction in the kilometers traveled by the trucks and an improvement in the efficiency of the waste collection service. Additionally, the system has demonstrated its capacity to dynamically adapt to operational setbacks in real time. Also, we carried out several scalability tests (see results in Table 1). As expected, the computational resources required increased with the number of trucks. Nevertheless, the simulator responded well for a good number of trucks.

Table 1. CPU and RAM usage percentages for different number of trucks

	5 trucks		25 trucks		50 trucks		60 trucks		75 trucks	
	CPU	RAM	CPU	RAM	CPU	RAM	CPU	RAM	CPU	RAM
Average	2.79	59.83	4.95	68.94	9.77	75.57	10.78	73.73	18.55	76.28
Minimum	0	56.1	0	56.8	0.4	56.7	0.4	51.9	0.5	44.5
Maximum	10.6	62.4	19.7	77.3	100	94.9	100	91.6	100	96.8

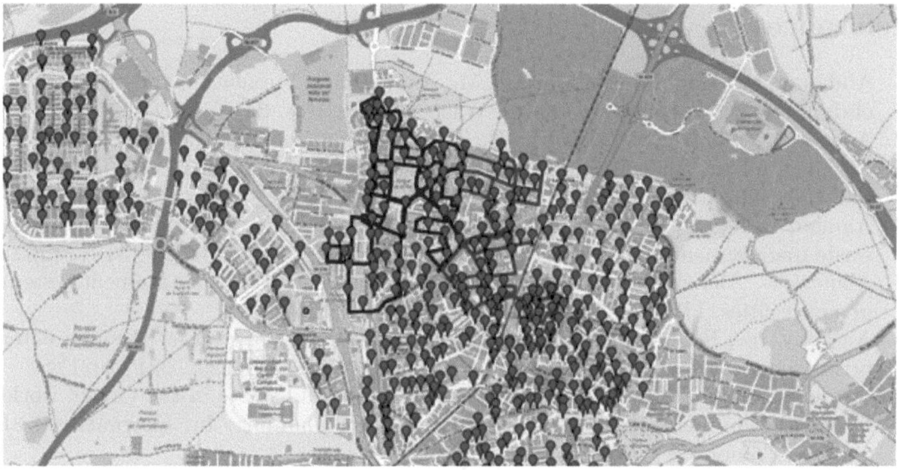

Fig. 5. Map with containers and two routes

6 Conclusions and Future Work

In this paper, we presented the concept of a distributed and decentralized digital twin for waste collection fleets and a simulator for their monitoring.

Using a decentralized digital twin framework, multiple WCFs operating in the same region can improve their operations and environmental impact through strategic information sharing. This approach not only enhances individual fleet efficiencies but also promotes collaboration among all stakeholders, transforming urban waste management.

Analysis of the preliminary simulation data suggests that the accuracy of route prediction and optimization improves with the continuous accumulation and analysis of data. The implementation of a fleet digital twin allows for detailed simulation and adjustment of operations before their actual execution.

Our vision encompasses the deployment of autonomous fleets in dynamic environments, facilitated by the utilization of digital twins. Evaluating the simulator's fidelity in future work will encompass comparative tests and simulations conducted with real fleets. In particular, we plan to apply the system to the city of Fuenlabrada (Madrid, Spain). These endeavors aim to provide insights into its operational performance and suitability for real-world applications, thereby advancing autonomous waste collection practices.

Acknowledgements. Work supported by the MCIN/AEI/10.13039/501100011033 and by the European Union's "NextGenerationEU/PRTR" under VAE grant: TED2021-131295B-C33; MCIN/AEI/10.13039/501100011033 and by "ERDF A way of making Europe" under grant COSASS: PID2021-123673OB-C32.

References

1. Abdallah, M., Adghim, M., Maraqa, M., Aldahab, E.: Simulation and optimization of dynamic waste collection routes. Waste Manag. Res. **37**(8), 793–802 (2019)
2. Addas, A., Khan, M.N., Naseer, F.: Waste management 2.0 leveraging internet of things for an efficient and eco-friendly smart city solution. PLoS ONE **19**(7), e0307608 (2024)
3. Ahmad, R.W., Salah, K., Jayaraman, R., Yaqoob, I., Omar, M.: Blockchain for waste management in smart cities: a survey. IEEE Access **9**, 131520–131541 (2021)
4. Alanazi, F., Alenezi, M.: Interoperability for intelligent traffic management systems in smart cities. IJECE **14**(2), 1864–1874 (2024)
5. Anthony Jnr, B.: Managing digital transformation of smart cities through enterprise architecture-a review and research agenda. EIS **15**(3), 299–331 (2021)
6. Cárdenas, I., Koeva, M., Davey, C., Nourian, P.: Solid waste in the virtual world: a digital twinning approach for waste collection planning. In: International 3D GeoInfo Conference, pp. 61–74. Springer (2023)
7. Di Salle, A., et al.: Waste management through digital twins and business process modeling. In: Proceedings of ACM/IEEE MODELS 2024, pp. 513–517 (2024)
8. Elia, V., Gnoni, M.G., Tornese, F.: Assessing the efficiency of a PSS solution for waste collection: a simulation based approach. Procedia Cirp **47**, 252–257 (2016)
9. Grieves, M.: Digital twin: manufacturing excellence through virtual factory replication. White Paper **1**(2014), 1–7 (2014)
10. Gruler, A., Fikar, C., Juan, A.A., Hirsch, P., Contreras-Bolton, C.: Supporting multi-depot and stochastic waste collection management in clustered urban areas via simulation-optimization. J. Simul. **11**(1), 11–19 (2017)
11. Guo, J., Bilal, M., Qiu, Y., et al.: Survey on digital twins for internet of vehicles: fundamentals, challenges, and opportunities. DCN **10**(2), 237–247 (2024)
12. Gutiérrez Cejudo, J., Enguix Andrés, F., Lujak, M., Carrascosa Casamayor, C., Fernandez, A., Hernández López, L.: Towards agrirobot digital twins: agri-RO5–a multi-agent architecture for dynamic fleet simulation. Electronics **13**(1), 80 (2023)
13. Hussain, I., Elomri, A., Kerbache, L., El Omri, A.: Smart city solutions: comparative analysis of waste management models in IoT-enabled environments using multiagent simulation. Sustain. Cities Soc. **103**, 105247 (2024)
14. López-Sánchez, A., Lujak, M., Semet, F., Billhardt, H.: Dynamic, fair, and efficient routing for cooperative autonomous vehicle fleets. ESWA **251**, 123964 (2024)
15. Lujak, M., Giordani, S., Omicini, A., Ossowski, S.: Decentralizing coordination in open vehicle fleets for scalable and dynamic task allocation. Complexity **2020**(1), 1047369 (2020)
16. Mes, M.: Using simulation to assess the opportunities of dynamic waste collection. In: Bangsow, S. (ed.) Use Cases of Discrete Event Simulation: Appliance and Research, pp. 277–307. Springer, Heidelberg (2012). https://doi.org/10.1007/978-3-642-28777-0_13
17. de Morais, C.S., Ramos, T.R.P., Lopes, M., Barbosa-Póvoa, A.P.: A data-driven optimization approach to plan smart waste collection operations. Int. Trans. Oper. Res. **31**(4), 2178–2208 (2024)
18. Szpilko, D., de la Torre Gallegos, A., Jimenez Naharro, F., Rzepka, A., Remiszewska, A.: Waste management in the smart city: current practices and future directions. Resources **12**(10), 115 (2023)
19. West, T.D., Blackburn, M.: Is digital thread/digital twin affordable? A systemic assessment of the cost of DoD's latest Manhattan project. Procedia Comput. Sci. **114**, 47–56 (2017)

Intelligent IoT Framework for Home Ambient Welfare

Marcelo Karanik, Iván Bernabé-Sánchez(✉), and Alberto Fernández

CETINIA, Universidad Rey Juan Carlos, Madrid, Spain
{marcelo.karanik,ivan.bernabe,alberto.fernandez}@urjc.es

Abstract. Internet of Things (IoT) devices have become popular in home environments. They provide various sensed data and make it possible to act on control systems to facilitate proper environmental welfare. This paper presents an architecture based on digital twins for integration into the Home Assistant platform, oriented to the automatic management of environmental sensors in smart home environments. The solution is applied to indoor air quality monitoring to preserve the well-being of home occupants. To this end, an infrastructure capable of virtually representing each physical sensor deployed is proposed, allowing it to maintain its functionality even in the event of communication failures or temporary disconnection of the actual sensors. In addition, the article proposes an environmental welfare model, which evaluates the adequacy of the measured values through a welfare index per room. The proposed model allows discriminating between normal, moderate or critical situations, triggering the necessary actions to restore the ideal conditions or alerting to possible sensor failures. A use case shows the functioning of the system.

Keywords: Digital Twins · Indoor Air Quality · Ambient Wefare

1 Introduction

Digital twins represent one of the most significant technological advances in recent years. They serve as virtual replicas of physical systems that can simulate, analyze, and predict the behavior of their real-world counterparts. Initially developed for complex industrial applications, digital twins have evolved to be applicable in smaller-scale environments, such as smart homes.

Digital twins have become an increasingly successful technology for engineering complex industrial and medical systems, with growing interest in standardizing their implementation in small and medium-sized systems through concise definition, understandable and easy-to-remember use cases, and standardized construction principles [4]. This standardization represents a fundamental step towards wider adoption in consumer-oriented applications like smart homes. Home automation, also known as smart home technology, encompasses advanced technological equipment and services in the home environment to improve the quality and empowerment of the elderly (in daily life) [6].

A. Nongaillard et al. (Eds.): PAAMS 2025, CCIS 2644, pp. 91–102, 2025.
https://doi.org/10.1007/978-3-032-05925-3_8

Another key aspect of using IoT (Internet of Things) indoors has been for environmental monitoring, allowing real-time collection of key data such as temperature, humidity, CO_2 concentration, volatile organic compounds (VOCs), among others. In this context, indoor air quality monitoring has become a central aspect to assess and ensure the well-being of occupants, especially considering that we spend more of our time indoors. IoT makes it easier to instrument living spaces, bringing intelligence to ventilation, heating and air purification systems through the use of distributed sensors and analysis platforms. In this scenario, the need arises to create more advanced models that collect environmental data and infer people's well-being and act accordingly.

The convergence of digital twins and home automation represents a promising frontier for enhancing smart home environments. By creating detailed virtual models of physical homes and their systems, digital twins enable advanced simulation, monitoring, optimization, and user interaction capabilities that traditional smart home systems alone cannot provide. Integrating these technologies offers potential benefits to various stakeholders, including homeowners, service providers and technology developers.

This paper presents an architecture for integrating digital twins in the Home Assistant platform to facilitate the automatic management of sensors oriented to maintaining environmental well-being. The proposed solution incorporates analysis, prediction, and correction mechanisms, supported by a configurable knowledge base, which allows maintaining optimal air quality conditions according to the needs of the people living in the space.

The rest of the article is divided into the following sections. Section 2 contains the state of the art. Section 3 presents an IoT framework for integrating IoT home devices to monitor and maintain ambient welfare within normal levels. Section 4 details the proposed ambient welfare model. Section 5 presents a use case scenario. Finally, Sect. 6 comments on some conclusions and future lines.

2 State of Art

Indoor air quality monitoring has become a growing interest due to its direct impact on people's health and well-being. In this context, multiple researchers have developed solutions based on IoT technologies that allow real-time monitoring of critical environmental parameters, adapted to different application environments. In this line, works such as [1–3,5,7,8,10,12,14] propose solutions oriented to monitor the main parameters related to environmental wellness (humidity, temperature, CO, CO_2, $TVCO$, etc.) through IoT sensors. Besides presenting the data communication infrastructure, these solutions also integrate network analysis mechanisms through neural networks (NN) and LSTM, statistical data analysis and advanced data visualization tools. One of the main ones we have detected in the analyzed works is the development of a custom-designed infrastructure. For example, in [5,7,12,14] a customized platform has been developed for data acquisition. In [2,8,9,11] integrate open source platforms to centralize the data collected in the deployed sensor network.

Most of these solutions require a manual configuration process to connect the sensors to the central platform and to configure the appropriate information flows from the data collected by the sensors to the relevant information analysis services. We propose an architecture that facilitates the integration of information from a sensor network through a widely used platform in the IoT domain. It also provides advanced mechanisms to manage the loss of communication between the central platform and the sensors. In addition, the proposed solution allows for managing different situations based on the measurements received from the deployed sensors.

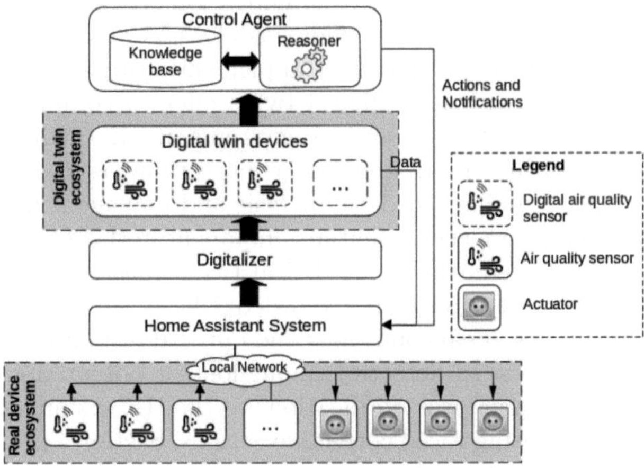

Fig. 1. Proposed IoT framework architecture.

3 IoT Framework

The IoT framework proposed in this paper is shown in Fig. 1. It is a framework focused on the management and control of sensors to monitor air quality in domotic environments. The solution implements complex mechanisms to manage the information obtained by the sensors, allowing the detection of anomalies in the sensor measurements and managing the disconnection or loss of communication with sensors. The solution uses digital twins to facilitate the implementation of these mechanisms. The framework comprises multiple interrelated components that ensure the collection, analysis and response to ambient welfare variations.

Physical sensors are strategically distributed in the environment to continuously monitor key parameters related to air quality, such as particle concentration, temperature, relative humidity and other critical variables. These sensors transmit the collected data to a centralised system called Home Assistant (HA)[1].

[1] https://www.home-assistant.io/.

The Home Assistant system is the central platform that records, manages and provides an API for accessing the data generated by the physical sensors. HA acts as a unified hub for all information from the physical environment, enhancing interaction and interoperability among diverse devices.

The measurements collected in HA are then transferred to the Digitalizer, a key component that automatically creates a corresponding digital twin for each physical sensor recorded in HA. The Digitalizer keeps these digital twins updated with real-time data provided by the physical sensors. Different device type implementations are needed for creating different types of physical devices connected to HA. For example, digital sensors are characterised by several parameters such as type of data, units, range of values, communication type (push/pull), etc. Such implementations must provide a behaviour as close as possible to the physical device. In this paper, we do not focus on implementing those components.

The Digitalizer's ecosystem of digital twins offers a comprehensive virtual representation of the monitored physical environment. Each digital twin functions autonomously within the HA environment, serving as an independent virtual sensor and offering enhanced data analysis and management flexibility.

The Control Agent is another essential component in this framework. Its task is to monitor the measurements of the digital twins constantly. This agent has direct access to a previously configured knowledge base, which contains information on acceptable ranges, ideal conditions and optimal responses to variations in environmental parameters. In detecting anomalous or potentially incorrect values, the Control Agent generates notifications to the HA system, alerting about the situation and facilitating rapid corrective actions. Section 4 proposes a model and mechanisms for detecting these situations. In addition, this agent continuously evaluates air conditions according to established criteria to ensure the health and well-being of people. When significant deviations are detected, the Control Agent can make autonomous decisions to activate actuators or specific actions to restore suitable environmental conditions.

Finally, to ensure the system's robustness and operational resilience, each digital twin integrates specific mechanisms that allow generating estimated values when the data transmission from the physical sensors is temporarily interrupted. This functionality guarantees operational continuity and maintains the integrity of the analysis and decisions made by the Control Agent, avoiding interruptions in the continuous monitoring of the environment.

4 Ambient Welfare Model

The proposed model utilises sensors in each room to monitor ambient welfare and respond accordingly. When sensors operate normally, any fluctuations in welfare parameters trigger actuators to make adjustments. The model also addresses abnormal situations, such as significant parameter variations or loss of data from sensors. This functionality is shown in Fig. 2.

The first process in Fig. 2 is determining the welfare parameters. In the context of a house composed of a set of rooms ($H = \{r_1, ..., r_i, ..., r_n\}$), the proposed

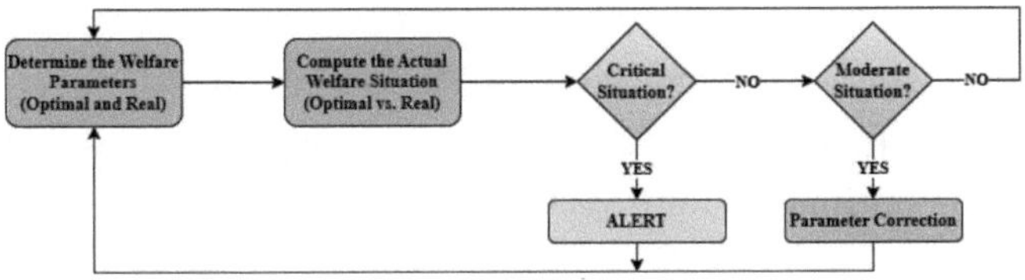

Fig. 2. Model functionality.

model uses a set of ambient variables $AV = \{av_1, ..., av_j, ...av_m\}$ where every av_j has a range of values; for example, temperature could vary between $[-10, 60]$ Celsius degrees. Using those ranges, the welfare value wv of room i at moment t of the day is defined by Eq. 1.

$$wv^{r_i}_{av_j}(x,t) = f(x, op^{r_i}_j(t), \rho_1, \rho_2, ...) \tag{1}$$

where x is the ambient value to compute the welfare, $op^{r_i}_j(t)$ is the optimal parameter for the ambient variable j in room i at moment t and $\rho_1, \rho_2, ...$ are a set of parameters for the specific function f. Resuming the temperature example, the characteristic welfare curve for temperature in room i at moment t could be a normalised Gaussian with a mean of 25 °C (optimal parameter for temperature) and a standard deviation of 10 (Fig. 3).

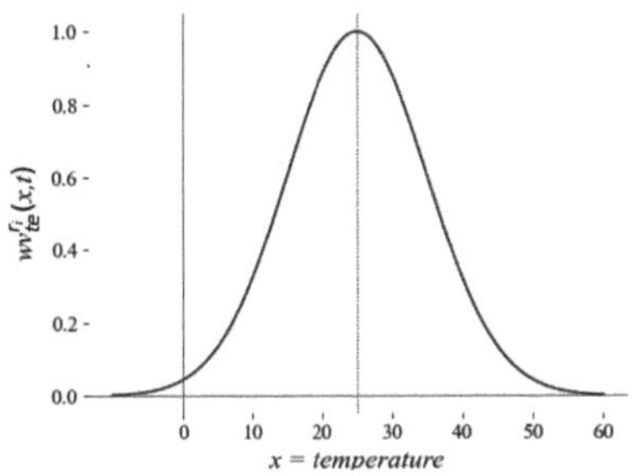

Fig. 3. Characteristic welfare curve for temperature.

Under these conditions, the optimal value for each ambient variable defines the vector of optimal welfare parameters for room i at moment t as:

$$OWP^{r_i}(t) = [op^{r_i}_1(t), ..., op^{r_i}_j(t), ..., op^{r_i}_m(t)] \tag{2}$$

Notice that this definition of the optimal welfare vector adapts the optimal value of each ambient variable to allow for changes in the characteristic curve throughout the day. Using the optimal parameters of the vector $OWP^{r_i}(t)$, the optimal welfare vector for room i at moment t (Eq. 3) is defined using Eq. 1.

$$OW^{r_i}(t) = [ow^{r_i}_1(t), ..., ow^{r_i}_j(t), ..., ow^{r_i}_m(t)] \tag{3}$$

where:

$$ow_j^{r_i}(t) = wv_{av_j}^{r_i}(op_j^{r_i}(t), t), \forall j \in \{1, ..., m\} \tag{4}$$

If all characteristic curves for every ambient variable are normalised between zero and one, the optimal welfare vector is:

$$OW^{r_i}(t) = [1, ..., 1, ..., 1] \tag{5}$$

The model also includes a set of sensors, $S = \{sav_1^{r_i}, ..., sav_j^{r_i}, ..., sav_m^{r_i}\}$, and their correspondent set of actuators $A = \{aav_1^{r_i}, ..., aav_j^{r_i}, ..., aav_m^{r_i}\}$. The sensors measure the real parameters of these variables to determine the actual welfare in each room i at moment t, and the actuators are used to modify the situation if necessary. In this way $sav_j^{r_i}$ returns the real parameter $rp_1^{r_i}(t)$ at moment t in room i. These values form the vector of real welfare parameters of room i at t:

$$RWP^{r_i}(t) = [rp_1^{r_i}(t), ..., rp_j^{r_i}(t), ..., rp_m^{r_i}(t)] \tag{6}$$

Again, using the Eq. 1, the real wefare vector is defined as:

$$RW^{r_i}(t) = [rw_1^{r_i}(t), ..., rw_j^{r_i}(t), ..., rw_m^{r_i}(t)] \tag{7}$$

where:

$$rw_j^{r_i}(t) = wv_{av_j}^{r_i}(rp_j^{r_i}(t), t), \forall j \in \{1, ..., m\} \tag{8}$$

Note that the elements of $RW^{r_i}(t)$ will be equal to one only if $rp_j^{r_i}(t) = op_j^{r_i}(t)$ and, in other case, there will be a deviation from optimal welfare value.

The second process of Fig. 2 is determining the welfare situation in the home. This implies computing the deviation between the real and optimal conditions. The approach adopted here is to calculate the welfare situation of each room in the house by computing the corresponding welfare index for each room. To compute the welfare index, the welfare deviation vector of room i at moment t is calculated as the difference between the optimal and the real welfare vector:

$$\Delta W^{r_i}(t) = OW^{r_i}(t) - RW^{r_i}(t) \tag{9}$$

where:

$$\Delta W^{r_i}(t) = [\delta w_1^{r_i}(t), ..., \delta w_j^{r_i}(t), ..., \delta w_m^{r_i}(t)] \tag{10}$$

and:

$$\delta_j^{r_i}(t) = ow_j^{r_i}(t) - rw_j^{r_i}(t) \tag{11}$$

Note that every $\delta_j^{r_i}(t)$ depends on the welfare value function (Eq. 1) for both the calculation of the optimal and the real values. Consequently, if the welfare value function is normalised between zero and one, then $\delta_j^{r_i}(t)$ will fall within the range $[0, 1]$. Here, 0 represents an optimal welfare situation, while 1 indicates the worst welfare situation for the ambient variable j in room i at time t. In this way, the situation of every ambient variable in a specific room and time can be categorised according to $\delta_j^{r_i}(t)$.

The model defines three categories for each ambient variable: *normal* ($Nor \in [0, 0.3]$), *moderate* ($Mod \in (0.3, 0.6]$) and *critical* ($Cri \in (0.6, 1]$). The model's response depends on specific categories of situations. Corrections aren't needed in normal situations, so the actuators remain unused. In moderate situations, corrections are essential using relevant actuators. Critical situations require alerts to prevent problematic outcomes. In this latter case, given the seriousness of the situation, no corrective action is taken, and the user is alerted to check the room.

To determine the situation in a room, simply aggregating all variables, for example, with the arithmetic mean, is inadequate. This approach may mask the critical state of one environmental variable due to the potential influence of normal values of the others. To deal with this problem, the model calculates a welfare index in room i at t using the OWA (Ordered Weighted Averaging) [13] operator, which gives more importance to critical values than to normal values. In this way, it is only necessary that when the value of one or several variables of the environment is critical, the index is triggered to the critical category, regardless of whether the rest of the values are normal or even optimal. For the rest of the cases, i.e., there are no critical values, and the category is adjusted as if it were a weighted average. In this way, the actuators will only be triggered in general moderate situations. So, given $\Delta W^{r_i}(t)$ the welfare index for the room i at moment t is defined as follows:

$$Widx^{r_i}(t) = OWA(\Delta W^{r_i}(t), w_1, ..., w_j, ..., w_m) \quad (12)$$

where $w_1, ..., w_j, ..., w_m$ are the weights for the deviation of every ambient variable in ascending order. Note that there is no specific formula to select the values for the weights, as a suggestion, they must be assigned following an exponential growth according to their position, and their sum must equal one. Finally, the house welfare vector is:

$$HW(t) = [Widx^{r_1}(t), ..., Widx^{r_i}(t), ..., Widx^{r_n}(t)] \quad (13)$$

The $HW(t)$ provides summary information about the welfare of each room in the house, enabling decisions to be made on a situation-by-situation basis.

The alert process starts when any $Widx^{r_i}(t)$ exceeds 0.6, indicating a critical category for at least one $\delta_j^{r_i}(t)$. This deviation may suggest either a serious environmental issue or a critical sensor error.

Two alerts are proposed to address this: one for serious situations and another for potential sensor malfunctions. When a critical condition is detected for sensor j in room i at time t, readings from other sensors in the same room and other rooms will be analysed to assess the overall context.

When the nearby sensor readings return abnormal values, serious situations are considered. This implies that there is a widespread problem, and therefore, the alert should specify this. On the other hand, if the reading of nearby sensors returns normal values, the problem is most likely local and corresponds to a malfunction of a particular sensor. Based on this proximity information, the corresponding alerts are sent accordingly.

The proposed strategy for corrections is based on the analysis of the welfare conditions of each room. Due to the OWA operator's characteristics, the value $Widx^{r_i}(t)$ shows that all deviations $\delta_j^{r_i}(t)$ will be below the welfare index, with the highest deviation close to it. In this way, if the model detects that all ambient variable deviations, represented by the $\Delta W^{r_i}(t)$ vector, are near to the lower limit (0.3), corrective actions are not required at this time and it is advisable to continue monitoring the situation. On the contrary, if many parameters are near the upper limit (0.6), the actuators should be activated to restore normal welfare levels. Note that this strategy tends to minimise the energy consumption.

Finally, if all rooms fall within the normal welfare category (i.e., $Widx^{r_i}(t) < 0.3\ \forall i$), no corrective actions are taken, minimising energy consumption too.

5 Use Case

This section describes the framework's functionality. The model aims to ensure environmental welfare by adjusting connected devices and alerting users of critical situations or sensor malfunctions.

5.1 Scenario Description

The house for this use case has five rooms (r_1, r_2, r_3, r_4 and r_5), a distribution hall (r_6) and a little hallway in the entrance (r_7). Four ambient variables are sensed in each space of the house: temperature (te), humidity (h), CO_2 level (CO_2) and $VOCs$ level ($VOCs$). Additionally, human presence (hp) is also sensed. These sensors return the corresponding parameters: pte, ph, pCO_2, $pVOCs$ and php. The characteristic curves of welfare for each of these ambient variables are modelled using Eqs. 14, 15, 16, 17:

$$wv_{te}^{r_i}(x,t) = \exp\left(-\frac{1}{2}\left(\frac{x-25}{10}\right)^2\right) \tag{14}$$

$$wv_{h}^{r_i}(x,t) = \exp\left(-\frac{1}{2}\left(\frac{x-50}{15}\right)^2\right) \tag{15}$$

$$wv_{CO_2}^{r_i}(x,t) = \begin{cases} 1 & \text{if } x \le 800 \\ \exp\left(-0.5\left(\frac{x-800}{250}\right)^2\right) & \text{if } x > 800 \end{cases} \tag{16}$$

$$wv_{VOCs}^{r_i}(x,t) = \begin{cases} 1 & \text{if } x \le 200 \\ \exp\left(-0.5\left(\frac{x-200}{200}\right)^2\right) & \text{if } x > 200 \end{cases} \tag{17}$$

Notice that hp is a binary variable for human presence, where 0 represents the absence of people in the room and 1 indicates their presence. Two normalized Gaussian functions are used, with $\mu = 25$ and $\sigma = 10$ for temperature (Eq. 14) and $\mu = 50$ and $\sigma = 15$ for humidity (Eq. 15). For CO_2, the first part is 1 if the parameter is less than or equal to 800, and for higher values, the second part is a normalised Gaussian function with $\mu = 800$ and $\sigma = 250$. Finally, for $VOCs$, the first part is equal to 1 if the parameter is less than or equal to 200 and for

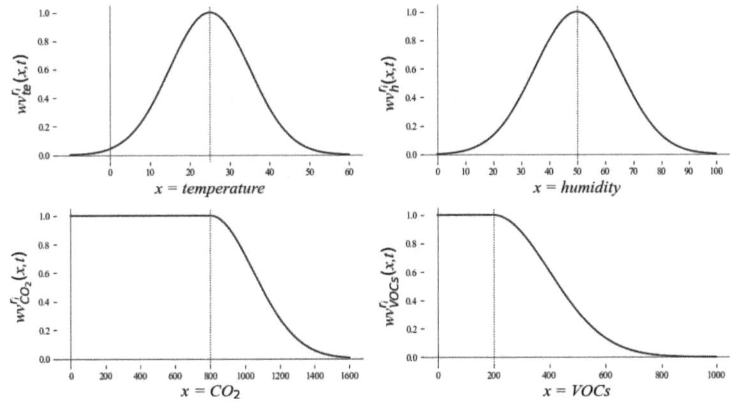

Fig. 4. Curves for *temperature*, *humidity*, CO_2 and $VOCs$.

higher values, the second part is a normalised Gaussian function with $\mu = 200$ and $\sigma = 200$. The characteristic curves are shown in Fig. 4.

The vector of optimal welfare parameters is defined using the optimal value of each ambient variable for every room i at moment t is:

$$OWP^{r_i}(t) = [opte^{r_i}(t), oph^{r_i}(t), opCO_2^{r_i}(t), opVOCs^{r_i}(t), ophp^{r_i}(t)] \quad (18)$$

Using Eq. 1 the optimal welfare vector is computed:

$$OW^{r_i}(t) = [ow_1^{r_i}(t), ow_2^{r_i}(t), ow_3^{r_i}(t), ow_4^{r_i}(t), ow_5^{r_i}(t)] \quad (19)$$

where $ow_j^{r_i}(t) = wv_{av_j}^{r_i}(op_j^{r_i}(t), t)$, $op_j^{r_i}(t)$ is the optimal parameter for $av_1 = te$, $av_2 = h$, $av_3 = CO_2$ and $av_4 = VOCs$ respectively.

Since all characteristic curves for every ambient variable are normalised between zero and one, the optimal welfare vector is $OW^{r_i}(t) = [1, 1, 1, 1, 1]$.

Notice that the $OW^{r_i}(t)$ considers the optimum value for human presence ($wv_{php}^{r_i}(ophp^{r_i}(t), t)$) equal to one, i.e., it is only necessary to monitor the ambient welfare if there are people inside room i at moment t. Finally, every room i is equipped with sensors that monitor the parameters at moment t of each ambient variable (ste^{r_i}, sh^{r_i}, $sCO_2^{r_i}$, $sVOCs^{r_i}$, and shp^{r_i}) and return the actual parameter for such rooms to define the vector of real welfare parameters:

$$RWP^{r_i}(t) = [rpte^{r_i}(t), rph^{r_i}(t), rpCO_2^{r_i}(t), rpVOCs^{r_i}(t), rphp^{r_i}(t)] \quad (20)$$

By using Eq. 1 the real welfare vector is obtained:

$$RW^{r_i}(t) = [rw_1^{r_i}(t), rw_2^{r_i}(t), rw_3^{r_i}(t), rw_4^{r_i}(t), rw_5^{r_i}(t)] \quad (21)$$

where $rw_j^{r_i}(t) = wv_{av_j}^{r_i}(rp_j^{r_i}(t), t)$, and $rp_j^{r_i}(t)$ is the real sensed parameter.

5.2 Ambient Welfare Computation

To illustrate how the model calculates welfare in each room of the house, the sensor values for each room are presented in Table 1. Using the sensed parameters, the welfare values for each variable in every room are calculated employing Eqs. 14, 15, 16, and 17 as appropriate. For example, the humidity in room 3 at moment t is 52% and, by using the Eq. 15 the welfare in room 3 is:

$$wv_2^{r_3}(52, t) = \exp\left(-\frac{1}{2}\left(\frac{52-50}{\cdot 15}\right)^2\right) = 0.991 \tag{22}$$

In this case, it is very close to the optimum, and the deviation is minimal. This deviation is calculated using Eq. 11. Since all the optimal values are equal to 1, all the deviations are computed as $1 - wv_j^{r_1}(rp_j, t)$, which results in the case of room 3, the humidity deviation is $1 - 0.991 = 0.009$. All welfare deviations are calculated similarly and summarised in Table 2.

Finally, the welfare index for every room at moment t ($Widx^{r_i}(t)$) is computed by using the OWA operator. As mentioned before, the suggestion is to assign the weights following an exponential growth according to their position, and their sum must equal one. Considering the scenario has four ambient variables, the selected weights for every position are $[0.001, 0.010, 0.100, 0.889]$.

Table 1. Real welfare parameters in t ($RWP^{r_i}(t)$)

	$rpte$	rph	$rpCO_2$	$rpVOCs$	$rphp$
room 1	27	46	764	272	1
room 2	15	45	855	222	1
room 3	17	52	890	178	1
room 4	31	31	885	169	0
room 5	24	40	766	163	1
room 6	28	58	791	270	1
room 7	19	48	855	256	1

Table 2 shows that room 4 requires attention, since the humidity has dropped to 31%. This should start the corresponding actuator to correct the humidity variable. Still, in the human presence column, the value is zero, i.e., no one is in room 4, so the corrective action is not initiated.

Now suppose that the temperature in room 6 increases to 45 degrees Celsius. Recalculating all the indices, the new welfare vector is:

$$HW(t) = [0.060, 0.355, 0.255, 0.508, 0.177, \mathbf{0.783}, 0.151] \tag{23}$$

According to Table 2, there is human presence in room 6 and the $Widx^{r_6}(t) = 0.783$. Since the other indices are relatively normal and do not need correction,

Table 2. Welfare deviations in t and $Widx^{r_i}(t)$ for each $room\ i$.

	$\delta w_1^{r_i}(t)$	$\delta w_2^{r_i}(t)$	$\delta w_3^{r_i}(t)$	$\delta w_4^{r_i}(t)$	$rphp$	$Widx^{r_i}(t)$
$room\ 1$	0.020	0.035	0.000	0.063	1	0.060
$room\ 2$	0.393	0.054	0.024	0.006	1	0.355
$room\ 3$	0.274	0.009	0.063	0.000	1	0.250
$room\ 4$	0.165	0.552	0.056	0.000	0	**0.508**
$room\ 5$	0.005	0.199	0.000	0.000	1	0.177
$room\ 6$	0.044	0.133	0.000	0.059	1	0.125
$room\ 7$	0.165	0.009	0.024	0.038	1	0.151

the model warns about the possible malfunction of the temperature sensor in room 6. As can be seen, the model enables comprehensive analyses by providing all necessary information to address the situation's severity.

6 Conclusions

This paper presents an architecture oriented to the intelligent management of ambient welfare in domestic environments, integrating digital twin technologies and open IoT platforms, such as Home Assistant.

The proposed solution allows for virtually representing each physical sensor using a digital twin that operates autonomously, ensuring the system's continuity in case of communication interruptions or failures in the real devices.

In addition, an environmental comfort assessment model has been introduced to detect deviations in the measured values concerning optimal conditions, classifying them as normal, moderate, or critical. This enables automatic decisions, such as activating actuators or issuing alerts, to restore the rooms' comfort.

The proposed solution is a modular and adaptable approach, allowing it to be deployed in different scenarios and improving the quality of life. Likewise, incorporating a configurable knowledge base facilitates customisation according to the environment's and users' specific needs.

Future research lines aim to define a formal model to enhance the framework, using data from adjacent rooms to identify critical situations, and exploring a decentralised approach for large buildings by connecting several frameworks.

Acknowledgments. Work been supported by grant VAE: TED2021-131295B-C33 funded by MCIN/AEI/10.13039/501100011033 and by the "European Union NextGenerationEU/PRTR", and by grant COSASS: PID2021-123673OB-C32 funded by MCIN/AEI/10.13039/501100011033 and by "ERDF A way of making Europe".

Disclosure of Interests. The authors have no competing interests to declare that are relevant to the content of this article.

References

1. Abraham, S., Li, X.: A cost-effective wireless sensor network system for indoor air quality monitoring applications. Procedia Comput. Sci. **34**, 165–171 (2014)
2. Benammar, M., Abdaoui, A., Ahmad, S.H., Touati, F., Kadri, A.: A modular IoT platform for real-time indoor air quality monitoring. Sensors **18**(2), 581 (2018)
3. Bhattacharya, S., Sridevi, S., Pitchiah, R.: Indoor air quality monitoring using wireless sensor network. In: 2012 Sixth International Conference on Sensing Technology (ICST), pp. 422–427. IEEE (2012)
4. Hauer, M., et al.: Integrating digital twins with BIM for enhanced building control strategies: a systematic literature review focusing on daylight and artificial lighting systems. Buildings (2024), https://api.semanticscholar.org/CorpusID:268494863
5. Liu, Y., Hassan, K.A., Karlsson, M., Weister, O., Gong, S.: Active plant wall for green indoor climate based on cloud and internet of things. IEEE Access **6**, 33631–33644 (2018)
6. Muhammadi, M.: The human dimension in intelligent living environment (2011). https://api.semanticscholar.org/CorpusID:111698134
7. Mumtaz, R., et al.: Internet of things (IoT) based indoor air quality sensing and predictive analytic—a COVID-19 perspective. Electronics **10**(2), 184 (2021)
8. Nasution, T.H., Hizriadi, A., Tanjung, K., Nurmayadi, F.: Design of indoor air quality monitoring systems. In: 2020 4rd International Conference on Electrical, Telecommunication and Computer Engineering, pp. 238–241. IEEE (2020)
9. Rani, S.U., Rajarajeswari, S., Jaimon, J.G., Ravichandran, R.: Real-time air quality monitoring system using MQ-135 and thingsboard. J, Critical Rev. **7**(18), 4107–4115 (2020)
10. Tiele, A., Esfahani, S., Covington, J.: Design and development of a low-cost, portable monitoring device for indoor environment quality. J. Sens. **2018**(1), 5353816 (2018)
11. Traboulsi, S., Knauth, S.: Towards implementation of an IoT analysis system for buildings environmental data and workplace well-being with an iot open software. Procedia Comput. Sci. **170**, 341–346 (2020)
12. Wall, D., McCullagh, P., Cleland, I., Bond, R.: Development of an internet of things solution to monitor and analyse indoor air quality. Internet Things **14** (2021)
13. Yager, R.R.: On ordered weighted averaging aggregation operators in multicriteria decisionmaking. IEEE Trans. Syst. Man Cybern. **18**(1), 183–190 (1988). https://doi.org/10.1109/21.87068
14. Yu, T.C., Lin, C.C.: An intelligent wireless sensing and control system to improve indoor air quality: monitoring, prediction, and preaction. Int. J. Distrib. Sens. Netw. **11**(8), 140978 (2015)

PAAMS - Workshop on Deep Learning Applications (DeLA)

Workshop on Deep Learning Applications (DeLA)

Deep learning is an artificial intelligence (AI) function that imitates the workings of the human brain in processing data and creating patterns for use in decision making. Deep learning is a subset of machine learning in artificial intelligence that has networks capable of learning unsupervised from data that is unstructured or unlabeled. It is also known as deep neural learning or deep neural networks.

The objective of the workshop on Deep Learning Applications was an opportunity for researchers to provide further insight into the problems solved at this stage, advantages and disadvantages of the various approaches used, lessons learned, and meaningful contributions to enhance applications based on deep learning. In this sense, the first workshop on Deep Learning Applications (DeLA) provided a forum for the presentation and discussion of novel research ideas or actual deployments focused on the development of advanced applications based on Deep Learning.

Topics that were relevant for the workshop included particularly applications, but also theoretical approaches, based on (but not limited to):

- Chatbots
- Natural Language Processing (NLP)
- Computer Vision
- Sentiment Analysis
- Speech Recognition
- Autonomous Vehicles
- Robotics
- Image Detection and Object Classification
- Deep Learning Business Applications
- Healthcare
- Entertainment
- Composing Music
- Pattern Recognition
- Action Recognition
- Virtual Assistants
- Facial Recognition Systems
- Fraud Detection
- Forecasting Solutions
- eXplainable Artificial Intelligence (XAI)

Organization

Organizing Committee

Dalila Durães	University of Minho, Portugal
Flávio A. O. Santos	Universidade Federal de Pernambuco, Brazil
Cleber Zanchettin	Universidade Federal de Pernambuco, Brazil
Leonardo Nogueira Matos	Universidade Federal de Sergipe, Brazil
Paulo Novais	University of Minho, Portugal

Program Committee

Maynara Donato de Souza	Universidade Federal de Pernambuco, Brazil
Michael Oliveira da Cruz	Universidade Federal Rural de Pernambuco, Brazil
Luís Conceição	GECAD-ISEP, Polytechnic Institute of Porto, Portugal
Diogo Martinho	GECAD-ISEP, Polytechnic Institute of Porto, Portugal
Francisco Marcondes	University of Minho, Portugal
Manuel Rodrigues	University of Minho, Portugal
Pedro Oliveira	University of Minho, Portugal
Hugo Peixoto	University of Minho, Portugal
Regina Sousa	University of Minho, Portugal

Hybrid Neuro-Symbolic Learning Agents: A Graph-Theoretic Approach to Interpretable Reinforcement Learning

Reem Alansary(✉) and Nourhan Ehab

Department of Computer Science and Engineering, German University in Cairo, Cairo, Egypt
{reem.adel,nourhan.ehab}@guc.edu.eg

Abstract. Recent advances in Reinforcement Learning (RL) have enabled agents to achieve remarkable performance in complex sequential decision problems. However, the opaque nature of RL models limits interpretability and generalization, prompting the need for hybrid neuro-symbolic approaches. In this paper, we propose an agent architecture that integrates reinforcement learning with a layered graph-based knowledge base (KB) offering a novel symbolic inference mechanism for inductive reasoning. The proposed architecture does not rely at all on knowledge provided by humans. The KB stores learned policies in a structured form, enabling explicit reasoning and generalization through a clique-based inference method applied to multigraphs with colored edges. We validate our approach on a grid-based environment, demonstrating improved learning efficiency and policy interpretability across deterministic and stochastic settings. Results indicate that agents leveraging the KB outperform purely sub-symbolic counterparts in cumulative reward and efficiency. Our findings suggest that combining reinforcement learning with structured symbolic reasoning offers a promising path toward explainable and adaptive decision-making systems.

Keywords: Reinforcement learning · Representation learning · Interpretable AI

1 Introduction

In the past century, efforts were poured into identifying elements of human cognition and incorporating them into machines. Two dominant approaches have emerged: symbolic reasoning, where expert knowledge is explicitly encoded into machines, and sub-symbolic learning, which approximates cognitive processes through neural networks and reinforcement mechanisms. However, "solutions that work" are no longer sufficient. It is now of great importance to have solutions that are interpretable, at least to a certain degree. A hybrid system integrating both symbolic and sub-symbolic components offers a promising direction toward this goal.

A. Nongaillard et al. (Eds.): PAAMS 2025, CCIS 2644, pp. 107–118, 2025.
https://doi.org/10.1007/978-3-032-05925-3_9

To address this, hybrid *neuro-symbolic* approaches have gained traction, combining learning and reasoning to achieve transparent and explainable decision-making. This paper proposes a novel graph-based neuro-symbolic RL agent that integrates reinforcement learning with structured symbolic reasoning. The agent maintains an interpretable knowledge base (KB), structured as a layered graph, and employs a clique-based inference method for inductive reasoning. The agent does not depend on and is not given knowledge, preprocessed or otherwise, from humans is any phase of its operation. Our contribution is three-fold.

1. We introduce a novel graph-based symbolic inference mechanism that enables inductive generalization through a clique-based approach applied to multi-graphs with colored edges.
2. We integrate this inference mechanism into an RL agent's knowledge base (KB), facilitating structured generalization and interpretability.
3. We empirically validate our approach in a grid-based environment, demonstrating significant improvements in cumulative reward and learning efficiency in the complete absence of knowledge provided by humans.

The remainder of this paper is organized as follows. Section 2 presents related work on sequential decision problems and knowledge-augmented learning agents. Section 3 describes the proposed hybrid system, including the structure and operations of the knowledge base. Section 4 introduces our purely symbolic inference mechanism and its theoretical foundation. Section 5 presents experimental results demonstrating the effectiveness of our approach in a grid-based environment. Section 6 concludes the paper with a discussion of findings and future research directions.

2 Problem Model and Related Work

In this section, we introduce the formal model for sequential decision problems, review agent-based approaches for learning abstract rules, and present relevant graph-theoretic concepts, particularly the clique problem, which forms the basis of our proposed inference method.

2.1 Abstract Problem Model

Before delving into the available approaches for tackling the problem of efficient and interpretable generalization in sequential decision problems, we introduce a simple model of such problems: the Markov Decision Process (MDP). An MDP M is formally defined as the 4-tuple $M = (S, T, A, R)$, where S is the state space, T is the transition model, A is the action space, and R is the reward function.

The transition model T usually has a probabilistic nature and the reward function is always defined with respect to some goal. In other words, for all states $s \in S$, where the goal is achieved, the reward is maximum. Any MDP M exhibits the Markovian Property that guarantees that the current state of the world is affected only by the most recent previous state.

A solution for M then would be the optimal global policy π^* found by an abstract embodiment of the solver as a rational agent which learns by reinforcement. This agent finds the optimal global policy by repeatedly observing state-action-reward sequences in the MDP and making predictions as to which actions would lead it to its goal.

2.2 Knowledge-Augmented Learning Agents

To address the challenge of interpretable generalization, researchers have explored model-based RL and knowledge-augmented learning approaches. Some techniques focus on representing environment dynamics to detect state regularities, while others abstract agent behavior.

One approach introduces Semi-MDPs (SMDPs) [3], where agents execute extended macro-actions, effectively segmenting behavior into hierarchical units. Alternatively, bisimulation metrics [1] abstract agent behavior by grouping states with similar optimal policies. Sub-symbolic methods also employ data mining [2] to accelerate policy learning.

Recent advances in neuro-symbolic RL leverage structured background knowledge to enhance learning efficiency. Deep RL, augmented with knowledge from humans to inhibit the generation of trivial action representations, is employed to learn mathematical functions as approximations for each action in the action space in a sequential manner [7]. Existing knowledge in the form demonstrations can also be used to enhance the agent's performance when data is scarce [9]. Additionally, declarative planning models have been used to improve RL in environments with sparse rewards [6]. In non-Markovian environments, learning deterministic finite automata (DFA) decomposes tasks into Markovian subproblems [5].

3 Proposed Hybrid System Description

We propose a hybrid agent architecture that integrates tabular Q-learning, which was chosen as the learning algorithm because it is guaranteed to converge to the optimal action-utility values, with a layered graph-based KB. This structure facilitates symbolic reasoning through inductive inference, preserving interpretability while enhancing learning efficiency.

3.1 KB Structure

Addressing the crux of efficient learning and generalization, we propose a graph-based Knowledge Base (KB) structured into layers. Each layer corresponds to the agent's sensors, forming a hierarchy that aids in efficient navigation, when the KB is searched for a particular rule, and representation of learned rules, since any node after level zero will be connected with a directed edge to another when both have similar rules. Rule structure is discussed in the next paragraph but we say that two rules are similar when they share literals in their antecedent. Rules are represented in the language of propositional logic. The graph data structure is chosen over the classical flat KB as it can separate the learned rules such that similar ones remain closer together.

The zeroth level of the KB is made up of one utility node that holds the structure together and is the entry point to it but that node is not representative of a rule specific to any decision problem; it will always hold the material conditional $\bot \implies \top$, which serves as a formalization of the fact that any agent situated in an unknown environment without prior knowledge will believe that it can execute any action and that all actions are equally preferable with respect to its goal, as indicated by the reward function. Any node, other than the utility node, holds a rule consisting of a conjunction of discretized state variables from an environment, as the antecedent, and the corresponding best action as the consequent of a material conditional. Furthermore, on the grounds that each rule is obtained through an inductive process that generates a belief that could be revised, we associate with each rule a weight measuring its relevance to the agent's goal. For nodes in the bottom level, this weight is based on the q-value of the rule, which comes directly from the learning algorithm. Each rule in any other level is induced and its weight is computed from the weights of the rules in the nodes that participated in its induction.

The levels of the KB are finite and directly correspond to the number of sensors of the agent; if the agent has m sensors (and m will be used exclusively to refer to the agent's number of sensors henceforth), then the graph has $m + 1$ levels, where the ith level has i sensor values forming the antecedent of every rule for $0 \leq i \leq m$. In the graphic example of Fig. 1, this means that any node in level i is reachable after traversing i directed edges from the utility node in level zero. Each rule maps either a full or partial state to the perceived optimal action; rules in the bottom level correspond to full states, but rules in any other level correspond to partial states as they are induced. This mapping, enforced by the rule format, helps in clarifying the agent's belief about the outcome of executing some action in some state and why the agent's beliefs may change with any change of an observation.

3.2 KB Operations

The KB supports four core operations.

Insert. This is a *TELL*-type operation invoked by an agent to add knowledge to the KB.
Infer. This is an *ASK*-type operation to apply an inference method for detecting implicit knowledge in the KB.
Search. This is an *ASK*-type operation for knowledge present explicitly in the KB. Search is implemented to be greedy where at each level only the subgraph under the node with the highest weight is explored further.
Prune. This is a utility operation to prevent cluttering the KB with unnecessary knowledge.

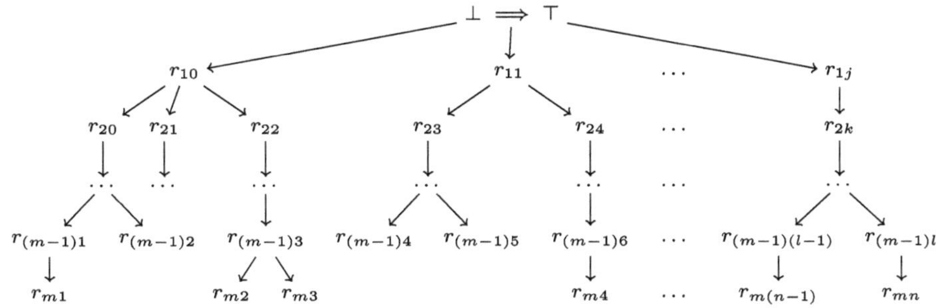

Fig. 1. An abstract example of the graph-based KB where each r_{ab} is a rule in level a and its index in that level is b. Out of all the contents of any node only the rule is shown here for simplicity.

4 A Purely Symbolic Mode of Inductive Inference

Although it is a mode of reasoning through which one cannot obtain necessary conclusions, inductive reasoning helps in obtaining patterns or similarities present in multiple observations. For the right patterns to be explicated, one has to combine the right observations and be able to discard the others. To operationalize induction in our agent, we frame it as a combinatorial problem: discovering structured patterns in observed data. This formulation naturally maps to the clique problem, where identifying cohesive subsets of knowledge elements enables rule generalization.

The inference procedure is designed with two abstract goals in mind; it should be *flexible* and *selective*. The former quality means that it is not obligatory to fill in the entire KB with a single invocation of the procedure so that memory consumption can be somewhat controlled in applications where this is required. The latter quality means that the agent or its controller will be able to select which part(s) of the KB will be filled.

The generation of new rules from existing ones will occur in the upwards directions of the KB; a rule in level i will be inferred using rules in level j where $i < j \leq m$. To infer a rule t from a set of rules R, we ensure that

1. the set of actions taken from each rule $r \in R$ is a singleton set, and
2. converting each antecedent of a rule $r \in R$ to a set of the propositions in that antecedent and applying the intersection operation on two or more of these sets results in the formation of a set of size i.

The application of the logical conjunction operator on two propositions indicates a relation between them that can be translated into an undirected edge between two nodes representing these propositions. This idea can be generalized to the application of conjunction on more than two propositions since this operator is commutative.

The propositions that appear in the antecedents of two or more rules with the same consequent will form a clique. To identify these cliques correctly, the antecedent of every rule will be assigned a distinct color and edges that result from transforming it to a graph will have that color. Therefore, propositions that show up together will be linked by edges of the same color. Consequently, the problem now is reduced to detecting two or more cliques, each of a uniform color, comprised of the same set of nodes. The transformation from a set of antecedents to the colored multigraph CMG_R is given in Definition 1 and the reduction to the k-clique problem in that multigraph is given in Theorem 1.

Definition 1 (CMG_R)**.** For some set of rules R, where all $r \in R$ share the same consequent, $CMG_R = (V, E)$ is the undirected multigraph formed by transforming all the propositions that appear in the colored antecedents of the rules in R to nodes and the conjunction applied on any pair of propositions to a colored edge between their corresponding nodes.

- Let $A = \{(a, c) \mid a \text{ is an antecedent colored in } c \text{ of any } r \in R\}$.
- $V = \{p \mid p \text{ is a proposition in } a \text{ of any } (a, c) \in A\}$.
- $E = \{\{p, q, c\} \mid p, q \text{ appear as } p \wedge q \text{ in } a \text{ of any } (a, c) \in A\}$.

Theorem 1. *A rule t in level i can be inferred if and only if CMG_R has n i-cliques, induced by the same set of nodes, of n colors for $n \geq 2$.*

Proof. Suppose a rule in level i can be inferred. This entails that there is a set of rules R, from which CMG_R will be constructed, such that all the rules share the same action and that the intersection of a subset of at least two antecedents of members of R is nonempty and has cardinality i. When any antecedent in level $i+1$ is transformed into a subgraph of CMG_R, it is guaranteed that the propositions of that antecedent will form an $i+1$-clique that in turn contains a total of $i+1$ induced i-cliques after the removal of a choice of one node at a time. At least one transformed antecedent will contain an i-clique that occurs in another transformed antecedent of a different color. Therefore, CMG_R will contain at least two i-cliques of two colors.

Suppose CMG_R has n i-cliques, induced by the same nodes, of n different colors, where $n \geq 2$. It directly follows from Definition 1 that the participating nodes come from n different antecedents. Accordingly, the intersection of these n different antecedents is nonempty and has cardinality i. Furthermore, since CMG_R can only be built using rules that share the same action, the two conditions required for inferring a rule are satisfied.

Repeated application of the theorem shows that a rule t of level i can be inferred if and only if CMG_R has n j-cliques induced by the same set of nodes, of n colors for $n \geq 2$ and $j > i$.

We adapt an algorithm, named COMPLETE which is attributed to Chiba and Nishizeki [4], that lists all complete subgraphs of order k of some simple graph to operate on multigraphs without loops instead by providing an extra input denoting the colors of edges. The major change done to the original algorithm is the adaptation of the *third* step. The modified algorithm, TWOCOLOR-COMPLETE, is shown in Algorithm 1.

Require: k, U, P
  if $k == 2$ **then**
    1: adjacents $= \{\} \cup C$
    for each labelled edge (x, y) of the subgraph induced by U and where y is adjacent to x at least twice **do**
      adjacents = adjacents $\cup \{x, y\}$
      results = results $\cup$ {adjacents}
      adjacents = adjacents $- \{x, y\}$
    end for
  else
    2: Sort the vertices in U such that $d_k(v_1) \geq d_k(v_2) \geq \ldots \geq d_k(v_{|U|})$ and store them in a list.
    for $i = 1$ to $|U|$ **do**
      Let U' be the set of all the vertices which are adjacent to v_i, where vertices are connected by edges that observe the requirements of Theorem 1, and labelled k.
      3: Relabel all the vertices adjacent to v_i "$k - 1$", while
        3.1: accumulating all colors of edges and which adjacents are associated with each color, then find the *true* adjacents which are connected to v_i by at least 2 differently colored edges and such that the colored edges are incident on at least $k - 1$ common nodes, then
        3.2: label the edges that should participate in U' "$k - 1$".
        3.3: Relabel the vertices adjacent to v_i, that do not have edges incident on v_i labelled $k - 1$, k.
      Store the colors that identify *true* adjacents only in list P.
      4: In the adjacency list of each vertex $u \in U'$, move the neighbors of u in U', identified by the labels of the neighbors and the connecting edges, at the first part. The vertices of G_{k-1} currently occupy the first parts of the adjacency lists of vertices in U', which realize the adjacency lists of G_{k-1}.
      5. Determine the degree $d_{k-1}(u)$ of each $u \in U'$ in G_{k-1}.
      6. Add the vertex v_i to C.
      7. TWOCOLOR-COMPLETE($k - 1$, U', P)
      8. Delete the top entry v_i from C.
      9. Relabel all the vertices in U' and their edges, currently labelled "$k - 1$", "k". This is the recovery step to G_k.
      10. Relabel v_i "$k + 1$".
      11. In the adjacency list of each vertex $u \in U'$, move the entries of v_i to the position next to the last entry containing an edge whose associated vertex is labelled "k".
    end for
  end if

Algorithm 1: TWOCOLOR-COMPLETE

Theorem 2. *Given a CMG_R constructed from R in level $i + 1$ in the KB, algorithm* TWOCOLOR-COMPLETE *finds the antecedents of inferred rule(s) using R in level j for $0 < j < i \leq m$.*

Proof. To prove the correctness of TWOCOLOR-COMPLETE, we draw upon the correctness proof of the original algorithm and augment it to show that U' is still formed correctly after the change to the *third* step.

Suppose that U' is *incorrectly* formed in some call of the algorithm. This means that one of two scenarios has taken place while some graph G_{k-1} is being processed:

- Edges of some colors that should not be members of the graph are considered. However, a set of permitted colors is passed as the third argument to eliminate this issue, so a simple set membership test using P would suffice.
- For the recursive call, after removing node n from G_k, where the size of P is three or more, there is a *detectable* k-clique with two or more edges between every pair of nodes such that the colors of these edges constitute a set of at least three elements. Let the former set contain exactly three colors, for simplicity, although the argument can be generalized for more, and let the violating clique be VC. Since the violating color, contributing to the formation of VC, is permitted, it must be the color of some edges in set E' that are incident on n and other nodes not in VC, and an edge e at least in VC. However, the ends of e must be connected to every end in E' by Definition 1. Further, as n is connected to every end of any edge in E' with an edge of the violating color, it must be connected to the ends of e with the same color. Therefore, e cannot be a member of any VC.

5 Empirical Validation

After having integrated the explicit knowledge component into the system, experiments were conducted to assess the performance of this agent in three versions of a grid-based environment, named The Gardener's World, created following the style of Frozen Lake [8].

The Gardener's World is an $n \times n$ grid where the agent is a gardener who collects flowers and makes sure that the soil remains healthy as a secondary task. A grid cell contains either a flower or a contaminated soil patch. In this environment, the agent can do one of six actions: move left, down, right, up, collect a flower, and decontaminate a soil patch. The environment may be modeled with deterministic or non-deterministic transition models for the movement actions; for example, if the agent chose to make a move in the upwards direction, it could end up sliding in either of the two perpendicular directions with a specified probability. The reward function of this environment gives the agent a reward of 5 units when it remedies a decontaminated soil patch, 10 units when it collects a flower, and 0 units for all else. To avoid having the agent execute an action that will never change the state signal, such as a collect when there is no flower or a decontaminate when the soil is clean, an action mask is provided with every state signal. Finally, a terminal state is reached in an episode when there are no more flowers to collect and an episode can also end when a truncation signal is observed by the agent. This is a signal that is issued after 200 steps. The agent starts in the top left-most cell at the beginning of any episode.

The Gardener's world was modeled twice with probabilistic transition models with differing probabilities and once with a deterministic transition model. In each experiment, the agent spent some episodes learning using the Q-Learning update rule then switches to the KB and refrained from learning again. More specifically, the agent was set to learn for 1000 episodes and it was forced to switch to the inferred knowledge in the KB after the third (75%), second (50%), and first (25%) quartiles of episodes, respectively. Results shown in Fig. 3 are the averaged results from 20 runs of the experiment.

The map in Fig. 2 was generated randomly and used for all experiments involving one deterministic transition model and two non-deterministic ones, each with a different probability distribution. An empty/white cell on the grid denotes a healthy soil patch without contamination and not containing a planted flower. A cell with the symbol marks a contaminated soil patch without a planted flower, and a cell with the symbol marks a healthy soil patch with a planted flower.

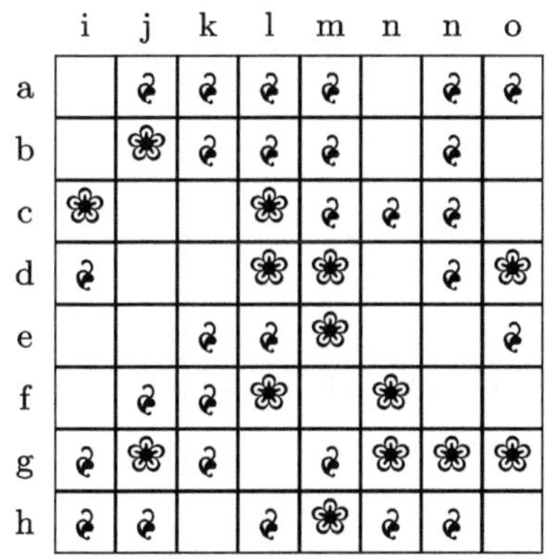

Fig. 2. 8 × 8 Gardener's World.

According to Fig. 3a, all the learning agents equipped with explicit knowledge and the inference system outperformed the learning agent, right after the switch to the explicit knowledge. The largest difference of more than 60000 units in total cumulative reward was observed between the agent that reverted to the explicit knowledge after 25% of the episodes in each run. The agents that switched after 50% and 75% recorded a difference in total cumulative reward of more than 20000 units. Two of the agents equipped with explicit knowledge also performed better when it came to time spent in an episode and the one with lowest total time was the agent that switched after 25% of the episodes and recorded the highest cumulative reward.

We now come to discuss the results of the first non-deterministic version of The Gardener's World (Fig. 3b). The transition model of this version assigned a

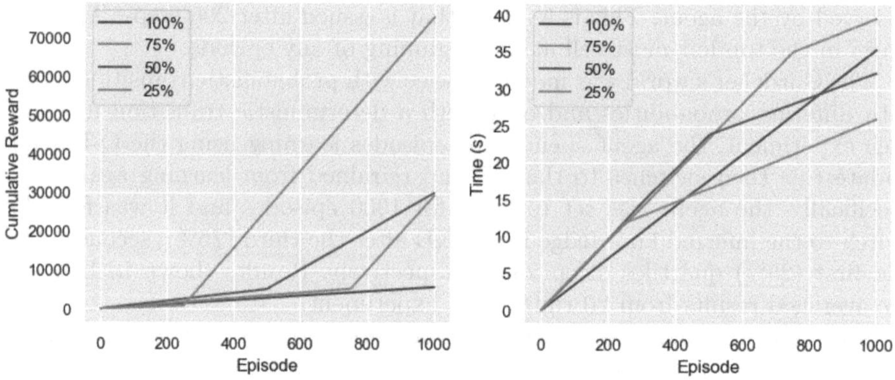

(a) Deterministic Gardener's World

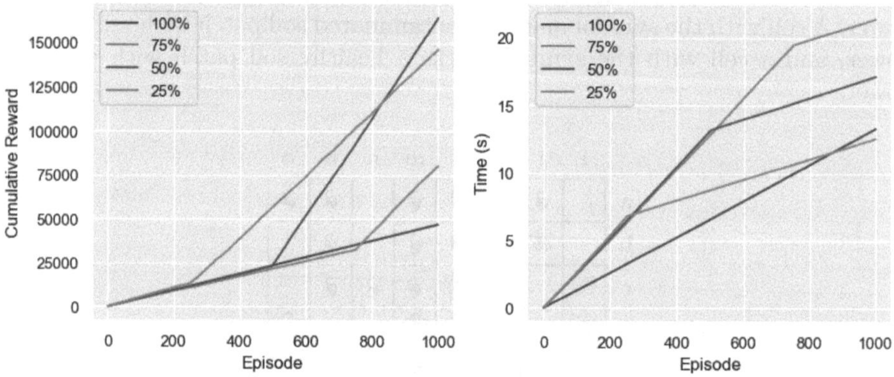

(b) Non-Deterministic Gardener's World - High Probability Assigned to Chosen Action

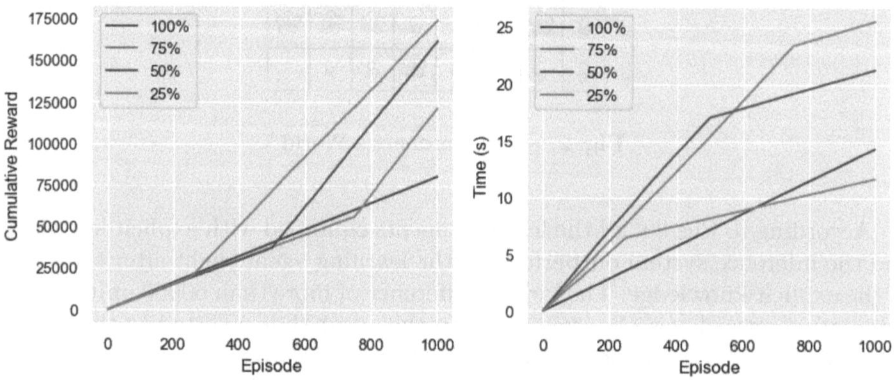

(c) Non-Deterministic Gardener's World - Equal Probabilities

Fig. 3. Cumulative reward obtained from and time spent in the Gardener's World under conditions of Experiment A and Experiment B.

probability of 0.8 to the movement action taken by the agent and 0.1 to either action that causes the agent to slide in one of the perpendicular directions, so the agent's actuators are still quite sound. The trend in results of the total cumulative reward gained by all four agents do not differ much than that observed during the use of the deterministic transition model. All learning agents that switch to explicit knowledge gain more reward directly after the switch. However, the second best-performing agent, that switched after 25% of the episodes per run, was the only agent that managed to spend less time in total than the learning agent.

The last version of the Gardener's World was equipped with a non-deterministic transition model that assigned equal probabilities to the movement action taken by the agent and the movements in both perpendicular directions; if the agent decides to move up, it can do so with probability $\frac{1}{3}$ and it can slide in a perpendicular direction with the same probability. The results in Fig. 3cshow that all learning agents with an accompanying KB performed better than the learning agent. The largest difference in total cumulative reward was recorded by the agent that switched after 25% of the episodes passed and this was also the agent that required the least time to reach this cumulative reward. The agents that switched after 50% and 75% of the episodes spent more time in the environment than agent without a KB.

6 Conclusion and Future Work

In this paper, we proposed a hybrid neuro-symbolic agent architecture augmenting learning agents with a KB and a purely symbolic process for inductive inference to enhance the outcome of learning in the complete absence of knowledge. We proved the effectiveness of this agent design by conducting three experiments on a randomly-generated grid-based environment, where the agent is coerced into falling back to the KB after a specified number of episodes. There were significant improvements in the cumulative reward received by the agent when it relied on the KB and sometimes, mostly when the transition model was deterministic, the time spent in the environment decreased as well. When the transition model is non-deterministic and becomes less and less reliable, the time spent in the environment increases for some instances of the proposed agent.

Future work can go in several directions. First, methods can be investigated for increasing the system's autonomy to remove the forced points of switching between the sub-symbolic and symbolic components. Further, the proposed neuro-symbolic system can be applied to partially-observable MDPs (POMDPs). Moreover, the complexity of the system could be enhanced by the design of approximate clique-listing algorithms to work on the multigraphs described in this paper. To address issues of scalability and the use of the proposed system with multiple agents, several instances of the agent can be created to operate on the same KB or each instance can operate on its own KB. However, when multiple KBs are used together, there should be a method to combine all into one if the knowledge obtained by all agents is to be analyzed.

References

1. Agarwal, R., Machado, M.C., Castro, P.S., Bellemare, M.G.: Contrastive behavioral similarity embeddings for generalization in reinforcement learning. ArXiv:abs/2101.05265 (2021). https://api.semanticscholar.org/CorpusID:231592776
2. Apeldoorn, D., Kern-Isberner, G.: Towards an understanding of what is learned: Extracting multi-abstraction-level knowledge from learning agents. In: Rus, V., Markov, Z. (eds.) Proceedings of the Thirtieth International Florida Artificial Intelligence Research Society Conference, FLAIRS 2017, Marco Island, Florida, USA, May 22-24, 2017, pp. 764–767. AAAI Press (2017)
3. Barto, A.G., Mahadevan, S.: Recent advances in hierarchical reinforcement learning. Discrete Event Dynamic Syst. **13**, 41–77 (2003). https://api.semanticscholar.org/CorpusID:386824
4. Chiba, N., Nishizeki, T.: Arboricity and subgraph listing algorithms. SIAM J. Comput. **14**(1), 210–223 (1985). https://doi.org/10.1137/0214017
5. Christoffersen, P.J.K., Li, A.C., Icarte, R.T., McIlraith, S.A.: Learning symbolic representations for reinforcement learning of non-markovian behavior (2023)
6. Guan, L., Sreedharan, S., Kambhampati, S.: Leveraging approximate symbolic models for reinforcement learning via skill diversity. CoRR arXiv:abs/2202.02886 (2022)
7. Landajuela, M., Petersen, B.K., Kim, S., Santiago, C.P., Glatt, R., Mundhenk, N., Pettit, J.F., Faissol, D.: Discovering symbolic policies with deep reinforcement learning. In: Meila, M., Zhang, T. (eds.) Proceedings of the 38th International Conference on Machine Learning. Proceedings of Machine Learning Research, vol. 139, pp. 5979–5989. PMLR (18–24 Jul 2021)
8. Towers, M., et al.: Gymnasium: a standard interface for reinforcement learning environments. CoRR abs/2407.17032 (2024). https://doi.org/10.48550/ARXIV.2407.17032
9. Wang, Z., Taylor, M.E.: Interactive reinforcement learning with dynamic reuse of prior knowledge from human/agent's demonstration. CoRR arXiv:abs/1805.04493 (2018)

An Explainable Approach to Predicting Academic Dropout: A Case Study at Faculdade Pernambucana de Saúde

Jefferson Rodrigues de Melo[1], Maynara Donato de Souza[1], Dalila Duraes[2](✉), and Flávio A. O. Santos[1]

[1] Centro de Informática, Universidade Federal de Pernambuco, Recife, Pernambuco, Brazil
{jrm,mds3,faos}@cin.ufpe.br

[2] LASI/ALGORITMI Centre, University of Minho, Braga, Portugal
b12166@algoritmi.uminho.pt

Abstract. Academic dropout is one of the main challenges faced by higher education institutions, affecting both the efficiency of the educational system and the development of qualified professionals. These studies suggest that effective school inclusion, especially for students with special needs, requires understanding individual differences, collaborative and well-trained support among educators and families, and that simply adding technology or policies is not enough without addressing broader social and educational factors. This study proposes a machine learning-based predictive model to identify key factors associated with student dropout in the state of Pernambuco, Brazil, supporting data-driven decision-making in educational management. The dataset, sourced from the Faculdade Pernambucana de Saúde, includes academic, socioeconomic, and demographic variables. The modeling pipeline involved data normalization, feature selection using Boruta with Random Forest, class balancing via SMOTEENN, and hyperparameter tuning with GridSearchCV and stratified cross-validation. Multiple models were evaluated—Decision Tree, SVM, Logistic Regression, and XGBoost—using accuracy, F1-score, and ROC AUC. Additionally, SHAP was applied to interpret model outputs and assess feature contributions. Results highlighted the importance of academic performance, distance to campus, and financial status in predicting dropout, offering valuable insights for the development of more effective institutional retention policies.

Keywords: Academic dropout · Interpretability · Machine learning

1 Introduction

Academic dropout in higher education is a highly relevant issue, directly affecting both social development and institutional efficiency. Furthermore, students from lower socioeconomic backgrounds often experience difficulties that reduce

A. Nongaillard et al. (Eds.): PAAMS 2025, CCIS 2644, pp. 119–131, 2025.
https://doi.org/10.1007/978-3-032-05925-3_10

their engagement in school activities and their overall academic performance, thereby increasing the likelihood of dropping out [15,16]. High dropout rates not only compromise students' educational attainment but also impose financial and operational challenges on educational institutions, which must deal with retention and academic performance management [13]. Therefore, understanding and predicting student dropout has become essential for improving educational policies and supporting proactive interventions.

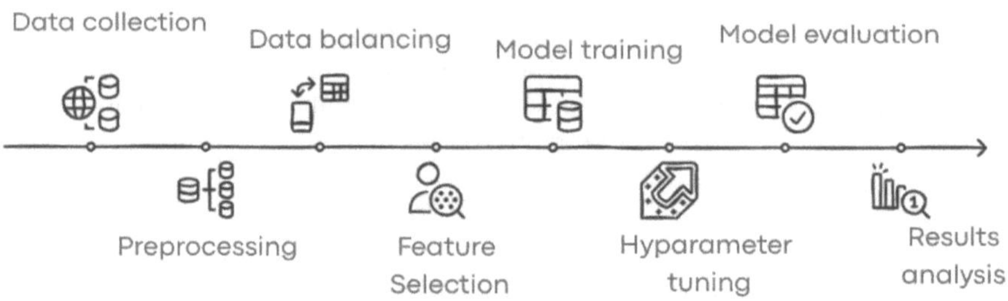

Fig. 1. End-to-end pipeline of the work: Starting with data collection, where academic and socioeconomic information was gathered, and ending with result interpretation. After data cleaning and standardization, class imbalance was addressed using the SMOTEENN technique. Feature selection was performed using the Boruta algorithm to identify the most relevant variables. Machine learning models—including Decision Tree, Support Vector Machine (SVM), Logistic Regression, and XGBoost—were trained and optimized using Grid Search and Random Search strategies. Model performance was evaluated using metrics such as AUC-ROC and F1-score, and supported by learning curves. Finally, the results were analyzed and visualized through graphs and tables, providing insights into the factors influencing academic dropout.

This study aims to develop and analyze predictive models for estimating the probability of university student dropout using various *Machine Learning* algorithms. To achieve this, we conducted a detailed exploration of a dataset comprising academic performance indicators, socioeconomic features, and students' historical engagement throughout their academic journey. To address class imbalance in the data, techniques such as SMOTEENN[1] were applied. Additionally, learning curves were generated to evaluate the training dynamics of the models. According to Pimentel et al. (2024), *"the application of advanced Machine Learning techniques in combination with Business Intelligence can enable the anticipation of potential dropout scenarios"* [14]. Figure 1 details our methodology.

Beyond achieving high predictive accuracy, this work seeks to identify the most relevant factors associated with academic dropout, offering actionable

[1] https://imbalanced-learn.org/stable/references/generated/imblearn.combine.SMOTEENN.html.

insights to support educational decision-makers in designing more effective student retention strategies. Machine learning models such as *Decision Tree* [3], *Support Vector Machine (SVM)* [5], *Logistic Regression* [8], and *XGBoost* [6] were trained and evaluated using metrics such as accuracy [2, p. 252], precision [12, p. 240], recall [7, p. 300], F1-score [7, p. 305], and ROC AUC [7, p. 310], ensuring a comprehensive assessment of each approach. Recent studies have shown that *"Random Forests and multilayer neural networks demonstrate strong performance in dropout prediction when combined with socioeconomic data"* [4].

To contribute to the academic literature, this study provides a detailed description of the entire development pipeline of a predictive dropout system. From data collection and preprocessing to model evaluation and interpretation, each step was rigorously executed. Our approach emphasizes not only high-performance models but also their interpretability and practical utility for educational management. For that, *Explainable AI (XAI)* techniques are applied to enhance transparency in model decisions and to support more informed and reliable decision-making [13].

This work aims to serve as both a technical and methodological reference for future research in the field, as well as a practical guide for higher education institutions seeking to develop data-driven strategies to mitigate student dropout.

2 Methodology

This study followed a structured pipeline for data processing and modeling, aiming to build robust and interpretable machine learning models for academic dropout prediction. The methodology can be summarized in five main stages: data collection, data preprocessing, feature selection, model training and evaluation, and interpretability analysis.

2.1 Data Modeling

Data Collection. The dataset was extracted from the Lyceum academic system of the Faculdade Pernambucana de Saúde (FPS), a Brazilian higher education institution. The system contains historical academic, financial, and demographic records of students, including information such as GPA, course load, scholarship status, payment agreements, and distance from home to university. A total of 30,716 records were collected, covering students from multiple semesters and courses.

Due to privacy and ethical considerations, the dataset used in this study—which contains sensitive academic, financial, and personal information of students—cannot be made publicly available. All data were obtained with institutional authorization and handled in accordance with data protection policies to ensure the confidentiality of the individuals involved.

Data Preprocessing. A series of preprocessing steps were applied to improve data quality and model performance:

- **Missing values:** Only one variable ('CrdSemester') had missing values (44 entries). These were removed due to their small proportion.
- **Outliers:** Winsorization is a statistical technique used to mitigate the influence of extreme values (outliers) by limiting observations to a specified percentile range. Rather than removing the outliers, this method replaces the values that exceed defined thresholds with the corresponding boundary values. This preserves the overall structure of the data distribution and prevents data loss. Mathematically, Winsorization can be defined as:

$$X_i^{\text{Winsor}} = \begin{cases} L_{\min}, & \text{if } X_i < L_{\min} \\ X_i, & \text{if } L_{\min} \leq X_i \leq L_{\max} \\ L_{\max}, & \text{if } X_i > L_{\max} \end{cases}$$

  where:
  - X_i denotes an individual observation of the variable,
  - $L_{\min}$ and $L_{\max}$ represent the lower and upper bounds defined by selected percentiles.

  This transformation ensures that extreme values are capped without distorting the core data distribution, thus enhancing the robustness of statistical analyses and machine learning models. The 'MeterDistance' feature showed extreme values (up to 12,682 km). Winsorization was applied at the 10% level to reduce the impact of these outliers while preserving data integrity.
- **Categorical encoding:** Categorical variables were encoded using One-Hot Encoding (e.g., gender, marital status, school type).
- **Label reclassification:** Students' status was grouped into binary classes—*Dropout* and *Non-dropout*—to facilitate binary classification.
- **Normalization:** Numerical features were normalized when required by the model.

Class Imbalance Handling. Since dropout cases represent a minority in the dataset, class imbalance was addressed using the SMOTEENN technique [1], — a hybrid of SMOTE (Synthetic Minority Oversampling Technique) and ENN (Edited Nearest Neighbors). This approach balances the dataset by oversampling the minority class and removing noisy examples from the majority class.

Feature Selection. To reduce complexity and improve model interpretability, feature selection was performed using the Boruta algorithm [10], which ranks features based on their importance in a Random Forest model. Its main idea is to compare the importance of each real feature with a randomized counterpart, known as a shadow feature. These shadow features are created by permuting the values of the original variables, thus removing any association with the target. By training a Random Forest model with both original and shadow features, Boruta assesses the importance of each variable. Features such as semester GPA, total course load, distance to university, school type, and scholarship information were selected as the most relevant predictors.

2.2 Model Training and Evaluation

The models chosen for this study were selected based on their ability to capture complex patterns in data and their widespread use in classification tasks. **Decision Tree:** An interpretable model that recursively splits the data into hierarchical segments, making it possible to understand the decision rules leading to a dropout prediction. **Support Vector Machine (SVM):** A robust algorithm that seeks to maximize the margin between classes, particularly effective for high-dimensional and non-linear datasets.**Logistic Regression:** A statistical model used to estimate the probability of a binary event, offering interpretability by quantifying the contribution of each feature. **XGBoost:** A gradient boosting algorithm that builds an ensemble of decision trees, known for its high predictive performance and scalability.

We trained all models using the preprocessed dataset, which included feature selection via the Boruta algorithm and normalization of numerical attributes when required. To ensure balanced representation of both classes during training and evaluation, we adopted a Stratified 10-Fold Cross-Validation strategy. It provides a reliable estimation of model performance across different class distributions [9]. We used GridSearchCV, to explore combinations of hyperparameters to identify the best configuration for each model.

Metrics. To compare the performance of the models, standard classification metrics were employed: **Accuracy**: Measures the proportion of correct predictions. **Precision and Recall**: Evaluate the model's ability to correctly identify dropouts while minimizing false positives. **F1-score**: Harmonic mean between precision and recall, useful for imbalanced datasets. **AUC-ROC**: Measures the model's ability to distinguish between dropout and non-dropout cases.

Given the class imbalance typically found in dropout prediction—where the number of non-dropouts (class 0) is significantly higher than dropouts (class 1)—metrics focused on the minority class are especially important. In this context, recall for class 1 is prioritized, as failing to identify an actual dropout (false negative) is more critical than incorrectly predicting a dropout (false positive). High recall ensures that at-risk students are identified, enabling earlier and potentially more effective intervention.

Interpretability. To enhance understanding of the models' decisions, the SHAP (SHapley Additive Explanations) method was applied to the best-performing model (XGBoost). To better understand the key factors associated with academic dropout, we applied a model interpretability analysis using SHAP (SHapley Additive Explanations). This technique quantifies the contribution of each feature to individual predictions, offering valuable insights for educational management.

SHAP, proposed by Lundberg and Lee [11], is a unified framework for interpreting machine learning models based on Shapley values from cooperative game theory. The Shapley value for a given feature i and instance x is defined as:

$$\phi_i(x) = \sum_{S \subseteq F \setminus \{i\}} \frac{|S|!(|F| - |S| - 1)!}{|F|!} [f(S \cup \{i\}) - f(S)]$$

where:

- F is the set of all features;
- S is a subset of features excluding i;
- $f(S)$ is the model prediction using only features in S;
- $|S|$ is the size of subset S;
- $|F|$ is the total number of features.

The value $\phi_i(x)$ represents the average marginal contribution of feature i to the model's prediction for instance x, compared to the average prediction. SHAP ensures desirable properties such as fairness, local accuracy, and consistency in feature attribution, making it a robust tool for model interpretability.

3 Dataset

3.1 Data Information

The dataset used in this study was sourced from the Lyceum academic database of the Faculdade Pernambucana de Saúde (FPS), a higher education institution in Brazil. This system contains detailed academic records of students, allowing for a comprehensive analysis of factors related to student dropout. The dataset integrates academic, financial, and demographic information across multiple semesters. Table 1 describes the features presents in the dataset.

In total, the dataset comprises 30,716 records, each representing a student's performance in a given semester. The variables include semester GPA, cumulative GPA, number of absences and failures, age, gender, marital status, total credit hours, type of high school, admission method, scholarship data, financial agreements, and even the distance from the student's home to the institution.

Some key variables and their statistics include: **Semester GPA:** mean = 8.51, SD = 1.58 **Cumulative GPA:** mean = 8.51, SD = 1.60 **Failures:** mean = 0.08, SD = 0.42 **Age:** mean = 23.3 years, SD = 4.56 **Distance from home:** mean = 183,859 m, SD ≈ 200,000 m **Dropout status:** 956 records labeled as "Dropout". The dataset also indicates categorical distributions such as gender (22,388 female, 8,328 male), and student status (17,569 graduated, 11,822 active, 956 dropped out, among others). These features enabled the application of machine learning models to explore patterns and predictors of student attrition.

Table 1. Description of the dataset fetaures

Feature	Description
GPASemester	Student's semester GPA (Grade Point Average).
GPAGeneral	Student's cumulative GPA.
LowestGrade	Lowest grade obtained by the student in any course.
Absenses	Number of absences during the semester.
Failure	Number of course failures in the semester.
Status	Student status at the end of the semester (*Dropout*, *Graduated*, *Active*, *Transferred*, *Withdrawn*).
Age	Student's age during the semester.
Sex	Student's gender (*F* for female, *M* for male).
Marital	Marital status (*Single*, *Married*, *Divorced*, *Widowed*, *Stable Union*, *Separated*).
CrdSemes	Total credit hours taken during the semester.
CrdCourse	Total credit hours of the entire degree program.
Scholarship	Indicates whether the student receives any scholarship.
Installments	Indicates whether the student has any negotiated payment installments.
MeterDistance	Distance from the student's residence to the institution (in meters).
Year	Academic year of the record.
Semester	Academic semester of the record.
Student	Unique identifier of the student.
HighSchool	Type of high school attended (*Public* or *Private*).
Admission	Admission type (*Entrance Exam*, *ENEM*, *Transfer*, etc.).
PreviousCourse	High school track/course attended, if applicable.
ScholarshipAverage	Average scholarship amount received during the program.
CrdIntegralized	Total credit hours completed by the student at the time of the record.
PctgComplete	Percentage of the program already completed.

3.2 Exploratory Data Analysis

In this section, we present the exploratory data analysis (EDA) performed to understand the key patterns and potential predictors of student dropout.

Analyzing the correlation between features as showed in Fig. 2, the key highlights include that GPASemester is negatively correlated with dropout, it means that lower academic performance increases the likelihood of abandonment. Also, absences and Failures are positively correlated with dropout, i.e., students with frequent absences or course failures are more prone to leave their studies.

Only the feature CrdSemester contained missing, with 44 records (0.15% of the dataset) missing total credit hours for the semester. Given its small proportion, these records were removed to preserve dataset integrity and avoid imputation bias. For modeling purposes, both *Withdrawn* and *Transferred* statuses were treated as *Dropped Out*, consolidating the dropout category. Table 2 describes the final counting for each student status.

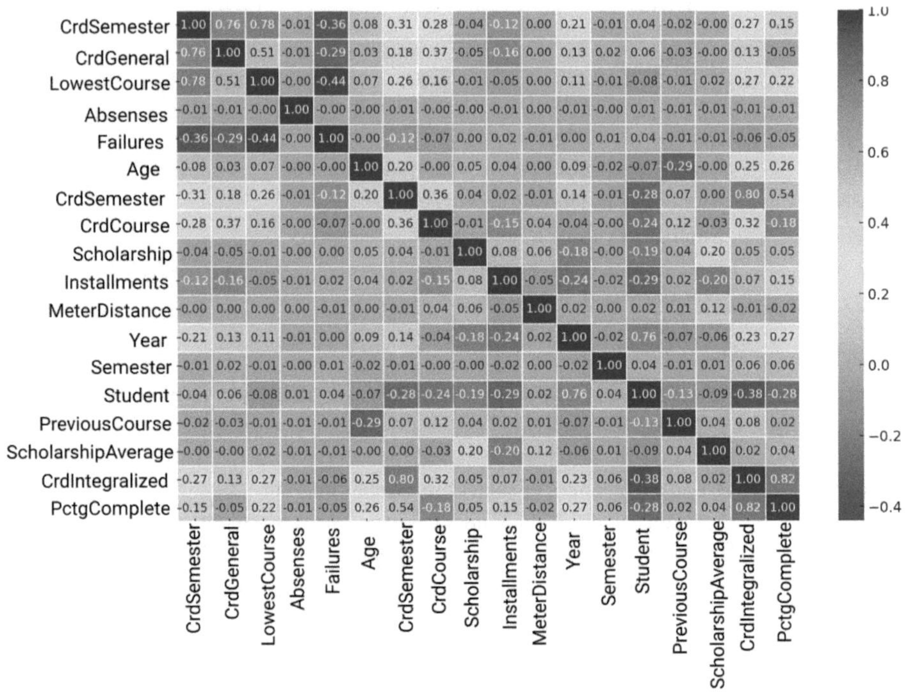

Fig. 2. Correlation matrix of numerical features. Semester GPA (*CRSemestral*) shows a strong negative correlation with dropout, while Absences (*Faltas*) and Failures (*Reprovado*) exhibit positive correlations, indicating that lower grades and more academic issues are associated with higher dropout risk.

3.3 Data Cleaning and Outlier Treatment

Following EDA and preliminary experiments, we applied the following data cleaning steps to ensure high-quality inputs for our machine learning models:

- Removed inconsistent records and handled missing values.
- Standardized and corrected categorical variables.

Table 2. Distribution of students by academic status

Student Status	Count
Graduated	17,573
Active	11,826
Dropped Out	948
Withdrawn	347
Transferred	22

- Identified and mitigated the impact of outliers.
- Reclassified student statuses into binary dropout labels.
- Encoded categorical features for model compatibility.

4 Results and Discussions

4.1 Model Performance and Results

The models showed varying levels of performance in predicting academic dropout. Among them, XGBoost achieved the best overall results, demonstrating strong generalization and predictive power. The key metrics for this model is displayed in Table 3. When compared to other models such as Decision Tree and Tuned Logistic Regression, XGBoost consistently delivered higher scores, demonstrating its robustness in identifying students at risk of dropout (high recall), while maintaining a low rate of false positives (high precision).

A learning curve was generated for the tuned XGBoost model to examine training and validation error rates and detect potential overfitting or underfitting issues [6]. The curve showed stable convergence, further validating the model's reliability.

4.2 Key Factors Associated with Dropout Risk

The SHAP analysis revealed several variables with strong influence on the model's dropout predictions. Figure 3 presents the most impactful features identified. Among them, the following stand out:

- **Semester GPA (CR Semestral)**: SHAP values showed a strong negative correlation between academic performance and dropout risk. Students with lower GPAs had higher dropout probabilities, highlighting the importance of academic support programs.
- **Distance from Home to Institution**: Students living farther from the university exhibited higher positive SHAP values for dropout. This suggests that logistical challenges, commuting costs, and reduced campus engagement may be contributing factors to attrition.
- **Socioeconomic Status**: Receiving a scholarship was associated with lower dropout risk according to SHAP values, indicating financial support as a protective factor. However, students with minimal scholarships still showed moderate dropout risk, suggesting ongoing economic challenges.
- **Course Completion Percentage**: Students with a lower percentage of course completion were more likely to drop out. This indicates that students in the early stages of their academic journey are more vulnerable to leaving the program compared to those who have progressed further.
- **Failure and Absence History**: A high number of academic failures—whether due to grades or attendance—was strongly associated with dropout. This finding reinforces the need for institutional support mechanisms to assist struggling students and monitor academic risk indicators.

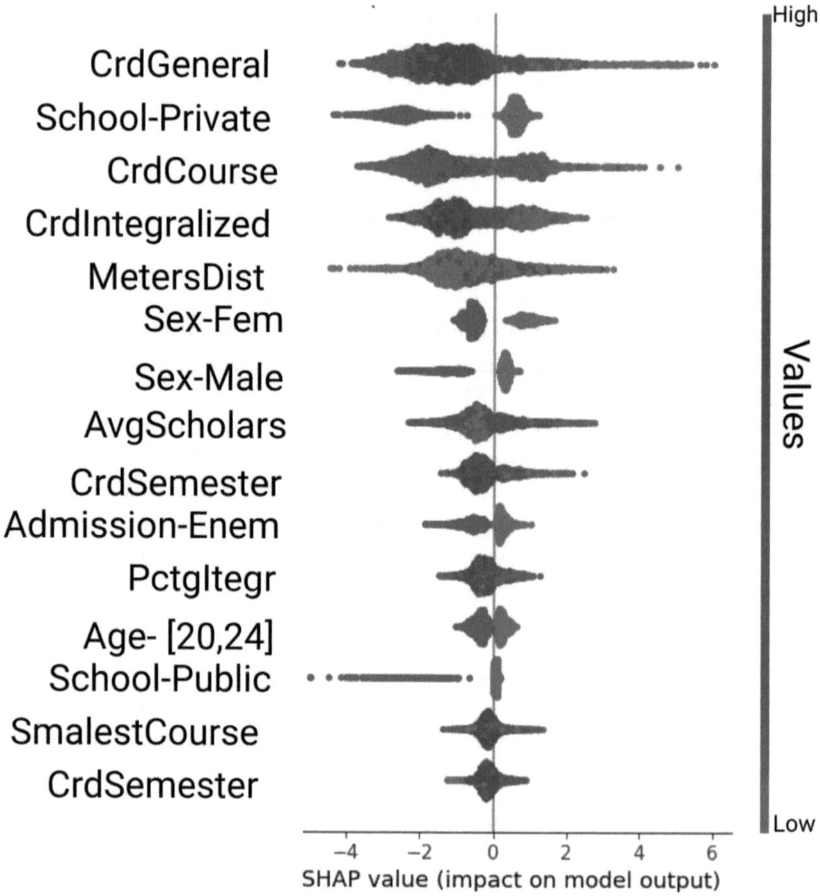

Fig. 3. This figure presents the importance of explanatory variables in the dropout prediction model using the SHAP (SHapley Additive exPlanations) method. The features are ranked by their impact on the model, with the most influential variables appearing at the top. The X-axis represents the SHAP values, indicating whether the presence of a given feature increases (positive SHAP) or decreases (negative SHAP) the probability of dropout. The color scale reflects the feature value: red tones represent higher values, while blue tones represent lower ones. For instance, a high cumulative GPA (`crGeral`) tends to reduce dropout risk (negative SHAP), whereas lower GPA values increase it. Similarly, greater distance from the student's residence to the campus (`distanciaMetros`) is associated with a higher dropout probability. This visualization helps interpret how academic, socioeconomic, and demographic characteristics influence dropout, providing insights for identifying meaningful patterns in student retention. (Color figure online)

Table 3. Performance comparison of classification models

Model	Accuracy	Precision	Recall	F1-score	ROC AUC
Decision Tree	89.98%	97.17%	91.48%	94.24%	84.28%
Logistic Regression	76.39%	95.68%	77.13%	85.41%	73.56%
Tuned Logistic Regression	79.56%	95.98%	80.56%	87.60%	75.76%
XGBoost	**94.04%**	**97.49%**	**95.81%**	**96.64%**	**87.29%**

4.3 Implications for Retention Policies

The results indicate that academic dropout does not stem from a single cause, but rather from a combination of academic, financial, and structural factors. Based on the findings, several recommendations can be made to help reduce dropout rates:

- **Academic interventions for students with low GPA:** Implementation of monitoring, tutoring, and academic reinforcement programs specifically targeting at-risk students.
- **Expansion of financial aid:** Reevaluation of scholarship criteria to ensure that financial support is sufficient to cover essential costs for students in socioeconomic vulnerability.
- **Monitoring of first-year students:** Development of initiatives aimed at facilitating the integration of freshmen into the university environment, thereby reducing early-stage dropout rates.

Understanding these contributing factors allows educational institutions to develop more effective strategies for student retention management, ultimately reducing dropout rates and promoting student academic success.

5 Conclusion

This study aimed to develop a predictive model for analyzing academic dropout in a higher education institution by applying advanced Machine Learning techniques and interpretability tools (XAI). With authorized access to the academic database of the Faculdade Pernambucana de Saúde (FPS), we carried out a complete data pipeline—from collection and preprocessing to modeling and interpretation—to identify the key factors associated with student dropout and to build a system capable of predicting at-risk students.

Currently, the identification of students at risk of dropout is conducted by the academic office based primarily on the experience and judgment of the administrative team. The purpose of this study is not to replace this team or automate the process entirely, but rather to provide an additional layer of analytical support. The predictive model offers a structured, data-driven approach to complement human expertise with actionable insights.

The implementation of interactive dashboards in Power BI will create a visual environment for strategic decision-making, while integration with an automated pipeline on the FPS server will ensure continuous data updates, enabling real-time and accurate monitoring of academic dropout.

Acknowledgements. This work is financed by National Funds through the Portuguese funding agency, FCT - Fundação para a Ciência e a Tecnologia within project "IA para a educação inclusiva: IA e Ciência de Dados para Necessidades Educativas Diversas para melhorar a Aprendizagem e a Equidade" e a referência 2024.07407.IACDC.

References

1. Batista, G.E.A.P.A., Prati, R.C., Monard, M.C.: A study of the behavior of several methods for balancing machine learning training data. SIGKDD Explorations **6**(1), 20–29 (2004)
2. Pattern Recognition and Machine Learning. ISS. Springer, New York (2006). https://doi.org/10.1007/978-0-387-45528-0_9
3. Breiman, L., Friedman, J.H., Olshen, R.A., Stone, C.J.: Classification and Regression Trees. Wadsworth International Group (1984)
4. Colak, H.: School Dropout Prediction in Malawi Using Household Panel Data Machine Learning Approach. Master's thesis, Tilburg University (2021)
5. Cristianini, N., Shawe-Taylor, J.: An Introduction to Support Vector Machines and Other Kernel-based Learning Methods. Cambridge University Press (2000)
6. Géron, A.: Hands-On Machine Learning with Scikit-Learn, Keras, and TensorFlow: Concepts, Tools, and Techniques to Build Intelligent Systems. O'Reilly Media (2019)
7. Hastie, T., Tibshirani, R., Friedman, J.: The Elements of Statistical Learning: Data Mining, Inference, and Prediction. Springer (2009)
8. Hosmer, D.W., Lemeshow, S., Sturdivant, R.X.: Applied Logistic Regression. Wiley (2013)
9. Kohavi, R.: A study of cross-validation and bootstrap for accuracy estimation and model selection. In: Proceedings of the 14th International Joint Conference on Artificial Intelligence (IJCAI), vol. 2, pp. 1137–1143. Morgan Kaufmann Publishers Inc. (1995)
10. Kursa, M.B., Rudnicki, W.R.: Feature selection with the boruta package. J. Stat. Softw. **36**(11), 1–13 (2010)
11. Lundberg, S.M., Lee, S.I.: A unified approach to interpreting model predictions. In: Advances in Neural Information Processing Systems, vol. 30 (2017)
12. Murphy, K.P.: Machine Learning: A Probabilistic Perspective. MIT Press (2012)
13. Nagy, M., Molontay, R.: Interpretable dropout prediction: towards xai-based personalized intervention. Int. J. Artif. Intell. Educ. **34**, 274–300 (2023). https://doi.org/10.1007/s40593-023-00331-8
14. Pimentel, K.G., Santos, R.E.C.: Previsão de evasão em cursos de graduação utilizando machine learning: Uma análise com alunos de uma instituição de ensino superior particular. Anais da SBC (2024). https://link.springer.com/article/10.1007/s11192-022-04538-4

15. Rodríguez-Triviño, J., Toro, R.M.M., Yela, M.T.A., Viteri-Chiriboga, E.: Socioeconomic status as a predictor of school dropout in high school students. South Eastern European Journal of Public Health (2024). https://doi.org/10.70135/seejph.vi.2013
16. Serem, F.K., Everlyn, C.: Socio-economic factors influencing repetition and dropout rates in primary schools in arid and semi-arid lands of Baringo county, Kenya (2017). https://doi.org/10.69641/afritvet.2017.2140

AI-Powered Automation in Healthcare: A Multi-agent Approach with LLM

Mariana Almeida, José Machado, Regina Sousa, and Hugo Peixoto(✉)

LASI/ALGORITMI, University of Minho, 4715 Braga, Portugal
pg54062@uminho.pt, {jmac,hpeixoto}@di.uminho.pt,
regina.sousa@algoritmi.uminho.pt

Abstract. The healthcare sector is undergoing rapid transformation with the integration of Artificial Intelligence (AI), particularly Large Language Models (LLMs). These models, with their exceptional capabilities in natural language processing and generation, offer innovative solutions to address challenges in managing clinical workflows. Traditional Clinical Decision Support Systems often lack flexibility and struggle with real-time data integration, highlighting the need for more advanced approaches. This work proposes a clinical chatbot that leverages LLMs within a multi-agent framework to automate the prescription of medical exams and efficiently retrieve clinical data from patient records. Unlike diagnostic systems, the chatbot focuses on automating repetitive workflows, reducing clinician workload, and enhancing operational efficiency. The multi-agent architecture enables dynamic collaboration among specialized agents, while LLMs process natural language inputs, construct Fast Healthcare Interoperability Resources (FHIR) and Structured Query Language (SQL) queries, and generate actionable responses in real-time. This research underscores the transformative potential of LLMs, demonstrating their ability to streamline clinical workflows and improve resource management in healthcare environments.

Keywords: Large Language Models · Clinical Decision Support · Healthcare Chatbots · Multi-Agent Framework

1 Introduction

The rapid growth of clinical data and the increasing complexity of healthcare workflows have created challenges for healthcare professionals, leading to inefficiencies in routine tasks and increased administrative burdens [1–3]. Studies report that physicians spend approximately 44.9% of their time on Electronic Health Records (EHRs), compared to only 27% on direct clinical face time with patients, which often contributes to burnout and a decreased care quality [4].

With the rapid development of Generative AI, LLMs have shown advanced capabilities in improving efficiency in various tasks. In the domain of Natural Language Processing (NLP), LLMs demonstrate their capacity to process and

A. Nongaillard et al. (Eds.): PAAMS 2025, CCIS 2644, pp. 132–143, 2025.
https://doi.org/10.1007/978-3-032-05925-3_11

generate text similar to human language [5]. Furthermore, these models can streamline workflows by converting natural language inputs into actionable tasks, functioning as effective task-oriented agents [6,7].

Despite their success across various domains, the application of LLM-powered systems in healthcare remains underexplored in automating routine clinical workflows [7]. In this paper, we aim to address this gap by proposing a novel LLM-based framework to automate clinical workflows, including the retrieval of patient data and the prescription of medical exams.

The proposed system integrates LLMs with a multi-agent architecture, facilitating collaboration between specialized agents to execute complex tasks autonomously. For example, one agent can use an LLM to build SQL queries, another to generate FHIR Uniform Resource Identifiers (URIs), and a third to interpret the data, transforming the results into natural language. The key contributions of this paper are as follows:

- An overview of the state-of-the-art LLMs in medical and healthcare applications.
- The integration of LLMs in generating FHIR URIs and SQL queries to enhance the efficiency and accuracy of clinical workflows.
- An LLM-powered, multi-agent framework to optimize routine clinical tasks, such as data retrieval and medical exam prescription.
- A two-phase evaluation plan, including simulation-based testing and real-world validation. The system will be assessed using accuracy, precision, and success rate for SQL and FHIR query generation, and coherence and correctness for natural language interpretations.

This work presents a conceptual architecture, yet to be implemented, serving as a foundation for future development and evaluation.

2 Background

This section provides the necessary background to understand the fundamentals of LLMs and Multi-Agent Systems (MAS), outlining their key components and characteristics.

2.1 Large Language Models and the Transformer Architecture

LLMs are AI tools based on deep neural networks trained on large datasets to process and generate natural language [8]. These models play an important role in various NLP tasks, including text generation, machine translation, summarization, and question-answering [9].

LLMs are built upon the Transformer architecture. The Transformer, introduced by Vaswani et al. in 2017 [10], revolutionized NLP by replacing the sequential processing of Recurrent Neural Networks with a fully parallel attention mechanism. According to the authors, the model employs a self-attention mechanism, which calculates the relevance between input tokens using query, key, and value vectors, normalized through a softmax function. This mechanism enables the efficient capture of long-range dependencies and prioritization of relevant parts of the sequence. The architecture follows an encoder-decoder structure. The encoder processes the input sequence into continuous representations through layers of self-attention and feed-forward networks, enhanced by residual connections and normalization for stability. The decoder generates the output sequence, utilizing masked multi-head attention to ensure predictions depend only on previously generated tokens, while an encoder-decoder attention mechanism aligns the input representations with the output sequence. To account for the order of tokens, Transformers use positional encodings, which are added to the input embeddings. These encodings allow the model to incorporate sequence structure, enabling it to process tokens with respect to their positional relationships [10].

2.2 Agents and Multi-Agent Systems

An agent is a computational system designed to perform tasks independently, acting on behalf of a user or another system [11,12]. This involves defining its own workflow and utilizing available tools to achieve its objectives [13]. MAS are systems that increase the capability of single agents by allowing cooperation among several agents to solve problems that would be impossible to solve by a single entity. Therefore, MAS can be defined as collections of computational entities that interact, share knowledge, and coordinate their actions to achieve common goals. Such systems are especially useful in scenarios involving distributed data, knowledge, or control [14].

3 Related Work

In recent years, integrating LLMs into healthcare has gained significant traction, showcasing their potential to streamline workflows and enhance decision-making [5,15].

The integration of LLMs in healthcare has become an area of growing interest, particularly in evaluating their ability to process and apply medical knowledge. ChatGPT, a large language model powered by GPT-3.5, was evaluated for its performance in answering medical exam questions from the United States Medical Licensing Examination (USMLE). The model achieved scores at or near the passing threshold across all three exam steps without any specialized training or reinforcement [16]. Additionally, the study demonstrated that GPT-4, using a simple 5-shot prompting method on the USMLE by more than 20 points, outperformed its predecessor, GPT-3.5, [17].

Several studies have investigated the application of foundational models fine-tuned on medical datasets. Notable examples include Med-PaLM [18] and Med-PaLM 2 [19], which are fine-tuned versions of Google's Flan-PaLM model. Med-PaLM 2 introduced the Ensemble Refinement (ER) technique to enhance reasoning capabilities by generating multiple response options and combining them into a cohesive and contextually accurate output. This approach enabled Med-PaLM 2 to achieve state-of-the-art performance on medical datasets such as MedQA and MMLU, significantly surpassing earlier models like Flan-PaLM and GPT-4 in specific tasks. These advancements highlight the ability of LLMs to perform exceptionally well in both multiple-choice and open-ended medical queries, as further corroborated by expert evaluations. Another study, conducted by Wu et al. [20], proposed the PMC-LLaMA model, an open-source language model fine-tuned on 4.8 million biomedical academic papers. This model was developed to enhance the accuracy of biomedical question answering and to improve the understanding of specialized concepts within the field.

The use of LLMs in healthcare faces significant challenges due to their limited knowledge in specialized medical domains and the inherent complexity of clinical tasks. Duong and Solomon [21] observed that ChatGPT's performance in answering genetic questions was comparable to human respondents but revealed notable gaps in medical expertise.

To overcome these limitations, Li et al. [22] developed ChatDoctor, a model based on LLaMA, which incorporates an autonomous information retrieval mechanism. This feature enables real-time access to external resources, such as Wikipedia, substantially improving its ability to comprehend patient queries and deliver accurate treatment recommendations. By fine-tuning ChatDoctor on large-scale datasets of medical-patient interactions and integrating real-time retrieval from external knowledge bases, the model demonstrated superior performance compared to general-purpose LLMs like ChatGPT. It excelled in metrics such as accuracy and F1 scores, highlighting its capacity to advance clinician-patient communication and support clinical decision-making.

Additionally, frameworks such as Almanac [23] have explored the integration of LLMs with external tools for secure and effective clinical applications. Utilizing models like GPT-3.5, Almanac excelled in factuality and reliability during adversarial scenarios, demonstrating robustness in clinical question-answering tasks. Similarly, OpenCHA [24] extended the utility of LLMs by introducing multimodal capabilities and dynamic orchestration, facilitating complex problem-solving and personalized recommendations in healthcare.

More recently, multi-agent architectures have gained attention for their ability to divide tasks among specialized agents. Frameworks such as MedAgents [25] and others have utilized LLMs to simulate multidisciplinary collaboration, enabling efficient task decomposition and execution. These systems have shown notable performance improvements in medical datasets like MedQA and PubMedQA, with GPT-4 outperforming earlier versions in accuracy and reasoning.

Despite these advancements, challenges persist in adapting LLMs for healthcare-specific tasks. Issues such as privacy, scalability, and integration with EHRs remain areas for further exploration. The proposed work seeks to address gaps in efficiency by leveraging a multi-agent, LLM-powered architecture tailored for automating routine clinical workflows thereby reducing the time healthcare professionals spend on repetitive tasks and improving overall workflow efficiency.

4 Proposed System

Prior works such as MedAgents [25] and ChatDoctor [22] have demonstrated the potential of multi-agent systems with LLMs in clinical reasoning and medical dialogue. However, these systems are often cloud-based and do not explicitly address the challenges of deploying LLM-powered agents in environments requiring strict data privacy, secure infrastructure, and robust integration with heterogeneous health information systems.

To mitigate these limitations, the proposed architecture supports the deployment of local LLMs, hosted entirely within the institution's infrastructure. This approach ensures that patient data never leaves the local environment, thus reducing the risk of third-party exposure and facilitating compliance with privacy regulations such as General Data Protection Regulation (GDPR) and Health Insurance Portability and Accountability Act (HIPAA) [26]. Local hosting also enables adaptation of the models to institution-specific language and practices, improving output relevance and reducing hallucinations.

From a security perspective, central orchestration ensures that all agent interactions are traceable, auditable, and subject to validation, minimizing risks related to uncontrolled autonomous behaviors or prompt injection attacks [27]. Furthermore, by combining a local PostgreSQL database with a fallback FHIR Retrieval Agent, the system remains operational and flexible even in the absence of complete FHIR infrastructure, addressing a common challenge in real-world deployments.

As illustrated in Fig. 1, the proposed system architecture comprises a Chatbot Interface, an Orchestrator and several specialized agents responsible for data retrieval, interpretation, and prescription management.

The adoption of a multi-agent architecture in the system is a deliberate design decision aimed at improving modularity, resilience, and maintainability. By assigning specific responsibilities to distinct agents—such as local retrieval, FHIR access, interpretation, and prescription—the system mirrors the compartmentalization of real clinical workflows. This not only allows each agent to be optimized independently but also facilitates scalability and fault isolation. If one agent fails or underperforms, the overall workflow remains operational through fallback mechanisms managed by the Orchestrator.

However, there are some common challenges associated with this kind of approach. Each agent interaction introduces additional latency, which can affect system responsiveness. The distribution of responsibilities across agents can make fault tracking more difficult, and ensuring data consistency between local databases and FHIR servers can also be challenging. To mitigate these issues, the current implementation uses a fixed number of specialized agents and centralizes all logging through the Orchestrator to support traceability. Additionally, as agents do not replicate or store data independently, but instead query shared sources in real time, consistency is ensured without requiring data synchronization mechanisms.

To ensure domain-specific performance, LLMs are fine-tuned for generating accurate SQL queries from free-text clinical questions, and constructing valid

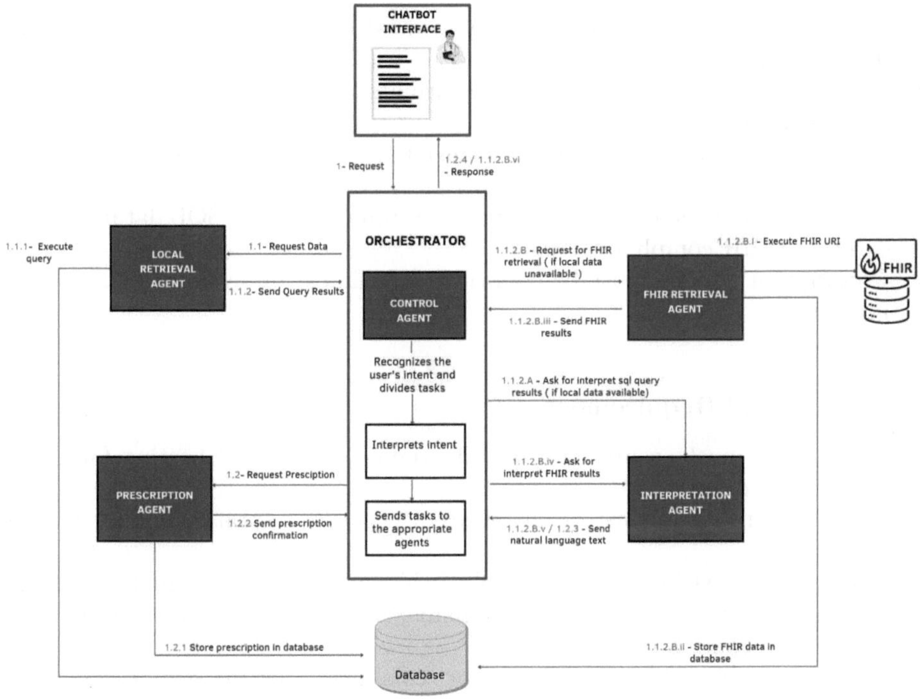

Fig. 1. Overview of the proposed system architecture.

FHIR URIs based on clinical input. Another model is used to transform structured outputs into appropriate natural language responses. The selection and tuning of these models are guided by performance metrics including query accuracy, relevance, and response time.

4.1 System Requirements

To support the proposed functionality, the system is defined by a set of functional and non-functional requirements that guide its implementation and ensure compliance with clinical standards. It is intended to be used by healthcare professionals, such as physicians and clinical staff, who are familiar with basic medical terminology and patient records.

These users interact with the system via natural language, without the need to understand technical formats like SQL or FHIR, and are responsible for validating actions such as medical exam prescriptions.

Functional Requirements

- Users should be able to query the system and request actions using natural language.

- The system must allow prescribing medical exams through conversational interaction.
- The system must support multiple formats and phrasings of semantically equivalent queries.
- Returned clinical data should be translated into clear and coherent natural language.
- The system must support retrieving data from both local SQL databases and external FHIR-compliant APIs.
- Prescription actions must be confirmed by clinical professionals before submission.

Non-functional Requirements

- The system must ensure data confidentiality, using local hosting for LLMs and clinical data.
- System interactions must occur within acceptable response time for clinical use.
- The system must be highly available, achieving an uptime target of 99.99%, and incorporate fault tolerance mechanisms such agent failover to maintain operational continuity.
- The architecture must be designed for scalability, allowing seamless addition and replication of agents to manage increasing workloads without compromising responsiveness or performance.
- The interface should be intuitive for clinical users with minimal training.
- The system must comply with data protection laws, including GDPR and HIPAA.
- All actions within the system must be comprehensively logged to ensure traceability and validation. Logging granularity must cover both user-initiated actions and automated system decisions, including outputs generated by LLMs.

4.2 System Components

Chatbot Interface: The Chatbot Interface serves as the primary entry point for user interactions. It receives a user's query and transmits it to the Orchestrator for further processing. Upon completion of a requested action or response generation by the system, the Chatbot Interface delivers the result back to the user.

Orchestrator: The Orchestrator is the core component of the system, using a locally hosted LLM for intent analysis. It parses user input into structured tasks like data retrieval or exam prescription. A two-step validation checks entity-action matching and prompts the user when input is incomplete. Agents operate asynchronously with fallback mechanisms and error handling. All interactions are logged, ensuring traceability and robust, reliable workflows.

Local Retrieval Agent: This agent is responsible for managing data stored in the local PostgreSQL database, leveraging an LLM to generate SQL queries based on user requirements. The agent formulates SQL commands to query structured data efficiently, ensuring precise and relevant data retrieval. Once the queries are executed against the local database, the retrieved records are transmitted to the Orchestrator. If the requested data are not found locally, the agent triggers a fallback mechanism that notifies the Orchestrator, which then delegates the request to the FHIR Retrieval Agent to obtain the necessary information from external sources.

FHIR Retrieval Agent: This agent utilizes an LLM to analyze the context of the user's request and generate the appropriate FHIR URI. The request is then sent to an FHIR server to retrieve relevant information, such as patient records and clinical observations. The acquired data are subsequently stored in the local PostgreSQL database to support future queries and improve the efficiency of subsequent requests.

Interpretation Agent: Data returned by the Local Retrieval Agent or the FHIR Retrieval Agent often lack readability or contextual clarity. The Interpretation Agent addresses this by leveraging an LLM to transform the results of executed SQL queries and FHIR URIs into coherent and user-friendly natural language descriptions.

Prescription Agent: When users request medical exam prescriptions, this agent validates and stores the necessary information. It uses an LLM to extract key details from the user's query, such as patient information, exam type, and required parameters. Once the healthcare professional confirms the prescription, it is saved in the local PostgreSQL database, and the user receives confirmation through the Orchestrator.

4.3 Process Flow

The typical workflow for user interaction within the system is outlined as follows:

1. **User Query:** The Chatbot Interface receives a request from the user (1). The system supports a wide range of queries including:
   - Retrieval of patient information by ID, name, or date of birth.
   - Access to consultations and medical appointments, filtered by date, physician, or time period.
   - Querying exams and lab results by type, date, status, or associated patient.
   - Listing medical staff and their specialties or schedules.
   - Prescription of specific medical exams with optional parameters.

The format of the queries is flexible and based on natural language. The system leverages LLMs to interpret diverse phrasing styles without requiring strict syntax or templates.

2. **Task Delegation by Orchestrator**: The Orchestrator interprets the user's query, identifies the intent, and delegates the necessary tasks to the appropriate agent(s) within the system (1.1 or 1.2).
3. **Data Retrieval**:
   - For local data, the Local Retrieval Agent employs an LLM capable of converting natural language queries into SQL commands. These commands are then executed on the local database to retrieve the required information (1.1.1).
   - If the requested data is not available locally, the Orchestrator activates the FHIR Retrieval Agent (1.1.2.B).
4. **Data Interpretation**: The Interpretation Agent converts retrieved data into a natural language response that is comprehensible for the user.
5. **Prescription Handling**: When the user request involves prescription generation (1.2), the Prescription Agent employs an LLM to analyze the request and extract the required information, while the final validation and possible adjustments are performed by the medical professionals. The agent then records the prescription in the database and confirms the successful completion of the task (1.2.1).
6. **Response Delivery**: The Orchestrator forwards the response received from the relevant agent directly to the user through the Chatbot Interface (1.2.4 /1.1.2.B.vi).

5 Conclusion and Future Work

In this work, a conceptual framework for a clinical chatbot was proposed, leveraging LLMs within a multi-agent architecture to address tasks such as the prescription of medical exams and the retrieval of clinical data. The framework places a strong emphasis on modularity, allowing specialized agents to collaborate dynamically, with the potential to streamline clinical workflows and enhance data accessibility in healthcare settings.

Future work will be directed towards implementing the framework by integrating a PostgreSQL database for local data management alongside an FHIR server for accessing external clinical information. The system will be evaluated in a simulated environment to assess the accuracy of data retrieval, the coherence of agent interactions, and the overall functionality of the architecture. Following this phase, gradual deployment in real-world healthcare settings is planned to validate performance under actual conditions and identify potential areas for further refinement and optimization.

To address the evaluation dimension, a structured validation procedure is planned. The assessment will include quantitative metrics including accuracy, precision, and success rate in the generation of SQL and FHIR queries from natural language inputs. Additionally, the coherence and correctness of natural language interpretations will be analysed, along with task completion time and the system's ability to handle incomplete or ambiguous inputs.

Although simulated testing enables controlled and repeatable experiments, its limitations in capturing the variability and complexity of real-world data and user interactions are acknowledged. For this reason, a second evaluation phase is envisaged in clinical settings, involving healthcare professionals to gather both technical performance indicators and practical feedback. This two-phase strategy aims to ensure both the robustness and the applicability of the proposed system in the real world.

Beyond technical validation, future iterations of the system will need to account for its scalability across different clinical environments, as well as its actual impact on clinician workload. While automation aims to reduce cognitive and administrative load for healthcare professionals, it is essential to assess whether it introduces new frictions or responsibilities. Institutional integration also poses challenges, particularly regarding interoperability with legacy systems and adherence to data governance policies. These aspects will be progressively explored during the transition from simulation to real-world deployment.

Acknowledgments. This work has been supported by FCT Fundação para a Ciência e Tecnologia within the R&D Units Project Scope: UID/00319/2023.

References

1. Hylock, R.H., Zeng, X.: A blockchain framework for patient-centered health records and exchange (healthchain): evaluation and proof-ofconcept study. J. Med. Internet Res. **21**(8) (2019). https://doi.org/10.2196/13592
2. Peixoto, H., Machado, J., Neves, J., Abelha, A.: Semantic interoperability and health records, vol. 335, pp. 236–237, Springer New York LLC. (2010). https://doi.org/10.1007/978-3-642-15515-4_30
3. Pimenta, N., Chaves, A., Sousa, R., Abelha, A., Peixoto, H.: Interoperability of Clinical Data through FHIR: a review. Procedia Comput. Sci. **220**, 856–861 (2023). The 14th International Conference on Ambient Systems, Networks and Technologies (ANT) and The 6th International Conference on Emerging Data and Industry 4.0 (EDI40). https://doi.org/10.1016/j.procs.2023.03.115
4. Toscano, F., et al.: How physicians spend their work time: an ecological momentary assessment. J. Gen. Intern. Med. **35**(11), 3166 (2020). https://doi.org/10.1007/S11606-020-06087-4
5. Zhou, H., et al.: A Survey of Large Language Models in Medicine: Progress, Application, and Challenge (2023). https://doi.org/10.48550/arXiv.2311.05112
6. De Maio, C., Furno, D., Grauso, T., Loia, V.: A Multi-Agent Architecture for Privacy-Preserving Natural Language Interaction with FHIR-Based Electronic Health Records. https://doi.org/10.23919/SoftCOM62040.2024.10721684
7. Gebreab, S.A., Salah, K., Jayaraman, R., Habib Ur Rehman, M., Ellaham, S.: LLM-based framework for administrative task automation in healthcare. In: 12th International Symposium on Digital Forensics and Security (ISDFS 2024). Institute of Electrical and Electronics Engineers Inc. (2024). https://doi.org/10.1109/ISDFS60797.2024.10527275

8. Lareyre, F., et al.: Large language models and artificial intelligence chatbots in vascular surgery. Semin. Vasc. Surg. **37**(3), 314–320 (2024). https://doi.org/10.1053/J.SEMVASCSURG.2024.06.001
9. Zhao, W.X., et al.: A Survey of Large Language Models (2023). https://doi.org/10.48550/arXiv.2303.18223
10. Vaswani, A., et al.: Attention Is All You Need. Advances in Neural Information Processing Systems, 5999–6009, December 2017. https://doi.org/10.48550/arXiv.1706.03762
11. Wooldridge, M., Jennings, N.R.: Intelligent agents: theory and practice. Knowl. Eng. Rev. **10**(2), 115–152 (1995). https://doi.org/10.1017/S0269888900008122
12. Sousa, R., Ferreira, D., Abelha, A., Machado, J.: Step towards monitoring intelligent agents in healthcare information systems. Advances in Intelligent Systems and Computing, vol. 1161, pp. 510–519. Springer. (2020). https://doi.org/10.1007/978-3-030-45697-9_50
13. Balaji, P.G., Srinivasan, D.: An introduction to multi-agent systems. Stud. Comput. Intell. **310**, 1–27 (2010). https://doi.org/10.1007/978-3-642-14435-6_1
14. Oliveira, E., Fischer, K., Stepankova, O.: Multi-agent systems: which research for which applications. Robot. Auton. Syst. **27**(1–2), 91–106 (1999). https://doi.org/10.1016/S0921-8890(98)00085-2
15. He, K., Lin, Q., Ruan, Y., Lan, X., Feng, M., Cambria, E.: A survey of large language models for healthcare: from data, technology, and applications to accountability and ethics (2023). https://doi.org/10.48550/arXiv.2310.05694
16. Kung, T.H., et al.: Performance of ChatGPT on USMLE: potential for AI-assisted medical education using large language models. PLOS Digital Health **2**(2), e0000198 (2023). https://doi.org/10.1371/JOURNAL.PDIG.0000198
17. Nori, H., King, N., McKinney, S.M., Carignan, D., Horvitz, E., OpenAI, M.: Capabilities of GPT-4 on Medical Challenge Problems (2023). https://doi.org/10.48550/arXiv.2303.13375
18. Singhal, K., Tu, T., Gottweis, J., et al.: Towards expert-level medical question answering with large language models (2023). https://doi.org/10.48550/arXiv.2305.09617
19. Singhal, K., Azizi, S., Tu, T., Mahdavi, S.S., et al.: Large language models encode clinical knowledge. Nature **620**(7972), 172–180 (2023). https://doi.org/10.1038/s41586-023-06291-2
20. Wu, C., Lin, W., Zhang, X., Zhang, Y., Xie, W., Wang, Y.: PMC-LLaMA: towards building open-source language models for medicine. J. Am. Med. Inform. Assoc. **31**(9), 1833–1843 (2023). https://doi.org/10.1093/jamia/ocae045
21. Duong, D., Solomon, B.D.: Analysis of large-language model versus human performance for genetics questions. Eur. J. Hum. Genet. **32**(4), 466–468 (2024). https://doi.org/10.1038/s41431-023-01396-8
22. Li, Y., Li, Z., Zhang, K., Dan, R., Jiang, S., Zhang, Y.: ChatDoctor: a medical chat model fine-tuned on a Large Language Model Meta-AI (LLaMA) using medical domain knowledge. Cureus (2023). https://doi.org/10.7759/cureus.40895
23. Zakka, C., et al.: Almanac: retrieval-augmented language models for clinical medicine. arXiv:2303.01229 (2023). https://doi.org/10.48550/arXiv.2303.01229
24. Abbasian, M., Azimi, I., Rahmani, A.M., Jain, R.: Conversational health agents: a personalized LLM-powered agent framework. arXiv:2310.02374 (2023). https://doi.org/10.48550/arXiv.2310.02374
25. Tang, X., et al.: MedAgents: large language models as collaborators for zero-shot medical reasoning. arXiv:2311.10537 (2023). https://doi.org/10.48550/arXiv.2311.10537

26. Dennstädt, F., Hastings, J., Putora, P.M., Schmerder, M., Cihoric, N.: Implementing large language models in healthcare while balancing control, collaboration, costs and security. NPJ Digital Medicine **8**(1), 143 (2025). https://doi.org/10.1038/s41746-025-01476-7
27. Gosmar, D., Dahl, D., Gosmar, D.: Prompt injection detection and mitigation via AI multi-agent NLP frameworks. arXiv preprint arXiv:2503.11517 (2025). https://doi.org/10.48550/arXiv.2503.11517

TLPSC: A Particle Swarm Clustering Algorithm with Transfer Learning

Rita Xavier[1(✉)], John Peller[2], Marco A. G. de Carvalho[1], and Leandro N. de Castro[1,2]

[1] School of Technology, Universidade Estadual de Campinas (UNICAMP), Paschoal Marmo St., Limeira, São Paulo, Brazil
r223447@dac.unicamp.br, magic@ft.unicamp.br

[2] Dendritic: A Human-Centered AI and Data Science Institute, U.A. Whitaker College of Engineering, Florida Gulf Coast University (FGCU), Fort Myers, USA
ldecastrosilva@fgcu.edu

Abstract. This paper introduces TLPSC, a novel clustering algorithm that combines Particle Swarm Clustering (PSC) with Prototype-Based Transfer Learning (PBTL). By leveraging knowledge transfer from a source domain, TLPSC enhances cluster quality, especially in scenarios with sparse or noisy data. Experimental results show TLPSC outperforms traditional clustering algorithms, such as K-Means, Gaussian Mixture Models (GMM), and the standard PSC, across some evaluation metrics, including NMI, ARI, Silhouette, and Davies-Bouldin. TLPSC shows its ability to maintain the data structure and generate cohesive clusters, proving to be a robust and efficient solution for clustering tasks.

Keywords: PSO · Clustering · Transfer Learning

1 Introduction

Clustering is a key task in Machine Learning (ML), grouping similar data points without prior class labels [1]. Traditional clustering methods, like K-Means and GMMs, are widely used due to their simplicity and effectiveness [18,19]. However, they struggle with sparse, noisy, or incomplete data, often failing to leverage prior knowledge in related domains where data is limited [1].

Transfer Learning (TL) addresses these issues by transferring knowledge between domains, enhancing model learning in low-data scenarios [2]. In clustering, TL can leverage previously learned structures to improve performance [3]. A notable TL strategy is PBTL, which uses source domain prototypes to guide clustering in a target domain, especially when data quality is poor [5,6].

Particle Swarm Optimization (PSO), a bioinspired optimization technique, has been adapted for clustering, leading to the proposal of the Particle Swarm Clustering (PSC) algorithm. PSC optimizes particle positions in feature space, where each particle represents a cluster prototype [7]. While PSC is effective, it

A. Nongaillard et al. (Eds.): PAAMS 2025, CCIS 2644, pp. 144–153, 2025.
https://doi.org/10.1007/978-3-032-05925-3_12

lacks transfer learning capabilities, limiting performance when prior knowledge could be beneficial.

This paper introduces TLPSC, a novel PSO-based clustering algorithm, integrating PBTL to enhance clustering by transferring prototypes from a source domain ($\mathcal{DS}$) to a target domain ($\mathcal{DT}$). TLPSC aims to overcome traditional clustering and PSC limitations by leveraging prior knowledge for improved clustering, particularly in low-data or domain-shift scenarios.

The paper is structured as follows: Sect. 2 reviews the conceptual research background, Sect. 3 details TLPSC, Sect. 4 presents the experimental setup and results, and Sect. 5 concludes with insights and future directions.

2 Theoretical Background

2.1 Particle Swarm Optimization: PSO

PSO is a swarm algorithm proposed in 1995 by Kennedy and Eberhart, following an extensive study on the swarm behaviors of living organisms [8,9]. In PSO, a set of particles moves within a constrained parameter space, interacting and adjusting their velocities and positions based on their own information and that of their neighbors, until an optimal solution is found.

The algorithm starts with particles randomly distributed, representing an initial solution to the problem. Each particle has two main parameters: velocity and position. During the search, particles continuously update their individual best values and share this information with the swarm. The optimal solution corresponds to the best individual found at that moment [9]. This process is described as follows. The movement of particle i in the space is determined by adding the velocity vector $\mathbf{v}_i$ to the current position vector $\mathbf{x}_i$:

$$\mathbf{x}_i\,(t+1) \;=\; \mathbf{x}_i\,(t) + \mathbf{v}_i\,(t+1) \tag{1}$$

The particle's velocity is updated considering the cognitive and social terms:

$$\mathbf{v}(t+1) = \omega.\mathbf{v}(t) + \mathbf{c}_1\mathbf{r}_1\left(\mathbf{p}_i(t) - \mathbf{x}_i(t)\right) + \mathbf{c}_2\mathbf{r}_2\left(\mathbf{p}_i(t) - \mathbf{x}_i(t)\right) \tag{2}$$

where $\mathbf{v}(t)$ and $\mathbf{x}(t)$ are the velocity and position of particle i in moment t, respectively; $\mathbf{p}_i$ is the individual optimal value of particle i found up to moment t; and $\mathbf{p}_j$ represents the global optimal value in the particle swarm found up to t; parameter ω is the inertia coefficient in the particle swarm; $\mathbf{c}_1$ and $\mathbf{c}_2$ are the cognitive and social coefficients, respectively, and $\mathbf{r}_1$ and $\mathbf{r}_2$ are the random parameters, which vary within a predefined range of values [8].

2.2 Particle Swarm Clustering: PSC

Clustering refers to the process of organizing or segmenting objects into groups of similar objects, called clusters, with two fundamental principles: 1) they must be homogeneous, meaning that objects within the same group should exhibit similarity to one another; 2) they must be distinct from one another, implying that objects within a cluster should be differentiable from objects in other clusters [1,7]. Cluster performance can be carried out externally, by comparing the obtained clusters with a predefined structure, or internally, by analyzing the compactness and/or separation of the clusters [10].

The PSC algorithm was introduced in [7]. Its main goal is to create a group of particles in the search space of the input data, causing these particles to move and become the prototypes that represent the original groups of the input data. As in PSO, the PSC also has its particles guided by the cognitive and social terms of the swarm [7].

Unlike PSO, however, PSC does not use a fitness function to evaluate the movements of the particles; they simply move to representative regions of the space, based on the input data distribution. Thus, each input object must be presented to the swarm, and for each object, the nearest particle should move towards it, being influenced by its best position up to the current moment [7]. The update rule for the PSC can be described as:

$$\mathbf{v}(t+1) = \omega.\mathbf{v}(t)\mathbf{c}_1\mathbf{r}_1\left(\mathbf{p}_i(t) - \mathbf{x}_i(t)\right) + \mathbf{c}_2\mathbf{r}_2\left(\mathbf{p}_i(t) - \mathbf{x}_i(t)\right) + \mathbf{c}_3\mathbf{r}_3\left(\mathbf{p}_j(t) - \mathbf{x}_j(t)\right) \tag{3}$$

in which the fourth term is introduced, where parameter $\mathbf{c}_3$ is the coefficient that will influence the self-organization of the particle swarm, and $\mathbf{r}_3$ is the random parameter for the new self-organizing term [7].

In the PSC algorithm, there are four hyperparameters: the maximum number of iterations for convergence; the maximum velocity of the particles; the number of particles; and the initialization value for the inertia.

2.3 Transfer Learning for Clustering

TL is based on the principle that knowledge acquired in a certain context can be transferred to another, enhancing the learning process. This approach reflects the idea that, just as humans build new knowledge from previous experiences, learning models should possess the same capability. The fundamental concept is to efficiently leverage previously acquired knowledge, allowing models to adapt and generalize to new tasks or domains [2].

TL is characterized by the adaptation of a model or system from a source domain, denoted $\mathcal{D}_S$, associated with a corresponding task $\mathcal{T}_S$, with the goal of enhancing the performance of a target task $\mathcal{T}_T$ in a target domain $\mathcal{D}_T$, where $\mathcal{D}_S \neq \mathcal{D}_T$ and $\mathcal{T}_S \neq \mathcal{T}_T$:

$$\mathcal{D}_S, \mathcal{T}_S \rightarrow \mathcal{D}_T, \mathcal{T}_T \tag{4}$$

where $\rightarrow$ represents the process of knowledge transfer.

Generally, in TL techniques, data sampling and the acquired knowledge typically occur in the source domain. Therefore, when discussing TL for clustering, it mainly refers to the unsupervised learning strategy. Due to the abundance of data, limited (or nonexistent) labeling, and distribution differences, direct clustering of the data is not feasible [5].

In previous research [3], various TL techniques for clustering were identified, such as Manifold TL [11], Auto-Adaptive TL [12] and Prototype-Based TL [5,6]. PBTL is a widely used technique for clustering algorithms, which uses clusters identified in $\mathcal{D}_\mathcal{S}$ as representative models to assist in the clustering of $\mathcal{D}_\mathcal{T}$. This technique is particularly beneficial when the data in $\mathcal{D}_\mathcal{T}$ is sparse or of low quality, enabling more effective data analysis across domains [6].

3 TLPSC: The Transfer Learning Particle Swarm Optimization for Data Clustering

PBTL is a technique used for various types of machine learning tasks, but it is especially employed for clustering [4]. This technique uses clusters identified in a $\mathcal{D}_\mathcal{S}$ as feature representation models to assist in clustering in a $\mathcal{D}_\mathcal{T}$. PBTL brings benefits when the data in $\mathcal{D}_\mathcal{S}$ is sparse or of lower quality, allowing for more efficient data analysis that can be applied across multiple domains [6].

The various TL techniques can be used in different ways to assist the learning process of the PSC algorithm. PBTL can help by enabling the algorithm to understand which relevant information should be transferred to improve the clustering performance. In this technique, the most important information to be transferred is the location of the cluster prototypes in $\mathcal{D}_\mathcal{S}$, which will assist the particles in their movement within $\mathcal{D}_\mathcal{T}$. Formally, PBTL is represented as [5,6]:

$$\Delta\left(\tilde{\boldsymbol{W}}_S, \mathbf{W}_T\right) = \sum_{k=1}^{o} \|\tilde{\boldsymbol{p}}_k - \mathbf{p}_c\|^2 \tag{5}$$

where $\widetilde{\mathbf{W}}_S$ is the set of prototypes found in $\mathcal{D}_\mathcal{S}$, $\mathbf{W}_T$ is the set of prototypes for $\mathcal{D}_\mathcal{T}$, $\widetilde{\mathbf{p}_k}$ is the centroid of the k-th cluster for $\mathcal{D}_\mathcal{S}$, and $\mathbf{p}_c$ is the centroid of the c-th cluster for $\mathcal{D}_\mathcal{T}$, and o is the number of clusters in $\mathcal{D}_\mathcal{S}$ and $\mathcal{D}_\mathcal{T}$, respectively. Therefore, it can be concluded that each vector of each particle represents the prototype of a cluster. Thus, Eq. 5 states that the PBTL process considers the prototypes from $\mathcal{D}_\mathcal{S}$ and moves the prototypes from $\mathcal{D}_\mathcal{T}$ towards their direction, as a way to transfer useful knowledge from one domain to another, assisting in the algorithm's learning process.

As presented in the previous sections, the PSC aims to group particles from a swarm within the search space of a dataset to be analyzed. In this process, the particles of the swarm will move and transform into representative prototypes of a cluster, and this is done based on the influence of the swarm's social and cognitive terms [7].

Based on the presentation of PSC and the PBTL process, the proposal for TLPSC was constructed, a particle swarm algorithm for data clustering with prototype-based transfer learning. For this implementation, it is necessary to insert a fourth term, which will represent an update of the weight vectors, taking into account, in addition to the social, cognitive, and self-organizing terms, the process of updating the particle velocities of $\mathcal{D}_\mathcal{T}$ according to the representative characteristics of the prototypes found in $\mathcal{D}_\mathcal{S}$. This update is performed by adding the following term to Eq. 5:

$$\lambda(t)\left[\widetilde{\mathbf{p}_k}(t) - \mathbf{x}_i(t)\right] \tag{6}$$

where $\lambda(t)$ is the influence of the TL parameter weight, and $\widetilde{\mathbf{p}_k}$ s the trained weight vector from $\mathcal{D}_\mathcal{T}$ that is closest to particle i, i.e., the prototype found in $\mathcal{D}_\mathcal{S}$. Algorithm 1 presents the pseudocode for TLPSC.

Algorithm 1. TLPSC: Transfer Learning-Based Particle Swarm for Clustering

function TLPSC(num_particles, num_iterations, max_vel, ω, c_1, c_2, c_3, λ)
    Initialize particles' positions, velocities, p_{best}, and g_{best}
for $t = 1$ **to** num_iterations **do**
    for each particle i **do**
        Generate r_1, r_2, r_3; select random particles j, k
        Update velocity, max_vel
        Update p_{best} if better
    end for
    Update g_{best}; check convergence
    if converged **then** break
    end if
end for
return g_{best}, final positions
end function

The TLPSC algorithm was developed in the Microsoft Virtual Studio Code environment, using the Python programming language, and utilizing the following libraries: Scikit-Learn for data analysis, importing datasets, and collecting evaluation measure results; Numpy for applying data science concepts and mathematical functions; Pandas for importing and reading datasets; Matplotlib and Seaborn for creating graphs and visualizations.

4 Performance Evaluation and Discussion

To test the performance of the TLPSC algorithm, experiments were conducted with widely used datasets from the literature for clustering task testing, comparing it with the PSC algorithm and traditional methods such as GMM and K-Means. The performance was measured using widely accepted cluster evaluation metrics commonly employed in similar experiments.

4.1 Methodology

The datasets used for the experiments were Iris [13], Wine [14], Habermans Survival (H.S.) [15], Breast Cancer Wisconsin (B.C.) [16], and Yeast [17]. These datasets were selected based on their characteristics, usability for clustering tasks, and suitability for transfer learning testing [3]. To conduct validation and robustness experiments of a new algorithm, it is important to compare its performance with other algorithms, whether they are traditional ones from the literature or state-of-the-art algorithms. In this study, for comparative purposes, the GMM [18] and K-Means [19] algorithms will be used due to their established concepts in the literature and academia, as well as the PSC algorithm [7], which represents the traditional version of the proposed algorithm, without the implementation of transfer learning.

The evaluation metrics used to analyze the performance of the algorithms were measured by NMI (Normalized Mutual Information), ARI (Adjusted Rand Index), Silhouette Score, and Davies-Bouldin Index. These metrics were chosen due to the nature of the TLPSC algorithm and its competitors, and are widely used to assess the quality of the clusterings resulting from the tested algorithms [3,5,6].

4.2 Hyperparameter Setting

The TLPSC algorithm includes the following hyperparameters to be explored in the experiments: maximum number of iterations for convergence, maximum particle velocity, number of particles in the swarm, initialization value for inertia, and transfer learning parameter value.

All algorithms were initialized randomly and TLPSC used the following hyperparameters: Inertia factor (ω): 0.90; Social coefficient ($\mathbf{c}_1$): 2.00; Self-cognition coefficient ($\mathbf{c}_2$): 2.00; Self-organization coefficient ($\mathbf{c}_3$): 2.00; Transfer learning coefficient (λ): 0.90; Number of rounds: 20.

These values were chosen based on experiments conducted in other previously published works [3,4,6], and have been extensively tested in various scenarios to identify the best and most suitable values for the competing algorithms.

4.3 Experiments and Results

The results were collected for each evaluation metric, with the average and standard deviation values from the 20 runs. For each of the metrics, across all datasets, the performance of the competing algorithms can be seen in Table 1.

Comparing the performance of TLPSC and its competitors, several trends and patterns can be observed regarding its performance in the clustering task. In the NMI and ARI metrics, which measure the consistency and similarity of the obtained clusters, TLPSC outperformed its competitors on the Iris, Breast Cancer Wisconsin, and Wine datasets; this shows that the algorithm was able to consistently preserve the structure of the dataset even after clustering. The PSC, that is, the algorithm without transfer learning, showed comparable results to TLPSC on the Yeast dataset, for example.

In the results of the Silhouette Score measure, TLPSC performed well on the Iris, Breast Cancer Wisconsin, Yeast, and Wine datasets. Thus, it is evident that the clusters formed by the proposed algorithm are more cohesive and well-separated compared to the performance of the competitors. These results can be seen in Fig. 1, which displays a graph showing the average values of the NMI, ARI, and Silhouette Score measures for each algorithm on each dataset.

Table 1. Average and standard deviation (Av±Std.) values for each algorithm, measure, and dataset.

Datasets - NMI	**PSC**	**TLPSC**	**K-MEANS**	**GMM**
Breast Cancer Wisconsin	0.84±0.01	**0.85±0.00**	0.7436±0.01	0.75±0.02
Habermans Survival	0.72±0.18	0.74±0.10	0.70±0.08	**0.78±0.02**
Iris	0.86±0.02	**0.88±0.01**	0.79±0.04	0.74±0.08
Wine	0.51±0.10	**0.53±0.06**	0.47±0.10	0.48±0.10
Yeast	0.50±0.00	**0.52±0.00**	0.40±0.00	0.40±0.00
Datasets - ARI	**PSC**	**TLPSC**	**K-MEANS**	**GMM**
Breast Cancer Wisconsin	0.85±0.10	**0.85±0.04**	0.74±0.10	0.75±0.22
Haberman's Survival	0.60±0.02	**0.60±0.00**	0.49±0.10	0.05±0.00
Iris	0.83±0.01	0.84±0.01	**0.84±0.00**	0.83±0.12
Wine	0.86±0.00	**0.87±0.04**	0.73±0.01	0.71±0.00
Yeast	0.50±0.00	**0.51±0.00**	0.50±0.08	0.51±0.01
Datasets - Silhouette Sc.	**PSC**	**TLPSC**	**K-MEANS**	**GMM**
Breast Cancer Wisconsin	0.64±0.00	**0.71±0.00**	0.70±0.01	0.69±0.00
Haberman's Survival	0.42±0.10	0.41±0.00	0.40±0.02	**0.42±0.01**
Iris	0.55±0.01	**0.58±0.04**	0.49±0.00	0.48±0.00
Wine	0.50±0.16	**0.59±0.02**	0.55±0.12	0.58±0.22
Yeast	0.52±0.08	**0.52±0.01**	0.47±0.00	0.44±0.00
Datasets - DBI	**PSC**	**TLPSC**	**K-MEANS**	**GMM**
Breast Cancer Wisconsin	0.50±0.02	**0.50±0.01**	2.16±0.11	1.98±0.03
Haberman's Survival	0.97±0.00	**0.65±0.00**	1.16±0.01	1.13±0.02
Iris	0.64±0.00	0.64±0.00	0.78±0.01	**0.58±0.00**
Wine	0.55±0.04	**0.55±0.01**	1.29±0.00	1.03±0.03
Yeast	2.04±0.05	**2.00±0.00**	3.28±0.04	4.20±0.08

In the Davies-Bouldin Index, which evaluates the quality of separation between clusters, TLPSC demonstrated competitive performance with consistency. These results can be seen in Fig. 2, where a larger bar indicates lower algorithm performance, as the Davies-Bouldin Index considers smaller values as the best performances.

Compared to the traditional algorithms K-Means and GMM, TLPSC exhibited slightly more robust performance in evaluation measures such as NMI, ARI, and Silhouette Score. Although PSC performed well, especially on the Yeast and Breast Cancer Wisconsin datasets, TLPSC leverages transfer learning to enhance the quality of clusters in both complex and simple scenarios. This highlights the efficiency and versatility of the proposed algorithm.

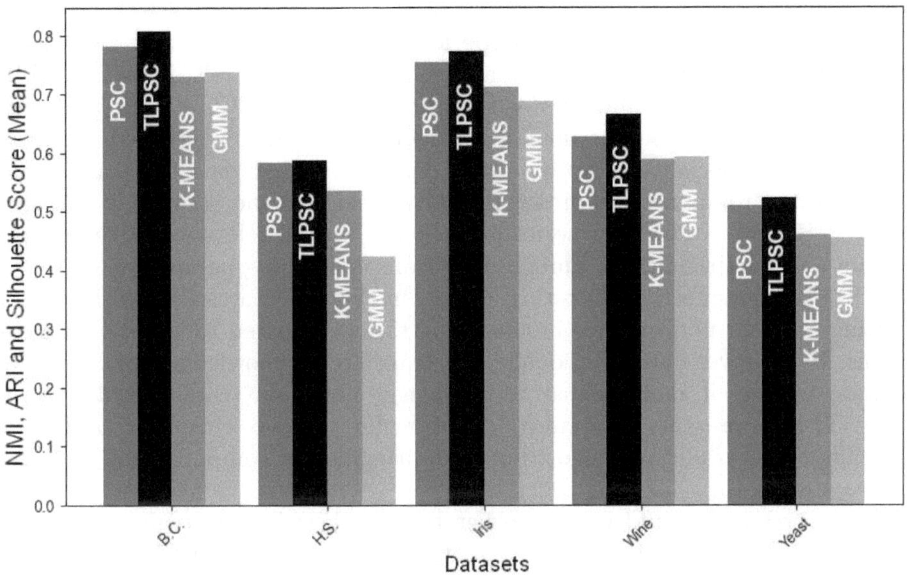

Fig. 1. Average NMI, ARI and Silhouette Score results values for algorithms across datasets.

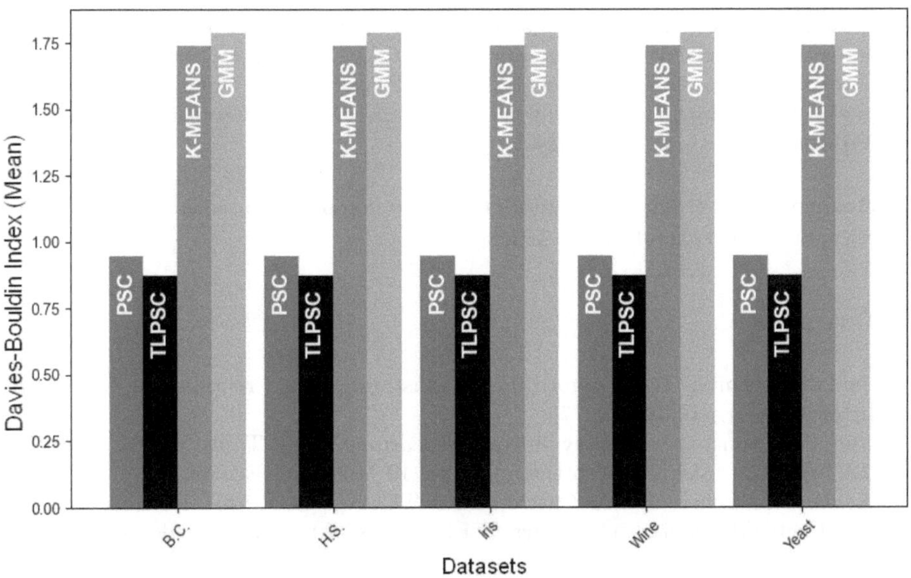

Fig. 2. Average Davies-Bouldin Index results values for algorithms across datasets.

5 Conclusions and Future Work

The results showed that TLPSC outperforms traditional clustering algorithms like K-Means, GMM, and the standard PSC in many metrics, including NMI, ARI, Silhouette Score, and Davies-Bouldin Index. TLPSC's ability to transfer knowledge from a source domain through PBTL significantly enhanced its performance, especially in datasets with sparse or noisy data. The algorithm demonstrated robustness in preserving data structure and producing cohesive clusters. However, TLPSC's performance relies on the relevance of the source domain and requires careful tuning of its transfer learning parameters.

TLPSC is an effective clustering algorithm that integrates PSC with PBTL, showing superior performance in clustering tasks compared to traditional algorithms. It improves clustering quality by transferring knowledge from a source domain, making it more robust to challenges like data scarcity and domain shifts. TLPSC presents a promising solution for complex clustering problems, especially when traditional algorithms fail, bringing low computational cost and more agility in the clustering proccess.

Future research could explore other transfer learning strategies to further enhance TLPSC, as well as adaptive methods for parameter tuning. Improving the algorithm's scalability to handle larger datasets and optimizing its computational efficiency are also important next steps. Additionally, testing TLPSC in real-world applications such as image segmentation, text clustering, and biomedical data analysis could provide further insights into its practical use and potential limitations.

Acknowledgments. This study was financed in part by the Coordenação de Aperfeiçoamento de Pessoal de Nível Superior Brasil (CAPES) Finance Code 001, in part by the São Paulo Research Foundation (FAPESP), Brasil. Process Number #2021/11905-0 and also funded by Conselho Nacional de Desenvolvimento Científico e Tecnológico (CNPq) under Proc. n.444999/2024-8.

Disclosure of Interests. The authors have no competing interests to declare that are relevant to the content of this article.

References

1. Jain, A.K., Dubes, R.C.: Algorithms for clustering data. Prentice-Hall, Inc. (1988). https://doi.org/10.5555/42779
2. Pan, S.J., Yang, Q.: A survey on transfer learning. IEEE Trans. Knowl. Data Eng. **22**(10), 1345–1359 (2010). https://doi.org/10.1109/TKDE.2009.191
3. Xavier, R., Peller, J., De Castro, L.N.: TRUNC: a transfer learning unsupervised network for data clustering. IEEE Access (2025). https://doi.org/10.1109/ACCESS.2025.3546787
4. Xavier, R., Peller, J., de Castro, L.N.: TRUNC: a transfer learning unsupervised. In: Distributed Computing and Artificial Intelligence, 21st International Conference, p. 170. Springer Nature. https://doi.org/10.1007/978-3-031-82073-1_17

5. Deng, Z., Jiang, Y., Chung, F.L., Ishibuchi, H., Choi, K.S., Wang, S.: Transfer prototype-based fuzzy clustering. IEEE Trans. Fuzzy Syst. **24**(5), 1210–1232 (2015). https://doi.org/10.1109/TFUZZ.2015.2505330
6. Zhao, F., Wang, C., Liu, H.: Differential evolution-based transfer rough clustering algorithm. Complex Intell. Syst. **9**(5), 5033–5047 (2023). https://doi.org/10.1007/s40747-023-00987-8
7. Cohen, S.C., de Castro, L.N.: Data clustering with particle swarms. In: 2006 IEEE International Conference on Evolutionary Computation, pp. 1792–1798. IEEE, July 2006. https://doi.org/10.1109/CEC.2006.1688524
8. Tang, J., Liu, G., Pan, Q.: A review on representative swarm intelligence algorithms for solving optimization problems: applications and trends. IEEE/CAA J. Automatica Sinica **8**(10), 1627–1643 (2021). https://doi.org/10.1109/JAS.2021.1004129
9. Kennedy, J., Eberhart, R.: Particle swarm optimization. In: Proceedings of ICNN'95-International Conference on Neural Networks, vol. 4, pp. 1942–1948, November 1995. https://doi.org/10.1109/ICNN.1995.488968
10. de Castro, L.N., Ferrari, D.G.: Introdução à mineração de dados. Saraiva Educação SA (2017)
11. Jiang, M., Wang, Z., Qiu, L., Guo, S., Gao, X., Tan, K.C.: A fast dynamic evolutionary multiobjective algorithm via manifold transfer learning. IEEE Trans. Cybern. **51**(7), 3417–3428 (2020). https://doi.org/10.1109/TCYB.2020.2989465
12. Zhang, X., Jin, Y., Qian, F.: A self-adaptive dynamic multi-objective optimization algorithm based on transfer learning and elitism-based mutation. Neurocomputing **559**, 126761 (2023). https://doi.org/10.1016/j.neucom.2023.126761
13. Fisher, R. (1936). Iris [Dataset]. UCI Machine Learning Repository. https://doi.org/10.24432/C56C76
14. Aeberhard, S., Forina, M.: Wine [Dataset]. UCI Machine Learning Repository (1992). https://doi.org/10.24432/C5PC7J
15. Haberman, S.: Haberman's Survival [Dataset]. UCI Machine Learning Repository (1976). https://doi.org/10.24432/C5XK51
16. Wolberg, W.: Breast Cancer Wisconsin (Original) [Dataset]. UCI Machine Learning Repository (1990). https://doi.org/10.24432/C5HP4Z
17. Nakai, K.: Yeast [Dataset]. UCI Machine Learning Repository (1991). https://doi.org/10.24432/C5KG68
18. Dempster, A.P., Laird, N.M., Rubin, D.B.: Maximum likelihood from incomplete data via the EM algorithm. J. Roy. Stat. Soc. Ser. B (Methodol.) **39**(1), 1–22 (1977). https://doi.org/10.1111/j.2517-6161.1977.tb01600.x
19. Forgy, E.W.: Cluster analysis of multivariate data: efficiency versus interpretability of classifications. Biometrics **21**, 768–769 (1965)

Towards Efficient Biogas Production: Deep Learning-Based Methane Forecasting in Anaerobic Digesters of Wastewater Treatment Plants

Duarte Lucas, Pedro Oliveira(✉), Afonso Bessa, Francisco S. Marcondes, and Manuel Rodrigues

LASI/ALGORITMI Centre, University of Minho, Braga, Portugal
{pg50345,pg53597}@alunos.uminho.pt,
{pedro.jose.oliveira,francisco.marcondes,
manuel.rodrigues}@algoritmi.uminho.pt

Abstract. Sustainability faces critical challenges, including the demand for renewable energy and the environmental impacts of pollution. Efficient wastewater treatment, combined with energy recovery, offers a strategic solution. Anaerobic sludge digesters in Wastewater Treatment Plants (WWTPs) convert organic waste into biogas, primarily methane (%CH_4), a renewable energy source. This study applies Deep Learning (DL) models to optimize operational efficiency and boost renewable energy production in Portuguese WWTPs. Using time series analysis, it forecasts %CH_4 in biogas production. Models evaluated include Convolutional Neural Networks (CNN), Long Short-Term Memory (LSTM), Temporal Convolutional Networks (TCN), and Gated Recurrent Units (GRU), employing a multistep recursive approach. CNNs performed best, achieving a low RMSE of 0.061%. These results demonstrate the potential of CNNs to enhance WWTP energy efficiency and contribute to environmental sustainability.

Keywords: Anaerobic Digestion · Artificial Intelligence · Deep Learning · Methane · Time Series Forecasting · Wastewater Treatment Plant

1 Introduction

Environmental sustainability is one of the biggest challenges of the 21st century, particularly in the face of population growth, urbanization and industrialization, which have significantly increased the impact of human activities on the environment [1]. Pollutants from these activities increase global problems such as climate change, air pollution, solid waste management and water contamination [2]. Water pollution is particularly alarming, being responsible for the deaths of 1.23 million people due to the consumption of unsafe water, which

A. Nongaillard et al. (Eds.): PAAMS 2025, CCIS 2644, pp. 154–165, 2025.
https://doi.org/10.1007/978-3-032-05925-3_13

places it among the 14 leading causes of death worldwide [3]. Water is essential for health, food safety, and environmental quality, and there is a continuous search for sustainable solutions. In this sense, alternative and renewable energy source, such as biogas produced through Anaerobic Digestion (AD), are emerging as a promising approach. AD is a four-stage microbial process, including hydrolysis, acidogenesis, acetogenesis and methanogenesis. In these stages, a complex microbial community uses biodegradable organic compounds in the absence of oxygen, producing biogas as byproduct. Biogas is an energy blend mainly composed of methane ($\%CH_4$, 50%–70%), the energy-carrying component, and carbon dioxide (CO_2, 30%–50%) [5]. Theoretically, 350 L of methane can be obtained per kg of chemical oxygen demand (COD), at standard temperature (i.e., 273.15 K) and pressure (101.33 kPa) conditions [4]. In wastewater treatment plants (WWTPs), AD can be used to stabilize and reduce the organic load of sludge surplus produced during the biological treatment of wastewater, while simultaneously recovering energy in the form of biogas [6]. This biogas can then be used to generate heat and electricity, reducing operational cost and contributing to the sustainability of wastewater treatment sector.

Artificial Intelligence (AI) techniques have proven valuable for optimizing operations in wastewater treatment processes. Specifically, AI enables predicting energy production based on historical data and operational variables [7]. In AD and biogas production, AI facilitates accurate performance predictions of sludge digester reactors, enhancing energy generation and waste management. Consequently, applying Deep Learning (DL) models to predict bioreactor energy production is gaining prominence, offering a combination of precision and efficiency [8]. This work aims to conceive, tune and evaluate the use of Long Short-Term Memory (LSTM), Gated Recurrent Unit (GRU), Convolutional Neural Networks (CNN) and Temporal Convolutional Networks (TCN) models to predict the $\%\mathrm{CH}_4$ resulting from the AD carried out in the digester for the next two days, applying a multistep recursive forecasting approach in a WWTP.

The paper is structured as follows: The next section reviews related work, contextualizing the existing literature. Section 3 outlines the materials and methods, including data collection, exploration, processing, model design, and performance evaluation metrics. Section 4 details the experimental setup, describing the environment and configurations. Section 5 presents the results and discussion, analyzing the findings and their implications. Finally, Sect. 6 concludes with a summary of key contributions and directions for future work.

2 State of the Art

The prediction of the $\%\mathrm{CH}_4$ resulting from AD in WWTPs is still little explored, but studies indicate that Machine Learning (ML) and techniques can improve energy efficiency and sustainability, given the importance of the $\%\mathrm{CH}_4$ generated.

The study by Gaoyang et al. [9] investigated the use of DL models to predict the treatment performance of real municipal wastewater using Anaerobic Membrane Bioreactors (AnMBRs) over a year-long operation. Data from two

AnMBRs were used to form a dataset with six experimental condition parameters, including reactor temperature, pH, and effluent Chemical Oxygen Demand (COD). Eight treatment evaluation parameters were also recorded, such as effluent pH. Three DL network structures were tested: ML fully connected network, CNN, and Densely Connected Convolutional Network (DenseNet) to model the relationship between conditions and outcomes. Results showed strong agreement between DL and experimental data, with DenseNet offering the fastest computation time (under 1 s) and the best overall performance, particularly for predicting $\%CH_4$ concentration in biogas.

Mahmood et al. [10] investigated the integration of Deep Neural Networks (DNN) with desirability analysis to optimize biogas purification in AD plants. The optimization of several substrate properties presents practical challenges, especially with limited datasets and many variables. A DNN model was developed to predict biogas compounds: $\%CH_4$, Carbon Dioxide (CO_2) and Hydrogen Sulfide (H_2S). All 14 slurry properties were used as input without feature selection. Hyperparameter optimization was conducted using a Genetic Algorithm (GA) to fine-tune the weights and biases of the DNN. The dataset was randomly divided into six subsets to enhance generalization during training. It was observed that high COD values decrease desirability, inhibiting biogas purification, while a pH slightly above neutral favours biogas quality. The model achieved a high R^2 value of 0.985, outperforming conventional approaches.

Jordan et al. [11] explored ML applications for optimizing the AD process in biogas plants, a highly complex system. Conventional models struggle with AD's non-linear dynamics, whereas ML approaches like Artificial Neural Networks (ANN), Fuzzy Logic (FL), Adaptive Fuzzy Inference System (ANFIS), Support Vector Machines (SVM), GA and Particle Swarm Optimization (PSO) offer better adaptability for real-time optimization. This work compared various ML techniques, emphasizing performance metrics such as R^2 and RMSE. Hybrid models, particularly GA-ANN and PSO-ANFIS, outperformed conventional methods. The GA-ANN model achieved an R^2 of 0.99 for biogas production prediction, indicating superior performance. These findings highlight the potential of hybrid models in enhancing prediction performance and operational efficiency in AD systems.

Several reviewed studies did not adequately address key validation practices, which may affect the robustness and generalizability of their results. In particular, some failed to apply appropriate cross-validation techniques tailored for temporal data, such as TimeSeriesSplit, which preserves the chronological order of observations and prevents data leakage. Incorporating such methods is essential to ensure a realistic evaluation of model performance and avoid overfitting to specific data subsets.

3 Materials and Methods

This section describes the materials and methods used, including the data collected, its exploration and manipulation, the DL models applied and the evaluation metrics employed.

3.1 Data Collection

A WWTP located in Portugal provided the data used in this study. This data comprises daily records of events collected over three years between January 1, 2020, and March 31, 2023. The database reflects the variation of the monitored parameters, providing a comprehensive and continuous representation of the reactor's operating conditions during this period.

3.2 Data Exploration

In the data exploration phase, the dataset was found to have a total of 1187 observations and 15 features. Table 1 summarizes the different characteristics present in the dataset, with a brief description and the units of measurement associated with each variable.

Since this is a time series problem, it is essential to check the consistency of the timestamps and the presence of missing values. Although the dataset does not contain missing values in the variables, there are 10 days without complete records, which generates minor interruptions in the temporal sequence. The treatment of these missing days will be dealt with within a later chapter, which will detail the methodology used to minimize the impact of these gaps and maintain the coherence of the analysis.

Table 1. Features of the Dataset.

Feature	Description	Data Type
Data	Measurement date	Object
Time lapse	Time interval between observations	Int64
Q(m^3/d)	Inflow rate	Float64
T(°C)	Temperature	Float64
Qgas produced (m^3/d)	Produced gas	Float64
Qgas cogenerator (m^3/d)	Gas used in cogenerator	Float64
E (kWh)	Energy	Float64
Pgas total	Total gas pressure	Float64
Pgas.CH4	Partial pressure of CH4	Float64
Pgas.CO2	Partial pressure of CO2	Float64
%CO2	Percentage of CO2 in gas	Float64
%CH_4	Percentage of CH4 in gas	Float64
VS	Volatile solids	Float64
X_I (mg/L)	Inorganic solids	Float64
Xc (mgO2/L)	Chemical oxygen demand	Float64

The line chart in Fig. 1 illustrates the temporal distribution of %CH_4 measurements over four years, with each year represented in a distinct color for clarity. The ten missing days are highlighted as purple dots positioned between

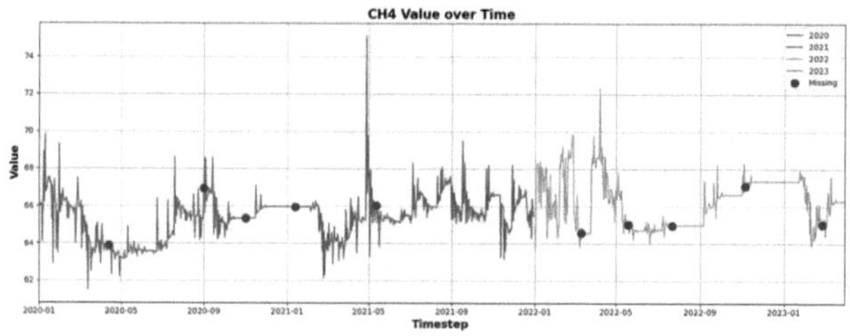

Fig. 1. Line Chart of $\%CH_4$ with 10 missing days

adjacent observations, revealing irregular gaps in the temporal sequence. Moreover, these gaps are relatively well distributed across the timeline. The years 2020 and 2022 account for the majority, each with four missing entries, while 2021 and 2023 register only one each. This pattern suggests that data loss occurred sporadically rather than in concentrated periods.

Table 2. Statistics of the $\%CH_4$ parameter.

Total	Mean	Standard Deviation	Minimum	Maximum	Median	Skewness	Kurtosis
1186	65.73	1.34	61.50	75.1	65.70	0.54	2.27

Subsequently, a statistical analysis was carried out on the target parameter, $\%CH_4$, as shown in Table 2. It can be seen that the minimum recorded value of $\%CH_4$ is 61.5, while the maximum value is 75.1. The mean $\%CH_4$ is 65.73, representing the central value of the distribution, with a standard deviation of 1.34, which indicates low variability around the mean. This low standard deviation suggests that most $\%CH_4$ values are close to the mean.

Further analysis of the distribution's symmetry and tail parameters, using skewness and kurtosis, indicated that the skewness value is 0.54, suggesting a slight asymmetry to the right due to higher values raising the average. The kurtosis value 2.27 indicates a slightly platykurtic distribution, i.e., less pointed than a normal distribution.

3.3 Data Preparation

The first step in data preparation was addressing missing timestamps. Although the dataset initially did not contain missing values in the variables, the absence of 10 days of records led to missing timestamps in the time series. These timestamps were reintroduced to rebuild the temporal sequence. Following this step, the observations corresponding to the missing timestamps were absent, creating missing values in the variables.

This issue was resolved using linear interpolation, a common and straightforward technique in time series analysis [12]. The method estimates the missing values by assuming a linear progression between the observed points immediately before and after the gaps. The time series retained its continuity by addressing missing timestamps and missing values, ensuring better input quality for subsequent analyses and modelling steps.

After addressing missing data, the next task was identifying and handling potential outliers in the dataset. The outliers were detected using an Interquartile Range (IQR) analysis, a robust statistical method. In this approach, the upper and lower bounds are calculated as:

$$\textit{Lower Bound: } Q1 - 1.5 \times \text{IQR} \quad (1) \qquad \textit{Upper Bound: } Q3 + 1.5 \times \text{IQR} \quad (2)$$

Where IQR is the difference between the third quartile (Q3) and the first quartile (Q1). Boxplot analysis was employed for the target variable $\%CH_4$ to visually identify extreme values that deviated significantly from the central distribution, as seen in Fig. 2.

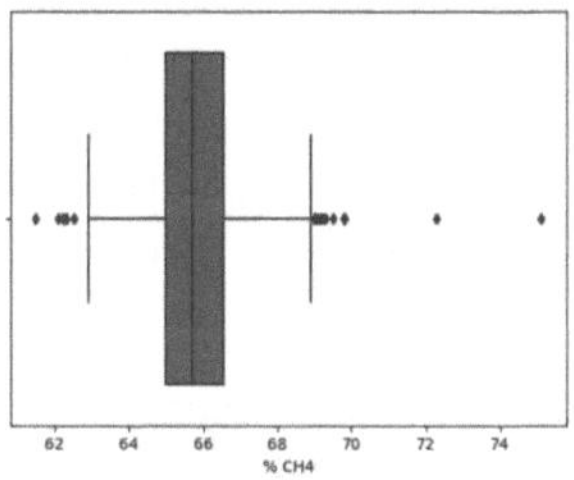

Fig. 2. *BoxPlot* of $\%CH_4$ before treatment.

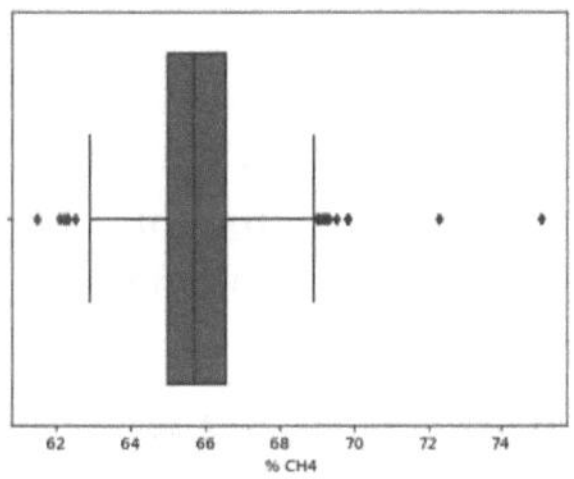

Fig. 3. *BoxPlot* of $\%CH_4$ after treatment.

Once identified, these outliers were converted into missing values to prevent their influence on the dataset. Subsequently, they were treated using linear interpolation. As shown in Fig. 3. This approach ensured a consistent and robust dataset, minimizing the risk of anomalies skewing model predictions or training processes.

Afterwards, feature engineering was applied to enhance the dataset's predictive power. This process involved creating new variables from existing data. For instance, the date feature was decomposed into day, month, and year components to capture temporal patterns better. These engineered features were designed to help the models identify trends and seasonal behaviours more effectively.

Lastly, data correlation analysis and feature selection were performed. To verify that none of the features exhibited a Gaussian distribution, the Kolmogorov-Smirnov (KS) test was applied, confirming the non-Gaussian nature of the data. Consequently, Spearman's correlation coefficient was selected as the most appropriate metric. This analysis revealed the most relevant features for predicting $\%CH_4$, including %CO2, Year, X_I (mg/L), and Xc. These selected features were subsequently normalized to ensure compatibility with the models. For LSTM-based models, data normalization ranged between −1 and 1. For other models, the range was set between 0 and 1.

3.4 Model Conception

As previous mentioned, several DL models were developed in this study to predict critical parameters in time series data. These models include the following:

LSTM. LSTM networks are distinctive Recurrent Neural Networks (RNNs) designed to capture long-term dependencies in sequential data, such as time series [13]. These networks address the vanishing gradient problem common in traditional RNNs thanks to their unique structure based on memory cells and three main gates [14]: input, forget, and output. This architecture enables the selective storage and discarding of information over time, effectively filtering relevant data. As a result, they are particularly suitable for modelling complex, long-term patterns in data.

GRU. As a simplified variant of LSTMs, GRU networks combine the input and forget gates functions into a single gate called the update gate, while the reset gate controls the amount of memory passed to the next state [15]. Due to their simplicity, GRUs are generally faster to train and require fewer computational resources, maintaining competitive performance in tasks such as time series forecasting. Compared to LSTMs, GRUs tend to be preferred in problems with less data or training time constraints.

CNN. Unlike RNN, CNNs process data by applying convolutions to identify local patterns in the data, such as trends or seasonalities in time series [16]. This approach makes CNNs highly efficient at detecting spatial and temporal characteristics, allowing for accurate analysis at a lower computational cost. In addition, CNNs do not rely on recurrent states, which reduces training complexity.

TCN. Built specifically for time series tasks, TCNs leverage causal and dilated convolutions to respect temporal order by considering only past information [17]. TCNs can model extended temporal contexts more efficiently than LSTMs or GRUs due to their dilated filters that expand the reception field without increasing the number of parameters [17]. However, TCNs can be more challenging to configure properly, requiring more outstanding care in the choice of hyperparameters.

3.5 Evaluation Metrics

This study addresses a regression problem evaluated using two metrics: Mean Absolute Error (MAE) and Root Mean Squared Error (RMSE). These metrics quantify performance by measuring the differences between predicted and actual values. MAE calculates the average size of errors based on absolute differences, providing a robust measure against outliers and indicating typical error magnitude. RMSE, on the other hand, is more sensitive to outliers, emphasizes larger errors by using squared differences before averaging and applying the square root. Their formulas are shown side by side below:

$$\mathrm{MAE} = \frac{1}{n}\sum_{i=1}^{n}|y_i - \hat{y}_i| \quad (3)$$

$$\mathrm{RMSE} = \sqrt{\frac{1}{n}\sum_{i=1}^{n}(y_i - \hat{y}_i)^2} \quad (4)$$

In both, y_i and $\hat{y}_i$ are actual and predicted values, and n is the number of data points. Together, these metrics provide a balanced evaluation, capturing both overall performance and sensitivity to large errors.

4 Experiments

During the development of the models, various key hyperparameters were systematically explored to increase their performance and generalization capabilities, as detailed in Table 3.

Table 3. Hyperparameters.

Hyperparameter	Values
Layers	[3, 4, 5]
Neurons	[34, 64, 128]
Dropout Rate	[0.0, 0.5]
Activation	['relu', 'tanh']
Timesteps	[7, 14, 21]
Batch Size	[5, 10, 20]
Filters	[16, 32]
Kernel Size	[3, 4, 5]
Pool Size	[2, 3]

The DL models were implemented in Python with TensorFlow library. Hyperparameter tuning was performed via grid search, allowing flexibility during training. Learning curves were analyzed to identify the optimal number of epochs, minimizing underfitting and overfitting.

Validation was performed using TimeSeriesSplit with three divisions, ensuring that the chronological order of the data was maintained throughout the process. As a result, the validation and test sets comprised future time intervals that were not present during training, enabling a realistic assessment of the models' ability to generalise to unseen time ranges. A fixed seed (91195003) guaranteed the reproducibility of the experiments. The RMSE metric was adopted as the loss function, and the Adam optimiser was selected due to its efficiency. A multi-step recursive forecasting approach was employed, where the first predicted value was used as input for the subsequent step.

5 Results and Discussion

Following the execution of the models, it is crucial to evaluate their performance and behaviour. Table 4 summarises the results. The table highlights the explored hyperparameter spaces for the best-performing models in each category and their respective scores based on the metrics previously mentioned. Additionally, it includes the training times for each model, allowing for a comprehensive assessment of their computational efficiency. In the case of error metrics, the best candidate model, in this case a CNN-based model, is highlighted, and the best candidate model in terms of training time (TCN-based) is also highlighted in this table.

Table 4. Top-five configurations for each model type (LSTM, GRU, CNN, TCN) and their respective metrics.

Layers	Neurons	Filters	Pool Size	Dropout	Activation	Timesteps	Batch	Kernel Size	Epochs	MAE	RMSE	Time (s)
LSTM Models												
3	128	–	–	0.5	relu	7	10	–	75	0.158	0.167	80.91
3	128	–	–	0.0	tanh	14	10	–	75	0.200	0.204	86.06
5	128	–	–	0.5	tanh	7	5	–	75	0.200	0.213	240.90
3	32	–	–	0.5	tanh	7	5	–	75	0.226	0.238	153.06
4	128	–	–	0.5	relu	14	10	–	75	0.247	0.249	107.78
GRU Models												
4	32	–	–	0.5	relu	14	5	–	130	0.073	0.074	148.18
5	64	–	–	0.5	tanh	21	5	–	130	0.117	0.124	176.69
5	32	–	–	0.0	tanh	7	5	–	130	0.124	0.126	168.65
5	64	–	–	0.5	relu	14	10	–	130	0.132	0.138	95.84
4	32	–	–	0.5	relu	21	10	–	130	0.135	0.145	92.89
CNN Models												
4	–	32	3	0.5	tanh	14	20	4	70	**0.061**	**0.067**	50.62
3	–	32	2	0.0	relu	14	20	5	70	0.063	0.068	32.70
3	–	16	2	0.5	relu	14	20	4	70	0.079	0.083	48.13
5	–	16	2	0.5	tanh	14	10	3	70	0.082	0.085	57.60
4	–	16	3	0.5	tanh	14	10	3	70	0.092	0.093	47.30
TCN Models												
3	–	–	–	0.0	tanh	7	20	3	40	0.287	0.295	45.93
3	–	–	–	0.0	relu	7	20	5	40	0.314	0.325	**43.47**
3	–	–	–	0.0	tanh	7	20	4	40	0.322	0.331	46.25
4	–	–	–	0.0	tanh	7	20	4	40	0.356	0.363	53.16
5	–	–	–	0.0	relu	7	10	3	40	0.360	0.367	70.37

Among the LSTM candidate models, the best result (MAE 0.158%, RMSE 0.167%, 80.91 s) was achieved with 3 layers, 128 neurons, 0.5 dropout rate, relu activation, and 7 timesteps, demonstrating a strong balance between simplicity and performance. This model had the fewest layers among the top performers, except for the second-best and fourth-best models, which also had 3 layers but different parameters. Results showed consistency with 128 neurons, except for one model with 32 neurons, which performed worse. 7 timesteps were often linked to lower error values, emphasizing their importance in performance. While relu and tanh activations showed mixed outcomes, relu yielded superior results in the best model.

On the other hand, the analysis of the GRU candidate models revealed that the best result was obtained with a MAE of 0.073% and RMSE of 0.074%, achieved in 148.18 s. This model used 4 layers, 32 neurons, dropout rate of 0.5, and relu activation. Most models used a batch size of 5, while the two worst used 10. In addition, relu activation was predominant among the best results, while tanh underperformed. The balance between precision and configuration highlighted the superior model.

The most efficient CNN model had an MAE of 0.061% and RMSE of 0.067%, with a run time of 50.62 s. This configuration combined 4 layers, 0.5 dropout rate, tanh activation, 32 filters, pool size of 3 and kernel size of 4. The second model had a shorter run time (32.70 s) but a higher error (MAE 0.063%). Notably, all five best-performing CNN models used 21 timesteps, underscoring the importance of this parameter in achieving lower errors. Moreover, in the filters and batch size hyperparameters, there was a consistent pattern among the top-performing models, with 32 filters for the first two and a batch size of 20 for the first three.

In the case of the TCN, the most efficient model, with the lowest MAE and RMSE (0.287% and 0.295%, respectively), was trained in 45.93 s. It featured 3 layers, a kernel size of 3, batch size of 20, 7 timesteps, a dropout rate of 0.0, and the tanh activation function, which was consistently used across all top models. Additionally, all models consistently used 7 timesteps and dropout rate of 0.0, highlighting their significance in achiveing the best result.

Finally, it can be concluded that the CNN model performed best, with the lowest RMSE, followed by the GRU model. After identifying the CNN as the most efficient for forecasting $\%CH_4$ production, Fig. 4 illustrates its recursive forecasts over four future timesteps, based on 14 input timesteps. The black line represents the actual $\%CH_4$ values, while the red points denote the model's predictions. Although the validation setup was limited to two-step forecasts, this figure highlights the model's capacity to extend predictions beyond the initial horizon. It is worth noting that the model remains stable and consistent even after a decline in actual values around timestep 14, reflecting its robustness and ability to smooth fluctuations.

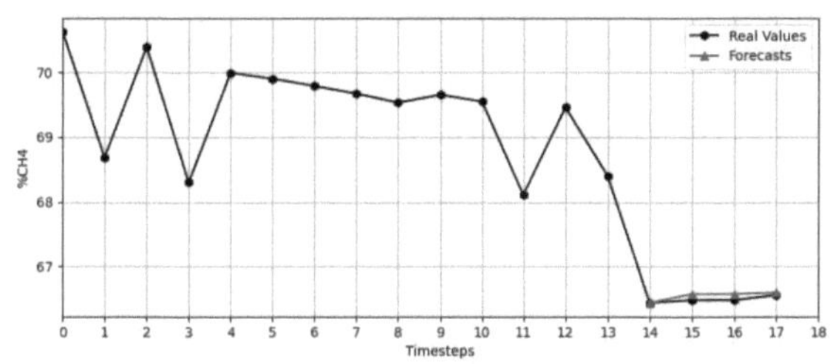

Fig. 4. Actual and forecasted $\%CH_4$ values over four future timesteps using the CNN model.

By analysing the results achieved, it is clear that CNNs outperformed the recurrent architectures in terms of forecasting performance. This can be largely explained by the characteristics of the $\%CH_4$ time series, which exhibits low variability (standard deviation of only 1.34) and well-defined local patterns. As previously discussed, CNNs are particularly well-suited for capturing such local structures through convolutional operations, making them highly effective in this specific context. In addition to their superior predictive performance, CNNs also demonstrated lower computational cost compared to recurrent models. Unlike

LSTM and GRU architectures, which require the maintenance of internal states across timesteps, CNNs operate without such dependencies, resulting in faster training times and reduced model complexity.

6 Conclusions

The growing environmental crisis from pollution impacts human health, mainly through water contamination caused by industrial, agricultural, and domestic activities. WWTPs, the key to water treatment via physical, chemical, and biological processes, contribute to pollution and offer solutions. The anaerobic reactor plays a vital role by reducing waste and producing biogas, a renewable energy source. Predicting $\%CH_4$ in the AD reactor is crucial for optimizing biogas production, reducing pollutants, and improving efficiency for sustainable solutions.

This study involved dataset preparation, model design, experimentation, and result comparison. The selection of $\%CH_4$ as the target is due to its importance in biogas production and pollutant reduction in WWTPs. Proper data preprocessing ensured high-performance and reliable multistep recursive forecasts. CNN models outperformed others, achieving an RMSE of 0.061% and an MAE of 0.067%. Future work could explore hybrid models combining neural networks with optimization techniques, like GA or Particle Swarm Optimization, to increase performance. Transformers, LSTMs, and AutoML could further improve prediction and automate hyperparameter tuning. Advanced sensors may also expand data availability, boosting prediction quality in anaerobic reactors.

Acknowledgements. This work is financed by National Funds through the Portuguese funding agency, FCT - Fundação para a Ciência e a Tecnologia within project 2022.06822.PTDC (https://doi.org/10.54499/2022.06822.PTDC). The work of Pedro Oliveira was supported by the doctoral Grant PRT/BD/154311/2022 financed by the Portuguese Foundation for Science and Technology (FCT), and with funds from European Union, under MIT Portugal Program.

References

1. Rockström, J., et al.: Planetary boundaries: exploring the safe operating space for humanity. In: Ecology and Society, vol. 14, no. 2. JSTOR (2009)
2. Mia, R., et al.: Review on various types of pollution problem in textile dyeing & printing industries of Bangladesh and recommendation for mitigation. In: Journal of Textile Engineering & Fashion Technology, vol. 5, no. 4, pp. 220–226. (2019). https://doi.org/10.15406/jteft.2019.05.00205
3. Fawell, J., Nieuwenhuijsen, M.J.: Contaminants in drinking water: environmental pollution and health. In: British Medical Bulletin, vol. 68, no. 1, pp. 199–208. (2003). https://doi.org/10.1093/bmb/ldg027
4. Oliveira, J.V., Costa, J.C., Cavaleiro, A.J., Pereira, M.A., Alves, M.M.: Effect of endogenous methane production: a step forward in the validation of biochemical methane potential (BMP) tests. Energies **15**(13), 4696 (2022). https://doi.org/10.3390/en15134696

5. Shen, Y., Linville, J.L., Urgun-Demirtas, M., Mintz, M.M., Snyder, S.W.: An overview of biogas production and utilization at full-scale wastewater treatment plants (WWTPs) in the United States: Challenges and opportunities towards energy-neutral WWTPs. Renew. Sustain. Energy Rev. **50**, 346–362 (2015). https://doi.org/10.1016/j.rser.2015.04.129
6. Appels, L., Baeyens, J., Degréve, J., Dewil, R.: Principles and potential of the anaerobic digestion of waste-activated sludge. In: Progress in Energy and Combustion Science, vol. 34, no. 6, pp. 755–781. Elsevier (2008). https://doi.org/10.1016/j.pecs.2008.06.002
7. Aghdam, E., Mohandes, S.R., Manu, P., Cheung, C., Yunusa-Kaltungo, A., Zayed, T.: Predicting quality parameters of wastewater treatment plants using artificial intelligence techniques. In: Journal of Cleaner Production, vol. 405, pp. 137019. Elsevier (2023). https://doi.org/10.1016/j.jclepro.2023.137019
8. Dairi, A., Cheng, T., Harrou, F., Sun, Y., Leiknes, T.O.: Deep learning approach for sustainable WWTP operation: a case study on data-driven influent conditions monitoring. In: Sustainable Cities and Society, vol. 50, pp. 101670. Elsevier (2019). https://doi.org/10.1016/j.scs.2019.101670
9. Li, G., et al.: Application of deep learning for predicting the treatment performance of real municipal wastewater based on one-year operation of two anaerobic membrane bioreactors. In: Science of The Total Environment, vol. 813, pp. 151920. Elsevier (2022). https://doi.org/10.1016/j.scitotenv.2021.151920
10. Mahmoodi-Eshkaftaki, M., Ebrahimi, R.: Integrated deep learning neural network and desirability analysis in biogas plants: a powerful tool to optimize biogas purification. In: Energy, vol. 231, pp. 121073. Elsevier (2021). https://doi.org/10.1016/j.energy.2021.121073
11. Ling, J.Y.X., et al.: Machine learning methods for the modelling and optimisation of biogas production from anaerobic digestion: a review. In: Environmental Science and Pollution Research, vol. 31, no. 13, pp. 19085–19104. Springer (2024). https://doi.org/10.1007/s11356-024-32435-6
12. Rehfeld, K., Marwan, N., Heitzig, J., Kurths, J.: Comparison of correlation analysis techniques for irregularly sampled time series. In: Nonlinear Processes in Geophysics, vol. 18, no. 3, pp. 389–404. Copernicus GmbH (2011). https://doi.org/10.5194/npg-18-389-2011
13. Lim, B., Zohren, S.: Time-series forecasting with deep learning: a survey. In: Philosophical Transactions of the Royal Society A, vol. 379, no. 2194, pp. 20200209. The Royal Society Publishing (2021). https://doi.org/10.1098/rsta.2020.0209
14. Sagheer, A., Kotb, M.: Time series forecasting of petroleum production using deep LSTM recurrent networks. In: Neurocomputing, vol. 323, pp. 203–213. Elsevier (2019). https://doi.org/10.1016/j.neucom.2018.09.082
15. Chung, J., Gulcehre, C., Cho, K., Bengio, Y.: Empirical evaluation of gated recurrent neural networks on sequence modeling. In: arXiv preprint arXiv:1412.3555 (2014). https://doi.org/10.48550/arXiv.1412.3555
16. Wang, Z., Oates, T.: Encoding time series as images for visual inspection and classification using tiled convolutional neural networks. In: Workshops at the Twenty-Ninth AAAI Conference on Artificial Intelligence. AAAI (2015)
17. Lea, C., Vidal, R., Reiter, A., Hager, G.D.: Temporal convolutional networks: a unified approach to action segmentation. In: Computer Vision–ECCV 2016 Workshops: Amsterdam, The Netherlands, October 8-10 and 15-16, 2016, Proceedings, Part III, vol. 14, pp. 47–54. Springer (2016). https://doi.org/10.1007/978-3-319-49409-8_7

PAAMS - Workshop on Digital Twinning for Training Purposes in Industry 4.0 (Twin4Train)

Workshop on Digital Twinning for Training Purposes in Industry 4.0 (Twin4Train)

Organizations all around the world are becoming more aware of the benefits and competitive advantages of providing and enhancing staff training. Traditional training methods have been shown to be effective throughout the years.

However, these strategies may not be appropriate for future organizational training developments. In some aspects, traditional training still has limits in terms of assisting learners in acquiring information and skills, such as costly methods that need significant resources and time. Demographic change, particularly in Europe, also means that new, more accessible and quicker to adapt training methods need to be brought into focus.

Extended reality technologies such as virtual reality (VR), augmented reality (AR) and mixed reality (MR) are widely used in various fields. They are increasingly used in organizational training interventions. VR, AR and MR have been used to train people in industries such as manufacturing, construction, automotive and medical. The integration of such technologies bridges the gap between the physical and digital worlds, allowing direct interaction with remote physical locations.

In comparison to traditional training, extended reality technologies may provide more professional immersion by seamlessly merging actual and virtual scenarios. Several studies have found that extended reality applications have a positive effect on the trainee's engagement and learning outcomes. AR, for example, reduced the difficulty and workload for mechanics during training and maintenance by adding extra labels and indicators to the machinery and also reduced the training costs.

Although VR training is not guaranteed to be less expensive, the benefits that these systems provide to the training audience may justify the investment costs. Depending on the domain, VR training may also provide a trainee with privacy, which is especially important in cases where a trainee may feel uneasy about his/her actions in a real-world training process due to the presence of observers. Moreover, VR training provides a safe environment with minimal exposure to dangerous situations.

These technologies also allow different training scenarios and use cases to be tested with less risk. And, an important point, training on digital twins can take place before the real twin is available. Furthermore, targeted training on the digital twin and hardware-in-the-loop makes it possible to optimize control system development and accelerate the commissioning processes for machines and systems.

Multiuser VR training is extremely beneficial in some domains. It has the potential to motivate and engage groups of learners. Additionally, positive peer pressure can be induced by multiuser training, in which individuals support one another during the training process.

Another positive aspect is the inclusion of older, highly experienced colleagues. Due to the demographic change described above, companies are under increasing pressure to pass on knowledge quickly and adequately. In a multi-user VR training environment, knowledge transfer can be integrated into a playful and user-centered environment.

Therefore, the focus of this workshop was to discuss the usage of extended reality technologies as tools for organizational training in several domains.

Moreover, it aimed to introduce some of the features that may affect extended reality organizational training applications. First, the multi-user feature as most organizations rely on teams not individuals. Second, the generalization feature to be able to use the same VR or AR app in several training programs or in different domains. Finally, the adaptivity feature that may be added in order to adapt training processes based on the user's capabilities, performance and needs.

Participants acquired knowledge about the types of extended reality and their real-world applications in the context of Industry 4.0, particularly organizational training.

- Human agent interaction, user interfaces
- Adaptation, learning and personalization
- E-learning and educational systems
- Virtual agents, animation and games
- Digital Twinning
- Human Computer Interaction
- Extended Reality Applications

Organization

Organizing Committee

Slim Andennadher	German International University, Egypt
Ute Dietrich	HTW Berlin, Germany
Nada Sharaf	German International University, Egypt
Nada Nasser	German University in Cairo, Egypt

Program Committee

Maggie Mashaly	German University in Cairo, Egypt
Eman Azab	German University in Cairo, Egypt
Sven-Olaf Schulze	LEXiCON, Germany***

Digital Twinning: Generative AI for Virtual Training Systems

Ahmed Refaat[2], Nada Nasser[1], Nada Sharaf[2(✉)], and Slim Abdennadher[2]

[1] German International University, Egypt, Egypt
nada.nasser@guc.edu.eg
[2] German University in Cairo, Cairo, Egypt
ahmed.elbarbary@student.giu-uni.de,
{nada.hamed,slim.abdennadher}@giu-uni.de

Abstract. Traditional training methods face challenges such as high costs, operational risks, and limited scalability. Digital twinning enables real-time simulation and optimization, while AI-driven assistants offer personalized instruction. This study explores the development and evaluation of an AI-powered virtual training system, emphasizing its benefits in knowledge acquisition and training performance. It presents the design and implementation of an AI-powered immersive virtual training system to enhance trainee learning in the assembly of machine parts in a virtual environment. The system provides real-time guidance and feedback by integrating Generative AI, Extended Reality (XR), and voice interaction. A virtual assistant, powered by OpenAI's ChatGPT API, interprets trainee queries and delivers step-by-step instructions. WhisperSpeech-to-Text (STT) and Google Text-to-Speech (TTS) facilitate seamless voice interaction. Built using Unity and tested with an HTC VIVE headset, the system allows trainees to interactively assemble a lathe machine without prior knowledge of its components. The experimental evaluation demonstrated significant improvements in user engagement, task performance, and knowledge retention compared to non-AI-supported training. These findings highlight the potential of AI-integrated digital twins in optimizing industrial training methodologies.

Keywords: Digital twinning · Extended Reality · Generative AI · Speech-to-Text · Text-to-Speech

1 Introduction

The rapid advancement of Artificial Intelligence (AI) and XR technologies has revolutionized various sectors, including industrial training and education. Traditional training methods, which rely on physical demonstrations, printed manuals, and hands-on experience, often present significant challenges, including high operational costs, safety risks, and limited access to real-world scenarios. As industries shift toward digital transformation, digital twinning has emerged as a powerful tool for enhancing training methodologies [1,2].

A. Nongaillard et al. (Eds.): PAAMS 2025, CCIS 2644, pp. 171–182, 2025.
https://doi.org/10.1007/978-3-032-05925-3_14

Digital Twins (DTs), virtual replicas of physical systems, provide a dynamic and interactive environment where trainees can engage in realistic simulations without physical constraints. By incorporating AI-driven virtual assistants and voice interaction, these training systems offer real-time feedback, adaptive learning paths, and enhanced engagement [3,4]. Unlike conventional training, AI-powered digital twins allow for scalable and repeatable training scenarios, ensuring higher knowledge retention and improved skill acquisition [14].

This paper explores the integration of generative AI and XR into digital twin-based training systems to make use of its full potential [5,12,13]. The proposed system makes use of AI for natural language processing, enabling trainees to receive step-by-step guidance in assembling complex machinery. The study evaluates the impact of AI-driven assistance on trainee performance, engagement, and learning outcomes. Through experimental analysis, this research aims to demonstrate the effectiveness of AI-enhanced training environments in optimizing industrial training methodologies [10].

2 Related Work

The integration of DTs, AI, and XR into training environments has been widely studied. Digital twins have proven beneficial in industrial applications by enabling real-time monitoring, predictive maintenance, and virtual prototyping [3]. AI-driven training systems have improved knowledge retention and skill acquisition, particularly in technical and engineering fields [4].

XR technologies, including Virtual Reality (VR) and Augmented Reality (AR), have significantly improved training simulations by providing immersive and interactive environments [14]. Prior studies have demonstrated the effectiveness of VR-based training in medical and industrial domains, allowing trainees to practice complex procedures without real-world risks [10].

Generative AI has further optimized training environments by enabling personalized learning paths and intelligent tutoring systems [8]. Conversational agents powered by AI and speech recognition systems have facilitated natural and adaptive interactions, improving user engagement and performance [9].

This paper builds on previous studies by presenting an AI-enhanced digital twin system for training applications. By leveraging generative AI for guidance and XR for interaction, the proposed system offers a novel approach to skill development and knowledge retention in assembly-based training scenarios.

3 System Architecture

The system architecture is designed to provide a seamless and interactive training experience. It consists of multiple interconnected modules to facilitate real-time AI-assisted guidance and immersive training.

The development of this organizational training system followed a structured, iterative workflow. It began with the design and creation of essential components, including the trainee interface module responsible for handling user interactions in the VR environment. Supports hand gestures, voice commands, and real-time feedback mechanisms. Then, the AI assistant module utilizes OpenAI's ChatGPT to understand trainee queries and generate context-aware guidance. Furthermore, the speech processing module in which Whisper STT was used to convert user speech into text and Google TTS for AI-generated verbal responses, ensuring an intuitive training experience. Furthermore, the simulation engine was built using the Unity game engine. This module ensures realistic physics, object snapping for correct part placements, and dynamic interaction between machine components. Finally, the data recording and performance tracking module records user actions, errors, and completion times for analysis and feedback. These elements were seamlessly integrated into a unified system, which was subsequently tested and assessed through user experiments and surveys.

3.1 Trainee Interface

A trainee interface was developed to facilitate intuitive and effective interaction. Since the training scenario involved only a single machine, the interface was designed to be minimalistic, avoiding complex menu systems. The machine's position within Virtual Environment (VE) was fixed, and all components required for assembly were placed in a designated area. Trainees interacted with the system by clicking on a part while engaging with the AI assistant, "Bob".

The AI assistant provides a brief description of the part's name and function. Following this, a guide line was rendered to indicate the correct placement of the part on the machine. This approach ensured that the trainees understood both the purpose and the correct position of each component, facilitating a smooth and structured assembly process. In addition, It provides real-time feedback during assembly. As the trainees interacted with different components, the AI continuously guided them, correcting errors, and reinforcing the correct actions. This step-by-step instructional support, combined with visual cues, improved the confidence and comprehension of the trainees about the assembly process.

3.2 AI Assistant

As mentioned above, an AI assistant, "Bob," was incorporated into the system to assist trainees throughout the assembly process as seen in Fig. 1. The assistant was powered by Large Language Models (LLMs), a type of artificial intelligence trained on vast datasets to understand and generate human-like text. LLMs are widely used to answer queries, provide explanations, and generate context-sensitive responses. ChatGPT API was selected due to its extensive adoption, continuous updates, and ability to handle a broad range of queries effectively. The AI assistant used this API to provide real-time guidance, respond to trainee inquiries, and deliver structured, step-by-step instructions throughout the training session.

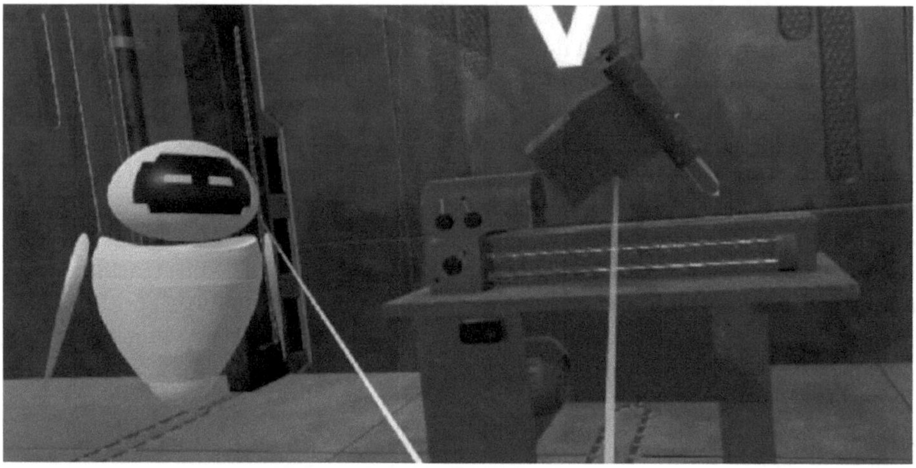

Fig. 1. The AI Assistant

3.3 Voice Recognition

The system utilized a voice-activated feature triggered by the phrase "Hey Bob." The system continuously recorded audio in 7-second intervals, analyzing each segment for the activation phrase. Upon detecting the trigger phrase, the AI assistant appeared and asked the trainee for a query. Speech input was then processed using OpenAI's Whisper STT model, which accurately transcribed the spoken query into text. The transcribed text was sent to the ChatGPT API for processing, and the AI-generated response was displayed in a text field while being converted into speech using Google TTS. This allowed the AI assistant to communicate verbally with the trainee, creating a more interactive experience. After delivering the response, the system resumed the recording loop, enabling continuous interaction. This open-ended voice interaction feature allowed trainees to seek clarification or additional guidance at any point during the training process.

3.4 Training Scenario

The training scenario involves assembling a lathe machine, which is shown in Fig. 2 in a virtual environment using AI guidance.

The workflow consists of the following steps. First, users enter the virtual training environment wearing an HTC VIVE headset. The AI assistant introduces the training module and provides an overview of the task. Then, the AI assistant prompts the trainee to pick up the machine parts in the correct sequence. The system highlights the correct components using visual markers. Trainees could begin by selecting any available part, prompting the AI assistant to provide an overview of its function and significance within the machine. Following this explanation, a guiding line was rendered to direct the trainee to

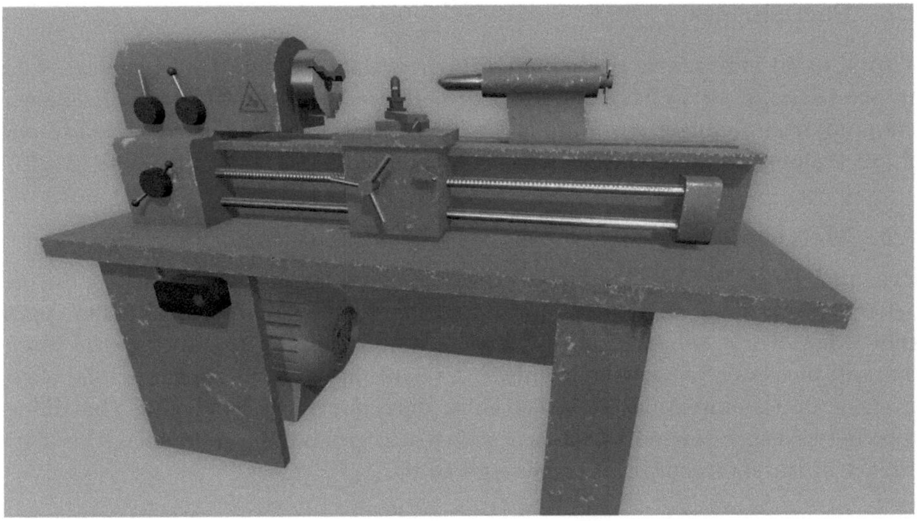

Fig. 2. The Lathe Machine

the correct placement of the part. Trainees then transported and positioned the component as instructed, repeating this process until the assembly was complete. If a user attempts to place a part incorrectly, the AI highlights the error, explains the mistake, and provides corrective actions. This structured workflow ensured that trainees not only understood the purpose of each component but also developed accuracy in its placement. The training scenario was designed to allow self-paced learning while emphasizing precision and comprehension. Trainees could issue voice commands anytime by saying, "Hey Bob," followed by a request for assistance. This feature provided an additional layer of support, ensuring that guidance was readily available whenever trainees encountered difficulties. After assembly, the system evaluates the performance of the trainee based on completion time, errors made, and adherence to the correct sequence. Users receive a performance summary with feedback on strengths and areas that need improvement.

4 Experimental Design

This experiment aims to evaluate the effectiveness of AI-driven guidance in a virtual training system for machine part assembly. Participants are divided into two groups: the control group completes the task without AI assistance, while the experimental group receives AI guidance. This approach ensures that prior knowledge or experience does not bias the results, as having the same individuals perform both tasks could introduce inconsistencies. The following section provides a detailed overview of the experimental design, outlining the procedures for both groups and the rationale behind this methodology.

4.1 Participants

A total of 40 individuals participated in the study (26 males, 14 females), with an age range of 18 to 24 years. Recruitment was conducted using convenience sampling from a university campus. Participants were randomly assigned to one of two training conditions, with each condition including 20 participants (n=20).

4.2 Metrics

Pre and Post Tests. The pre-test serves as an initial assessment conducted before the training, or experimental treatment to evaluate participants' prior knowledge of the subject matter. The post-test, administered after the intervention, measures knowledge acquisition resulting from the training. The effectiveness of the intervention is typically determined by analyzing the difference between pre-test and post-test scores–the greater the difference, the more impactful the intervention is considered to be.

Engagement Level. Engagement refers to the sense of presence or the feeling of being fully immersed in an experience. Key factors that define engagement include involvement, immersion, arousal, attention, curiosity, identification, enjoyment, effort, and flow. Various methods exist to measure engagement, with self-reported surveys being among the most commonly used.

Immersion Level. Telepresence assesses the extent to which an individual perceives themselves as being inside a virtual environment, effectively detaching from their physical surroundings. This perception is primarily influenced by sensory experiences such as sight, sound, and touch. The questionnaire in this study examines the degree to which participants felt immersed in the virtual environment.

NASA Task Load Index. NASA-TLX is a widely used tool for evaluating a user's perceived workload. It assesses mental, temporal, and physical demands, along with perceived performance, effort, and frustration levels when completing a task.

System Usability Scale. The System Usability Scale (SUS) is a standardized tool designed to assess the usability of a system, product, or service. It provides a simple yet reliable method for measuring user satisfaction and overall usability. The questionnaire captures users' subjective evaluations after interacting with a system, making it an effective metric for usability assessment.

4.3 Procedure

The experiment follows a structured process to ensure consistency and reliability in data collection. Before starting the task, all participants began by signing a consent form. Then, they complete a pre-experiment survey to assess their prior knowledge, abilities, and expectations. This ensures baseline consistency between the two groups. Participants were then assigned to one of the two training conditions. During the training sessions, participants interacted with the system to complete a machine assembly task.

After completing the task, regardless of whether they successfully assembled the machine–participants fill out a post-experiment survey assessing their learning outcomes, task performance, and overall experience. Additionally, participants' performance metrics were recorded throughout the training. Furthermore, they were given some standard questionnaires to fill them for later analysis.

5 Results

5.1 Learning Outcome

Participants' knowledge of the lathe machine was assessed in the pre-and post-survey. The results are summarized and visualized in Fig. 3. Results revealed that participants had significantly higher learning outcome in the AI-assisted training with a p-value < 0.05.

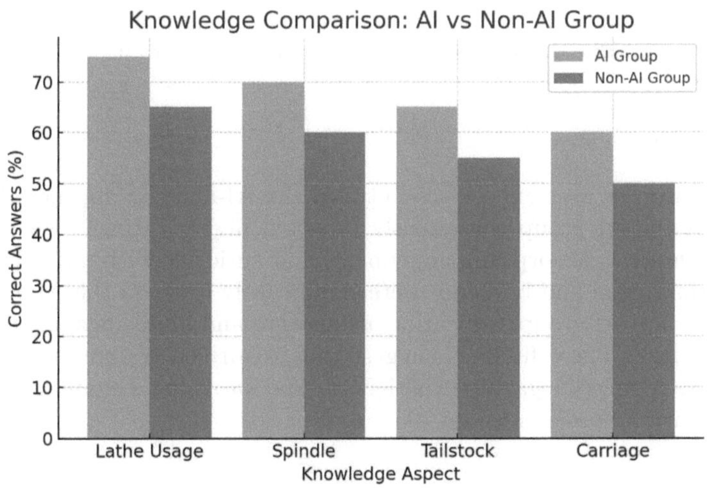

Fig. 3. Knowledge Improvement After the Experiment

5.2 Task Perceptions

The AI-assisted users significantly experienced lower cognitive and physical strain, less frustration, and higher success rates compared to those without AI support with a p-value < 0.05. The results of the participants' workload are visualized in Fig. 4.

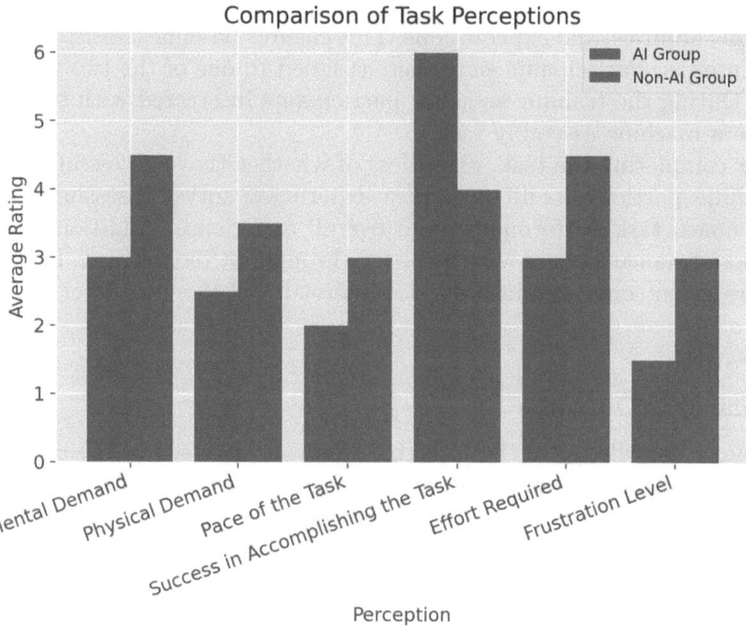

Fig. 4. Task Perceptions: AI vs Non-AI Groups

5.3 User Experience

The comparison of user experience between the AI-assisted and non-AI groups reveals that the AI group consistently reported higher ratings in aspects such as control, interest, absorption, enjoyment, and curiosity with a p value < 0.05. Notably, frustration and boredom were significantly lower in the AI group compared to the non-AI group, indicating a smoother and more engaging experience as seen in Fig. 6. These findings suggest that AI-driven training enhances user engagement, reduces negative experiences, and provides a more intuitive and enjoyable learning process.

5.4 System Usability Scale

Based on the system usability scale scoring, we can consider the two training applications usable as their usability scores are greater than 68. The results also indicate that AI-assisted training was easier and more usable than the normal VR training as shown in Fig. 5.

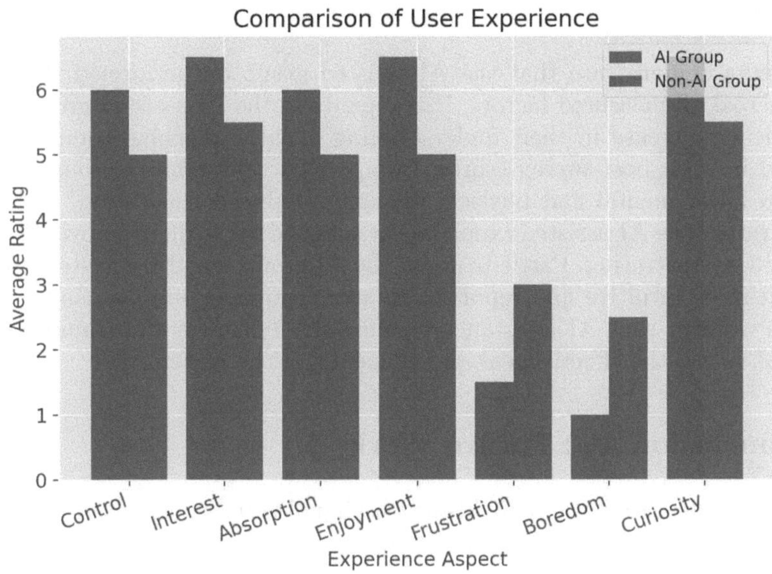

Fig. 5. System Usability: AI vs Non-AI Groups

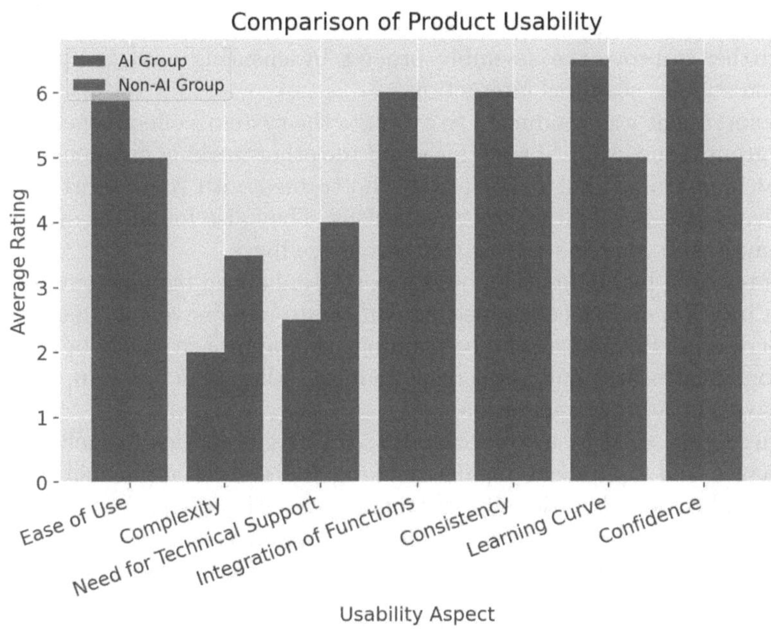

Fig. 6. User Experience: AI vs Non-AI Groups

6 Discussion

The results demonstrate that the AI-assisted group outperformed the non-AI group across all measured factors: Participants in the AI-assisted group showed a significant increase in their understanding of lathe machine components, as reflected in their post-survey scores. Compared to the non-AI group, AI users reported lower mental and physical demands, reduced frustration, and higher success rates. The AI-assisted experience was perceived as more enjoyable, engaging, and less frustrating. Participants in the AI group found the system easier to use, and more intuitive and reported greater confidence in operating it. These findings confirm that AI assistance significantly enhances the training experience, validating the effectiveness and efficiency of the system.

7 Conclusion and Future Work

This study aimed to develop an AI-driven virtual training system that enhances learning in machine assembly through the integration of extended reality (XR), voice interaction, and artificial intelligence. Extended Reality has already proven to be effective in different educational, training and simulation settings [6,7,11].

The system features an AI assistant, "Bob," which provides real-time feedback using OpenAI's ChatGPT for answering queries, Whisper for speech-to-text conversion, and Google Text-to-Speech for delivering instructions. XR components further improve the assembly process by ensuring accuracy, while voice activation enables seamless interaction.

An experiment was conducted to evaluate the system's effectiveness, comparing two groups: one using AI assistance and the other working independently. The results demonstrated that participants who trained with AI support performed better, learned faster, and felt more confident. They also found the system more user-friendly and appreciated the continuous feedback.

This research highlights the potential of AI-enhanced training environments, showing how XR and voice-enabled AI can create immersive and effective learning experiences. Beyond assembly training, this approach could be applied in education, healthcare, and industrial training, offering a modern, hands-free alternative to traditional methods.

Future work could focus on expanding training scenarios to include routine maintenance and equipment repairs, making the system applicable to a wider range of industries. Additionally, enhancing the AI assistant's capabilities by incorporating features such as error detection, adaptive learning–where instructions adjust based on user feedback–and multimodal interaction through gestures and eye tracking could further improve the training experience.

Another key area for development is optimizing usability by integrating performance monitoring, automated evaluation reports, and compatibility with existing corporate training programs. Incorporating Internet of Things (IoT) devices could also enhance realism by providing real-time machine data within the simulation. Lastly, longitudinal studies should be conducted to assess long-term skill retention and the effectiveness of AI-driven training in real-world applications.

Acknowledgments. We acknowledge the use of generative AI tools in the work and the writing. However, everything was revised.

References

1. Bordukova, M., Makarov, N., Rodriguez-Esteban, R., Schmich, F., Menden, M.P.: Generative artificial intelligence empowers digital twins in drug discovery and clinical trials. Expert Opin. Drug Discov. **19**(1), 33–42 (2024)
2. Bosché, F., Abdel-Wahab, M., Carozza, L.: Towards a mixed reality system for construction trade training. J. Comput. Civ. Eng. **30**(2), 04015016 (2016)
3. Chen, J., Lu, W., Ghansah, F.A., Peng, Z.: Defect digital twinning: a technical framework to integrate robotics, AI and BIM for facility management and renovation. In: IOP Conference Series: Earth and Environmental Science, vol. 1101, p. 022041. IOP Publishing (2022)
4. Dietrich, U., Zwanzig, D.: Ditact-digital twin for automated, customized training documents generation: a project to develop a generative digital twin for training materials. In: International Conference on Practical Applications of Agents and Multi-Agent Systems, pp. 361–368. Springer (2024)
5. Elkhadrawy, Z., Amr, K., Nasser, N., Sharaf, N., Abdennadher, S.: Interactive learning in pharmaceutical engineering: deploying augmented reality for enhanced understanding of mixer granulators. In: González-Briones, A., et al. (eds.) Highlights in Practical Applications of Agents, Multi-Agent Systems, and Digital Twins: The PAAMS Collection - International Workshops of PAAMS 2024, Salamanca, Spain, June 26-28, 2024, Proceedings, volume 2149 of Communications in Computer and Information Science, pp. 369–377. Springer (2024)
6. Elshahawy, M., Magdy, S., Sharaf, N.: ARTour: an augmented reality collaborative experience for enhancing tourism. Inf. Technol. Tourism **25**(4), 549–563 (2023)
7. Farouk, P., Faransawy, N., Sharaf, N.: Using hololens for remote collaboration in extended data visualization. In 2022 26th International Conference Information Visualisation (IV), pp. 209–214. IEEE (2022)
8. Jauhiainen, J.S., Guerra, A.G.: Generative AI and ChatGPT in school children's education: evidence from a school lesson. Sustainability **15**(18), 14025 (2023)
9. Kehoe, F.: Leveraging generative AI tools for enhanced lesson planning in initial teacher education at post primary. Irish J. Technol. Enhanced Learn. **7**(2), 172–182 (2023)
10. MacNeil, S., et al.: Automatically generating CS learning materials with large language models. arXiv preprint arXiv:2212.05113 (2022)
11. Adly, N.N.M., Sharaf, N.: PHYAR: Introducing a mixed/augmented reality platform for physics concepts (2021)
12. Nasser, N., Sharaf, N., Abdennadher, S.: Transforming organizational training: a study of extended reality applications in industry 4.0. In: González-Briones, A., et al. (ed.) Highlights in Practical Applications of Agents, Multi-Agent Systems, and Digital Twins: The PAAMS Collection - International Workshops of PAAMS 2024, Salamanca, Spain, June 26-28, 2024, Proceedings, volume 2149 of Communications in Computer and Information Science, pp. 385–393. Springer (2024)

13. Radwan, Y.M., Amr, K., Nasser, N., Sharaf, N.: From simulation to application: the transformative role of augmented reality in industry 4.0 training. In: González-Briones, A., et al. (eds.) Highlights in Practical Applications of Agents, Multi-Agent Systems, and Digital Twins: The PAAMS Collection - International Workshops of PAAMS 2024, Salamanca, Spain, June 26-28, 2024, Proceedings, volume 2149 of Communications in Computer and Information Science, pp. 378–384. Springer (2024)
14. Roullier, B., McQuade, F., Anjum, A., Bower, C., Liu, L.: Automated visual quality assessment for virtual and augmented reality based digital twins. J. Cloud Comput. **13**(1), 51 (2024)

The Role of Collaboration in Virtual Quality Control Training: Effects on Engagement and Effectiveness

Seif ElFayoumy[1], Nada Nasser[1(✉)], Nada Sharaf[2], and Slim Abdennadher[2]

[1] German University in Cairo, Cairo, Egypt
seif.elfayoumy@student.guc.edu.eg, nada.nasser@guc.edu.eg
[2] German International University, Cairo, Egypt
{nada.hamed,slim.abdennadher}@giu-uni.de

Abstract. Virtual Reality (VR) technology significantly improves workforce training by offering realistic and immersive simulations. Despite their potential, most VR-based industrial training focuses on individual scenarios, while real-world industrial tasks often require collaboration. In this study, collaborative interactions within VR quality control training were investigated to address this gap. Using a between-subjects experiment, we compared solo and collaborative conditions in a realistic conveyor belt inspection scenario. Metrics such as immersion, enjoyment, cognitive workload, usability, learning outcomes, co-presence, and social presence were evaluated. Although not statistically significant, the results suggested beneficial trends in collaborative VR in immersion, workload, and learning improvements, while enjoyment was significantly higher in solo conditions. High copresence and social presence scores highlight VR's effectiveness for realistic collaborative interactions. These findings underscore the potential of collaborative VR training and recommend further exploration in diverse industrial contexts.

Keywords: Extended Reality · Virtual Reality · Collaboration · Quality Control · Training · Industry 4.0 · Immersive Learning

1 Introduction

Training is widely recognized as a critical component in workforce development, ensuring that individuals possess the necessary skills, knowledge, and competencies to perform effectively in their respective roles. With the rapid advancement of technology, industries are increasingly taking advantage of digital tools to enhance the quality and efficiency of training programs. Among these technological solutions, Extended Reality (XR), which includes VR, Augmented Reality (AR), and Mixed Reality (MR), has emerged prominently as a powerful training modality [3,11]. XR technologies provide immersive, interactive and engaging learning environments capable of bridging theoretical knowledge and

A. Nongaillard et al. (Eds.): PAAMS 2025, CCIS 2644, pp. 183–194, 2025.
https://doi.org/10.1007/978-3-032-05925-3_15

practical skills through realistic simulations without inherent risks and logistical constraints associated with physical settings [1,12].

In particular, VR has become a significant asset for industrial training due to its immersive capabilities and its ability to replicate real-world scenarios with high fidelity [1]. VR-based training applications have demonstrated considerable potential in diverse sectors such as healthcare [1,4,9], automotive [7], manufacturing [13], and emergency response [8], due to their capability to simulate complex or hazardous tasks safely.

Traditional industrial training typically relies on face-to-face, hands-on methods. However, such traditional methods often involve significant logistical constraints, risks, and costs associated with physical simulations. VR technologies overcome these limitations by creating safe, controlled, repeatable virtual environments, significantly enhancing training efficiency and effectiveness [1,13].

Collaboration has been an element of study for extended and virtual reality applications in different settings [2,5,6,10].

2 Related Work

Most existing studies primarily explore individual (solo) trainee interactions within VR scenarios. Limited research has addressed collaborative VR training, despite collaboration being a critical component in many real-world industrial settings, significantly influencing learning outcomes, engagement, cognitive load, and usability perceptions [6,14]. Recent studies underline the effectiveness of collaborative VR applications, demonstrating improved user engagement, more effective task performance, and enhanced immersion and enjoyment levels [14].

To address this research gap, this paper investigates the impact of collaboration within a VR-based quality control training scenario, comparing solo and collaborative conditions in a conveyor belt inspection task–a representative industrial scenario. Participants either independently or collaboratively sorted defective items in an immersive VR environment, employing visual and verbal interaction.

This research aims to examine whether collaborative training significantly enhances user engagement, task efficiency, and overall effectiveness compared to solo training. Using a between-subjects experimental design, multiple dependent variables, including training performance, cognitive workload, immersion, social presence, enjoyment, usability, and subjective co-presence, are measured to comprehensively assess training impacts. The outcomes of this study contribute valuable empirical evidence regarding the integration of collaborative interactions into VR-based quality control training. Furthermore, the findings offer significant implications for designing effective industrial training programs, highlighting the promising potential of collaborative XR scenarios to enhance workforce development, engagement, and training effectiveness.

3 Methodology

The training scenario selected takes place in a factory, specifically at the conveyor belt checkpoint. This scenario was chosen as it is one of the most common tasks in quality control training. In this scenario, the trainee is a factory worker positioned at the conveyor belt checkpoint. The objective is to inspect bolts running on the conveyor belt. There are two types of bolts: gold and silver. The trainee's task is to pick up each gold bolt and place it outside the conveyor belt while allowing every silver bolt to pass as shown in Fig. 1.

This scenario was designed to simulate real-world quality control procedures, where workers must quickly and accurately identify defective items in a production line. By incorporating this repetitive yet critical task, the training aims to enhance the user's ability to recognize defects efficiently while maintaining coordination and speed. The VR environment provides a controlled setting where participants can engage with the task without external distractions, ensuring consistency across all training sessions.

To assess the role of collaboration in virtual quality control training, two different training conditions were developed and implemented. These conditions were designed to compare the effectiveness, engagement, and teamwork of trainees when completing the task alone versus in a collaborative setting.

In both training sessions, the session included 25 s of low difficulty, followed by 25 s of medium difficulty, and then 25 s of high difficulty. The difficulty was determined by the speed of the conveyor belt and the likelihood of a defective bolt (gold bolt) appearing on the conveyor.

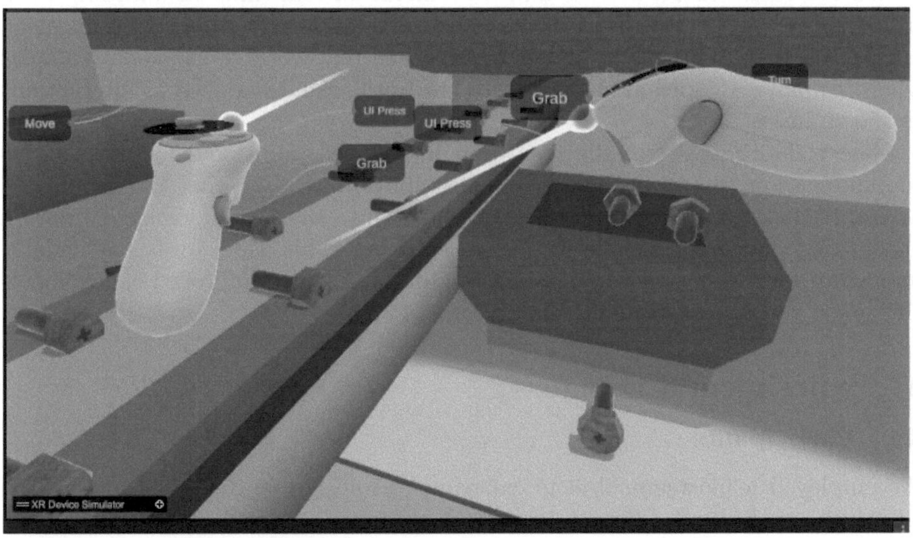

Fig. 1. The conveyor belt in the VR environment.

3.1 Solo Training Condition

In the solo condition, each participant completed the VR training individually. The trainee was positioned alone at the conveyor belt, where they had to inspect and sort the bolts without any external assistance. The virtual environment remained consistent throughout the session, with a steady flow of bolts moving along the conveyor belt. This condition served as a baseline to measure individual performance, engagement, and task efficiency without the influence of collaboration.

The solo training emphasized independent decision-making, reaction time, and accuracy. Since the participant was solely responsible for sorting the bolts, their cognitive load was potentially higher compared to the collaborative condition. This version was essential to understanding how well individuals could adapt to the VR training scenario without support from a partner.

3.2 Collaborative Training Condition

In the collaborative condition, two participants engaged in the training simultaneously. Each trainee was positioned on one side of the conveyor belt, and both worked together to remove defective (gold) bolts. This setup required real-time coordination, as trainees had to distribute the workload efficiently to ensure all defective bolts were removed while minimizing errors.

To enhance the collaborative experience, both participants wore VR headsets that enabled them to see each other's avatars within the virtual environment. The avatars included VR-tracked hand representations, allowing trainees to observe each other's actions and movements in real-time. In addition, both trainees were physically placed in the same room, allowing verbal communication during the task. This setup aimed to replicate real-world workplace dynamics where employees coordinate tasks through both visual and verbal interactions as shown in Fig. 2.

The collaborative training condition introduced additional factors such as communication, teamwork, and role distribution. Unlike the solo condition, where trainees relied solely on their judgment, the collaborative condition encouraged discussion and joint decision-making. This aspect was particularly important for evaluating whether working in pairs led to improved engagement, efficiency, and overall training effectiveness.

4 Experimental Design

4.1 Participants

We employed a between-subjects experimental design to directly compare the effectiveness of the 2 different training techniques. A total of 60 participants were recruited for the study (30 males, 30 females; age range: 18–24 years). Participants were recruited from a university campus using convenience sampling. Participants were randomly assigned to one of the two training conditions (Solo and Collaborative), with 30 participants per condition (total N = 60).

Fig. 2. Participants doing the Collaborative Quality Control VR Training.

4.2 Metrics

Score Calculation. The score is calculated as a percentage and is expressed like this:

$$\text{score} = \left(\frac{\text{silverBoltsPassed} - \text{errorsMade}}{\text{totalSilverBoltsSpawned}} \right) \times 100 \tag{1}$$

where *totalSilverBoltsSpawned* is a count of all the silver bolts spawned at the right end of the conveyor belt, *silverBoltsPassed* is the count of all silver bolts reaching the left end of the conveyor belt, and *errorsMade* is the count of all gold bolts reaching the left end of the conveyor belt.

Pre and Post Tests. A pre-test is an assessment conducted before the intervention, training, or experimental treatment. It aims to measure the learner's existing knowledge, skills, or abilities on the topic being studied. In the context of Quality Control VR training, pre-tests help evaluate baseline competencies in defect identification, adherence to standardized procedures, and performance under challenging conditions. In this study, the pre-test consisted of a more difficult version of the training, conducted in a SOLO (non-collaborative) setting, where bolts moved at high speeds along the conveyor belt, and the probability of encountering defective bolts was significantly increased.

A post-test is an assessment conducted after the intervention, training, or experimental treatment. It measures the change in knowledge, skills, or behavior resulting from the intervention. Similar to the pre-test, the post-test in this study was also a more challenging SOLO version of the training, designed to assess improvements in error detection, reaction time, and overall performance following the training.

The difference between pre-test and post-test results is often used to measure the effectiveness of an intervention or training program. The larger the difference, the more effective the intervention is considered. In this study, pre-tests and post-tests were essential in evaluating the impact of collaborative training on Quality Control performance by comparing individual improvements after experiencing SOLO pre-tests, collaborative training, and SOLO post-tests. This approach provides valuable insights into whether collaboration enhances defect detection skills and performance under high-pressure conditions.

Co-presence Questionnaire. Co-presence refers to the extent to which individuals perceive others as being physically or virtually present in a shared environment. In the context of VR training, co-presence assesses how aware and connected participants feel with their collaborators, even when physically distant. This questionnaire evaluates factors such as perceived proximity, mutual awareness, and the realism of interactions within the virtual space.

Social Presence Questionnaire. Social presence measures the sense of meaningful interaction and connection between participants in a virtual environment. Unlike co-presence, which focuses on awareness, social presence emphasizes the depth of interpersonal engagement, including emotional connection and responsiveness. This questionnaire examines how effectively the virtual environment facilitates natural communication, teamwork, and collaboration during the training experience.

Enjoyment and Engagement Questionnaire. The notion of presence or a sensation of being there is called engagement. The criteria that constitute engagement are involvement, immersion, arousal, attention, curiosity, identification, enjoyment, effort, and flow. There are a variety of methods for measuring involvement, but self-reports on surveys are the most used (Lombard & Ditton, 1997). Hence, a self-reported questionnaire is employed in this study.

Telepresence and Immersion Questionnaire. Telepresence is a measure of a person's perception of being within a virtual environment, or of being there and disconnecting their senses from the physical location in which it is located. Perception in this context mainly refers to the senses of sight, hearing, and touch. This metric is derived from creating a metric for presence as immersion (Lombard & Ditton, 1999). The questions tackled how immersed the participants were in the experiment. This questionnaire is rooted in the work of Lombard and Ditton (1997).

NASA Task Workload Index. NASA Task Load Index (NASA-TLX) was developed by Hart and Staveland in 1988. This is used to measure the users' perceived workload in terms of mental, temporal, and physical demand as well as the perceived performance, effort, and frustration rates while doing a certain task.

System Usability Scale Questionnaire. SUS stands for System Usability Scale, which is a widely used tool for assessing the usability of a system, product, or service. It is a simple, reliable, and effective questionnaire designed to evaluate user satisfaction and overall usability based on users' subjective opinions after interacting with a system. The SUS provides a quick measure of a user's overall experience with a system and can be applied to websites, software applications, hardware devices, or any user interface.

4.3 Procedure

The experiment involved two training conditions: Solo and Collaborative. Initially, all participants provided informed consent, granting permission to utilize their data for research purposes. Subsequently, participants completed a pre-test designed to assess baseline skills and knowledge in quality control tasks within a challenging VR scenario.

Following the pre-test, participants were randomly assigned to either the Solo or Collaborative training condition. Participants in the Collaborative condition generally consisted of pairs who were friends; however, a few pairs comprised strangers. The independent variable in this experiment was the training condition (Solo vs. Collaborative). Dependent variables included learning outcomes, immersion level, enjoyment and engagement level, perceived workload (measured by NASA-TLX), and system usability (evaluated via the System Usability Scale).

Each training session lasted approximately 30 min, during which participants were tasked with identifying and sorting defective bolts on a conveyor belt within the VR environment. After completing the training, all participants undertook a post-test identical to the pre-test to evaluate improvements in their defect identification skills and performance.

Throughout both training and testing phases, participant performance metrics, including accuracy in detecting defective bolts, were continuously recorded. Upon completion of the post-test, participants filled out several standardized questionnaires to measure immersion, enjoyment, workload, social and co-presence, and usability, enabling further detailed analysis of their experiences and performance.

5 Results

This section presents the results comparing Collaborative and Solo VR training conditions across various metrics. An independent samples T-Test was used to analyze differences between conditions. Table 1 presents descriptive statistics for Immersion, Enjoyment, Workload, Usability, and Learning scores, while Table 2 summarizes the statistical significance of differences. Additionally, Table 3 provides descriptive statistics for Co-Presence and Social Presence metrics, collected exclusively from the Collaborative condition.

5.1 Immersion

Levene's test indicated unequal variances between conditions ($F = 11.898$, $p = 0.001$). Using the appropriate t-test assuming unequal variances, immersion scores between Collaborative ($M = 83.33$, $SD = 11.40$) and Solo ($M = 82.80$, $SD = 7.14$) conditions did not differ significantly ($t(48.71) = 0.217$, $p = 0.829$). Thus, both training conditions yielded comparable immersive experiences.

5.2 Enjoyment

There was a statistically significant difference in Enjoyment scores between the Collaborative condition ($M = 81.89$, $SD = 12.34$) and the Solo condition ($M = 88.12$, $SD = 6.76$); $t(58) = -2.424$, $p = 0.019$. Notably, the Solo training participants reported significantly higher enjoyment compared to participants in the Collaborative condition.

5.3 Workload

The Workload metric indicated that participants in the Collaborative condition ($M = 43.56$, $SD = 12.10$) perceived a lower workload compared to those in the Solo condition ($M = 49.56$, $SD = 12.83$). This difference approached statistical significance but did not cross the standard threshold of significance ($t(58) = -1.864$, $p = 0.067$). Considering workload as an inversely desirable metric (lower scores reflect less cognitive load), these results suggest a trend where collaboration might reduce participants' perceived cognitive load during the VR training tasks.

5.4 Usability

Participants rated usability similarly for both conditions, with Collaborative training ($M = 84.00$, $SD = 10.16$) and Solo training ($M = 86.08$, $SD = 11.37$) yielding no significant difference ($t(58) = -0.748$, $p = 0.457$). This indicates that both training modes offered comparable usability and were perceived as user-friendly and intuitive.

5.5 Learning Outcomes

Learning outcomes, measured by improvements between pre- and post-training tests, did not show statistically significant differences between conditions. However, participants in the Collaborative condition ($M = 14.42$, $SD = 13.49$) demonstrated a numerically higher mean learning improvement compared to participants in the Solo condition ($M = 9.94$, $SD = 12.31$), although this difference was not statistically significant ($t(58) = 1.342$, $p = 0.185$).

5.6 Co-presence and Social Presence

As collaboration inherently involves interaction with others, Co-Presence and Social Presence metrics were measured exclusively in the Collaborative condition. Results in Table 3 show high mean scores for both Co-Presence ($M = 80.12$, $SD = 15.03$) and Social Presence ($M = 74.17$, $SD = 15.32$), indicating that participants experienced a strong sense of connection, interaction realism, and social engagement within the virtual environment. These high scores underscore the effectiveness of the VR collaborative setting in simulating realistic social interactions and fostering meaningful team experiences.

6 Discussion

This study compared collaborative and solo VR-based quality control training across various key metrics. Although statistical significance was not reached, collaborative training showed numerically better results in immersion, workload

Table 1. Group Statistics for Immersion, Enjoyment, Workload, Usability, and Learning Scores.

Metric	Group	N	Mean	Std. Deviation
Immersion	Collaborative	30	83.33	11.40
	Solo	30	82.80	7.14
Enjoyment	Collaborative	30	81.89	12.34
	Solo	30	88.12	6.76
Workload	Collaborative	30	43.56	12.10
	Solo	30	49.56	12.83
Usability	Collaborative	30	84.00	10.16
	Solo	30	86.08	11.37
Learning	Collaborative	30	14.42	13.49
	Solo	30	9.94	12.31

Table 2. Independent Samples T-Test Results Comparing Collaborative and Solo Conditions.

Metric	Variance Equality	F	Sig.	t	df	Sig. (2-tailed)	Mean Difference	95% CI of Difference
Immersion	Equal variances assumed	11.898	.001	.217	58	.829	.53333	[−4.38086, 5.44753]
	Equal variances not assumed			.217	48.710	.829	.53333	[−4.40090, 5.46756]
Enjoyment	Equal variances assumed	10.569	.002	−2.424	58	.019	−6.22727	[−11.37037, −1.08418]
	Equal variances not assumed			−2.424	44.987	.019	−6.22727	[−11.40223, −1.05231]
Workload	Equal variances assumed	.045	.833	−1.864	58	.067	−6.00000	[−12.44360, .44360]
	Equal variances not assumed			−1.864	57.801	.067	−6.00000	[−12.44397, .44397]
Usability	Equal variances assumed	.053	.818	−.748	58	.457	−2.08333	[−7.65528, 3.48861]
	Equal variances not assumed			−.748	57.289	.457	−2.08333	[−7.65675, 3.49008]
Learning	Equal variances assumed	.007	.935	1.342	58	.185	4.47567	[−2.51765, 11.14098]
	Equal variances not assumed			1.342	57.776	.185	4.47567	[−2.13824, 11.08958]

Table 3. Means and Standard Deviations for Co-Presence and Social Presence.

Metric	Mean	Std. Deviation
Co-Presence	80.12	15.03
Social Presence	74.17	15.32

(lower perceived cognitive load), and learning outcomes compared to solo training. These findings suggest the potential benefits of collaborative interactions in distributing cognitive demands and enhancing the overall training experience.

However, enjoyment was significantly higher in the solo condition. This unexpected finding might be related to additional coordination and communication challenges in collaborative scenarios, possibly affecting immediate enjoyment.

High reported co-presence and social presence scores emphasize that collaborative VR setups successfully foster realistic interactions and meaningful interpersonal engagement, reinforcing VR's potential as a valuable collaborative training tool.

7 Conclusion and Future Work

In conclusion, our findings suggest collaborative VR training has potential advantages over solo training, particularly regarding immersion, workload distribution, and learning outcomes, although these advantages were not statistically significant in this study. The reduced enjoyment in collaborative settings highlights a potential trade-off warranting further investigation.

The study encountered limitations, notably minor technical issues such as gameplay lag potentially caused by high internet bandwidth requirements. Additionally, our participant sample lacked demographic diversity, consisting predominantly of university students from a similar age group, limiting the generalizability of findings.

Future research could address these technical limitations through network optimization or local network implementations. Additionally, future studies should involve more diverse demographics, examine long-term learning retention, and explore various collaborative task structures and team dynamics. Addressing these factors can enhance the understanding and effectiveness of collaborative VR training scenarios in industrial settings.

Acknowledgments. We acknowledge the use of different Generative AI tools in the work and writing. All the outputs were reviewed.

References

1. Abbas, J.R., et al.: What is virtual reality? A healthcare-focused systematic review of definitions. Health Policy Technol. **12**(2), 100741 (2023). https://doi.org/10.1016/j.hlpt.2023.100741, https://www.sciencedirect.com/science/article/pii/S2211883723000199
2. Abdelhamed, H., El-Faransawy, N., Sharaf, N.: In-place collaboration in extended reality data visualization. In: 2022 26th International Conference Information Visualisation (IV), pp. 215–220. IEEE (2022)
3. Cárdenas-Robledo, L.A., Hernández-Uribe, Ó., Reta, C., Cantoral-Ceballos, J.A.: Extended reality applications in industry 4.0.–a systematic literature review. Telematics Inf. **73**, 101863 (2022)
4. Cecil, J., Gupta, A., Pirela-Cruz, M., Ramanathan, P.: A network-based virtual reality simulation training approach for orthopedic surgery. ACM Trans. Multimedia Comput. Commun. Appl. **14**(3) (2018). https://doi.org/10.1145/3232678
5. Elshahawy, M., Magdy, S., Sharaf, N.: ARTour: an augmented reality collaborative experience for enhancing tourism. Inf. Technol. Tourism **25**(4), 549–563 (2023)
6. Farouk, P., Faransawy, N., Sharaf, N.: Using hololens for remote collaboration in extended data visualization. 2022 26th International Conference Information Visualisation (IV), pp. 209–214 (2022). https://api.semanticscholar.org/CorpusID:256214642

7. Lan, G., Lai, Q., Bai, B., Zhao, Z., Hao, Q.: A virtual reality training system for automotive engines assembly and disassembly. IEEE Trans. Learn. Technol. **17**, 754–764 (2024). https://doi.org/10.1109/TLT.2023.3330471
8. Lerner, D., Mohr, S., Schild, J., Göring, M., Luiz, T.: An immersive multi-user virtual reality for emergency simulation training: usability study. JMIR Serious Games **8**, e18822 (2020).https://doi.org/10.2196/18822
9. Mao, R.Q., et al.: Immersive virtual reality for surgical training: a systematic review. J. Surg. Res. **268**, 40–58 (2021). https://doi.org/10.1016/j.jss.2021.06.045, https://www.sciencedirect.com/science/article/pii/S0022480421004169
10. Nasser, N., Makled, E., Sharaf, N., Abdennadher, S.: Social interaction in virtual shopping. In: 2021 IEEE International Symposium on Multimedia (ISM), pp. 204–205. IEEE (2021)
11. Nasser, N., Sharaf, N., Abdennadher, S.: Transforming organizational training: a study of extended reality applications in industry 4.0. In: González-Briones, A., et al. (eds.) Highlights in Practical Applications of Agents, Multi-Agent Systems, and Digital Twins: The PAAMS Collection - International Workshops of PAAMS 2024, Salamanca, Spain, June 26-28, 2024, Proceedings. Communications in Computer and Information Science, vol. 2149, pp. 385–393. Springer (2024). https://doi.org/10.1007/978-3-031-73058-0_32
12. Rutkowski, S., et al.: Use of virtual reality-based training in different fields of rehabilitation: a systematic review and meta-analysis. J. Rehabil. Med. Official J. UEMS Eur. Board Phys. Rehabil. Med. **52**, jrm00121 (2020). https://doi.org/10.2340/16501977-2755
13. Wolfartsberger, J., Zimmermann, R., Obermeier, G., Niedermayr, D.: Analyzing the potential of virtual reality-supported training for industrial assembly tasks. Comput. Ind. **147**, 103838 (2023). https://doi.org/10.1016/j.compind.2022.103838, https://www.sciencedirect.com/science/article/pii/S0166361522002342
14. Yildiz, E., Melo, M., Møller, C., Bessa, M.: Designing collaborative and coordinated virtual reality training integrated with virtual and physical factories. In: 2019 International Conference on Graphics and Interaction (ICGI), pp. 48–55 (2019). https://doi.org/10.1109/ICGI47575.2019.8955033

RAI: Flexible Agent Framework for Embodied AI

Kajetan Rachwał[1(✉)], Maciej Majek[1], Bartłomiej Boczek[1], Kacper Dąbrowski[1], Paweł Liberadzki[1], Adam Dąbrowski[1], and Maria Ganzha[2]

[1] Robotec.AI, Warsaw, Poland
{kajetan.rachwal,maciej.majek,bartlomiej.boczek,kacper.dabrowski,pawel.liberadzki,adam.dabrowski}@robotec.ai

[2] Faculty of Mathematics and Information Science, Warsaw University of Technology, Warsaw, Poland
maria.ganzha@pw.edu.pl

Abstract. With an increase in the capabilities of generative language models, a growing interest in embodied AI has followed. This contribution introduces RAI – a framework for creating embodied Multi Agent Systems for robotics. The proposed framework implements tools for Agents' integration with robotic stacks, Large Language Models, and simulations. It provides out-of-the-box integration with state-of-the-art systems like ROS 2. It also comes with dedicated mechanisms for the embodiment of Agents. These mechanisms have been tested on a physical robot, Husarion ROSBot XL, which was coupled with its digital twin, for rapid prototyping. Furthermore, these mechanisms have been deployed in two simulations: (1) robot arm manipulator and (2) tractor controller. All of these deployments have been evaluated in terms of their control capabilities, effectiveness of embodiment, and perception ability. The proposed framework has been used successfully to build systems with multiple agents. It has demonstrated effectiveness in all the aforementioned tasks. It also enabled identifying and addressing the shortcomings of the generative models used for embodied AI.

Keywords: Embodied AI · Multi-Agent Systems · Robotics · Generative AI · Digital Twin · Simulations

1 Introduction

Since the advent of Large Language Models (LLMs), there has been a growing interest in their applications in embodied AI agents [10,17]. This effort has accelerated with the introduction of tool or function calling mechanisms, leading to the creation of more complex embodied AI systems [22]. These systems often rely heavily on custom implementations that enable integration with foreign APIs and AI models.

A. Nongaillard et al. (Eds.): PAAMS 2025, CCIS 2644, pp. 195–206, 2025.
https://doi.org/10.1007/978-3-032-05925-3_16

Some existing solutions facilitate the development of tools for API integration, such as ModelScope [11]. Systems such as ROSA [20] are tightly coupled with particular solutions (in this case ROS and ROS 2 [15]), but do not offer solutions for integration with other communication stacks. Frameworks such as AgentGYM [23] offer agents a standardized environment and evaluate LLM-based agents within that environment. These LLM-based solutions are generally designed for single-agent deployments. However, all of the above inherit common limitations of LLMs, including hallucinations [9], a lack of interpretability and explainability [26], and susceptibility to jailbreak attacks [24]. These constraints often lead to serious functional and ethical concerns.

It is worth mentioning that before the rise in popularity of LLMs, several frameworks were already developed for building robotic agents. For example, FABRIC [21] has been introduced to develop robotic agents that utilize reusable components for seamless integration with ROS. Likewise, MARC [4] has been designed for Multi-Agent Systems (MAS) based on reinforcement learning. In addition to these, some frameworks have been proposed for specific robotic applications [12,19,27], ranging from designs based on multi-robot cooperation to human-robot interaction with multiple people. An important contribution toward creating a generalized framework applicable across various robotic domains is the G++ architecture [6]. All of the aforementioned approaches lack the flexibility and potential for human-robot interaction offered by native integration with LLMs.

In this context, this paper presents RAI, a framework designed for creating Multi-Agent Systems (MAS) with built-in capabilities for integration with LLMs, robotic stacks, external APIs, and human-robot interaction mechanisms. It also comes with components which support embodiment, such as tools for understanding Agent's physical form. Generality is achieved through a modular and scalable architecture, which is based on the M-Agent model [1]. This model defines an agent through its reasoning system, sensors, and actuators.

In RAI, these abstractions are streamlined into the agent's core logic and connectors – utility components that allow the agent to both observe and interact with a broadly defined environment. RAI agents can be virtual (interacting solely with a digital environment), physical, or exist within a virtual-physical continuum, seamlessly integrating both domains. By being in a single MAS, the virtual and physical agents can communicate with each other to better achieve their goals. The details of these mechanisms are described in Sect. 2.

This paper presents three deployments in different environments to validate the viability of RAI. The performance of the system in an edge computing setup within a physical environment has been tested using ROSBotXL, a ROS 2 autonomous mobile robot platform. RAI agents have been deployed on the platform to observe the environment, control robot movement, and enable human-robot interaction (HRI) capabilities. Details of this experiment are presented in Sect. 3.1. In addition, two pure virtual (simulation-based) experiments have been performed. These RAI agents have been utilized for manipulation tasks with a simulated robotic arm and controlling a tractor. The details are described in Sect. 3.

2 Architecture

RAI architecture defines high level abstract classes, that allow for concise and flexible Agent definition. The current section focuses on details of these interfaces and describes example use cases.

2.1 Component Definitions

At the highest level, RAI uses three abstractions – *Agents*, *Connectors*, and *Tools*.
Agents are the basic building blocks of a MAS. RAI *Agent* implements a simple interface containing two methods, `run()` and `stop()`. *Agents* are also guaranteed to possess *Connectors* – mechanisms for observing and actuating their environment. It is up to the user to define the internal model of the environment and the decision-making process for selecting actions. Some RAI *Agents* use simple rules-based systems, while others can utilize mechanisms such as LLMs for the decision-making process.
Connectors are an abstraction that represents the sensors and actuators of the *Agents*. They enable three modes of communication: publish-subscribe, service-based, and action-based. Previous experiences [8] have shown that relying only on one mode of communication can be limiting, so with RAI, we decided on an approach similar to ROS 2 communication. The publish-subscribe mode provides utilities for publishing and receiving messages from other hosts. In most implementations (e.g., ROS 2, MQTT, XMPP), this method of communication is efficient and performant. However, its reliability is limited as there is no guarantee that a sent message will be received. The service-based mode addresses this limitation by providing the API caller with information on the message delivery and the result of the call. This type of communication is usually less performant than the publish-subscribe mode (given the need to receive a response), but provides more reliability. Finally, the action-based mode is modeled after the ROS 2 Actions API, which informs users about the acceptance and outcome of actions. In addition, it provides continuous feedback on the execution state.

A specific RAI *Connector* can implement all of these modes or combine any of them depending on the particular communication mechanism it encapsulates.
Tools are an abstraction inspired by LLMs and their tool-calling mechanisms. A specific *Tool* implements a way to create or parse data sent or received through a *Connector*. These implementations are compatible with langchain[1], enabling seamless integration with tool-calling-enabled LLMs. They can also be used by *Agents* utilizing other decision-making mechanisms.

[1] https://www.langchain.com/.

2.2 Embodiment

Robotic embodiment lacks a clear and broadly accepted definition. Some researchers [7] argue that simply having information on ways to interact with an environment is sufficient to constitute embodiment. Others [5] think that more information is needed, such as a certain understanding of an environment and a robot's own "body". RAI follows the latter view by enabling the creation of an agent's embodied identity from versatile data sources. The proposed RAI framework enables users to experiment with different types and configurations of embodiment mechanisms. The dedicated `RAI_whoami` package provides an easy-to-configure way to incorporate embodying information into the *Agents*. This package includes features to automatically convert text, PDFs, and other documents into a vector database. RAI supports multiple vector databases and was deployed with Faiss [3] as a robust solution. The vector database can then enable LLMs with Retrieval Augmented Generation (RAG). The functionality to store other embodiment-related data, such as images or URDFs, is also provided. All of this data is accessible to a RAI *Agent* and can be used to semi-automate the creation of system prompts. It can also be used during the *Agent's* runtime to retrieve additional information, e.g. when handling a user requesting information about the robot's capabilities.

2.3 Example of System Configuration

To better understand these abstractions, consider a simple embodied deployment illustrated in Fig. 1. In the illustrated example, we have access to a robot, its documentation, and a ROS 2 service that uses an open-set segmentation model GroundingDINO [13]. These can be easily connected to create an embodied *Agent* using RAI. Such an *Agent* would be designed to have two ROS 2 *Connectors* – one for connection with the robot and one with the GroundingDINO ROS 2 Node. The first *Connector* would be coupled with *Tools* designed for robot control, and the second one with a *Tool* for parsing GroundingDINO output into LLM understandable input. The *Agent* could be a simple conversational LLM, or a more advanced system (see Sect. 3 for more complex examples).

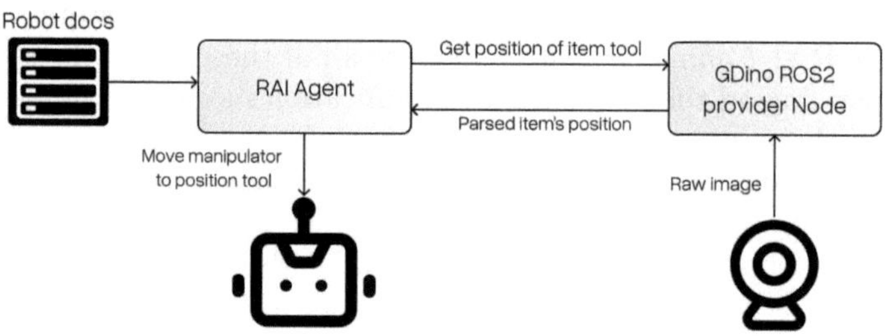

Fig. 1. Simple embodied agent setup

2.4 Flexibility and Extensibility

To simplify the deployment of abstractions from Sect. 2.1, RAI comes with a library of configurable components. Currently, there are four pre-packaged deployable agents:

- `VoiceRecognition` – coupled with configurable models for speech processing pipelines, enabling automatic speech recognition and transcription for human-robot interaction, as well as microphone integration;
- `TextToSpeech` – equipped with direct speaker integration and coupled with text-to-speech (TTS) model;
- `Conversational` (Fig. 2) – an agent based on ReAct [25] LLM architecture which utilizes connectors to send and receive multimodal inputs;
- `StateBased` (Fig. 3) – an agent based on a finite state machine – a mechanism similar to SPADE's [16] **FSMBehaviour**, which integrates LLM based reasoning with procedural approaches, which can be utilized for more complex tasks.

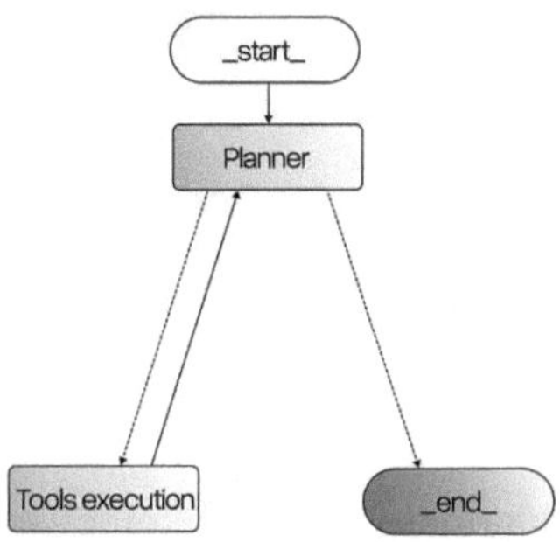

Fig. 2. Conversational Agent

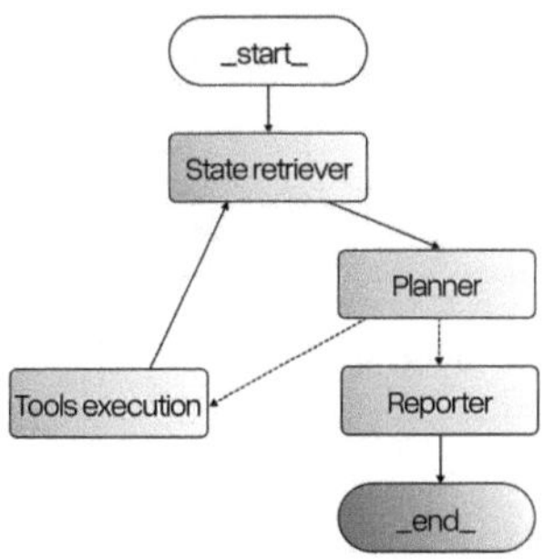

Fig. 3. StateBased Agent

The provided *Agents* come with a set of connectors that enable interoperability through communication protocols (e.g. `ROS2Connector`) and direct peripheral access (e.g. `SoundDeviceConnector`). Connectors are coupled with tools for low-level communication e.g. `CallROS2Service` or `ReceiveROS2Message`. The library also includes *Tools* for data processing, like `GetDistanceToObjects` for spatial analysis of camera and depth data. It should be noted that the RAI components library is under active and continuous development, so the pool of available components is constantly growing. In Sect. 4 plans for further work are described.

3 Applications

3.1 Navigation and Human-Robot-Integration: Autonomous Mobile Robot

Overview. The Husarion ROSBot XL was selected for indoor navigation and HRI experiments. It is an autonomous mobile robot platform for indoor applications. It comes equipped with an Intel RealSense Camera, a Slamtec RPLIDAR

S3, and a Bosch BNO055 IMU. Navigation is controlled through the ROS 2 nav2 [14] stack. Two environments were used for the tests: a physical office setting (Fig. 4) and a simulated household implemented in Open 3D Engine (O3DE)[2] (Fig. 5) with a digital twin of the robot. The double deployment accelerated prototyping and enabled testing of the system's robustness during the transfer from simulation to the real world. In addition, the MAS deployment included a flexible human-robot interface that supports both S2S and text-based interactions via a web user interface.

In the experiments, RAI *Agents* were equipped with open-set detection and generic ROS 2 tools used by the *Agents* for the discovery of robot interfaces and the execution of navigation objectives. To achieve embodiment, the system prompt was initialized with the robot's identity, and a tool for RAG querying was provided utilizing the mechanism described in Sect. 2.2.

Fig. 4. Physical office setting

Fig. 5. Household with the digital twin

Configuration. A series of experiments was conducted using different architecture configurations. Initially, a single state-based agent (described in Sect. 2.4) was implemented to handle human interaction, camera image interpretation, and tool invocation. This configuration resulted in advantages such as lower latency, full context retention, and easier debugging. However, it also showed drawbacks: while the robot was performing a mission, the HRI interface was less responsive, as the LLM risked losing track of the mission goal when handling concurrent user queries. To overcome these issues, a multi-agent setup was applied – shown in Fig. 6. The Conversational *Agent* responded to Human text based input, and commanded the Robot Control *Agent*, which was responsible for execution of the mission. The mission was defined by a human prompt (e.g. "Navigate to the chair"). Its execution was performed through ROS 2 based tooling using actions. The *Agent* was also responsible for deciding when to report completion or failure to the user.

Conclusions. The Robot Control *Agent* utilized the ROS 2 nav2 stack and the open-set detection tools, to fulfill navigation commands (e.g. navigate to the

[2] https://o3de.org.

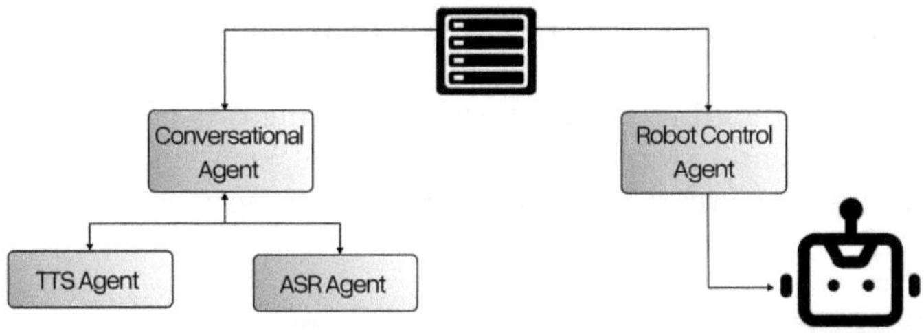

Fig. 6. Multi-agent architecture for S2S and navigation

kitchen). The system was able to handle commands such as navigating to specified locations or positioning itself relative to environmental objects. The digital twin environment proved invaluable for rapid prototyping, and the subsequent transfer to the real robot confirmed the robustness of the design. In general, the MAS-based setup provided a balanced approach between efficient mission execution and effective human-robot interaction. The framework proved itself to be flexible enough for testing different complex agent setups, where the user can examine the influence of each pipeline component.

Challenges. Several challenges were encountered during system integration. Difficulties were experienced in achieving a clear understanding of agent embodiment, and issues were observed in the multi-agent architecture. In particular, inconsistencies in the understanding of embodiment were occasionally observed between the two LLM-based *Agents*. It has also been noted, that the decision to make LLM-based *Agents* responsible for synchronization of information regarding the state of the mission led to some inconsistencies. Similar problems were also encountered with long-running background tasks executed by the robotic stack. This could be addressed by incorporating rule-based synchronization mechanisms in future work. Furthermore, while Robot Control *Agent* could use the navigation stack successfully, error handling and mission success detection were inconsistent.

3.2 Manipulation: Robotic Arm

Overview. An *Agent* controlling a robotic arm was deployed in O3DE, where it received a task defined using natural language. *Agent's* perception was limited to a camera stream. The received images were processed using an open-set segmentation model [18], which provided additional information about the view. The observed environment included a desk with colorful blocks and vegetables. The interaction with the environment was performed with *Tools* utilizing MoveIt 2 [2] for motion planning and execution.

Experiments. To evaluate its performance, the *Agent* was tested in three key manipulation tasks:

1. Sorting Objects – classifying objects before placing them in corresponding groups (Fig. 7);
2. Stacking Items – building stable stacks by placing objects on each other;
3. Object Replacement – swapping pairs of objects, strategically using an intermediate position to prevent collisions and ensure proper placement.

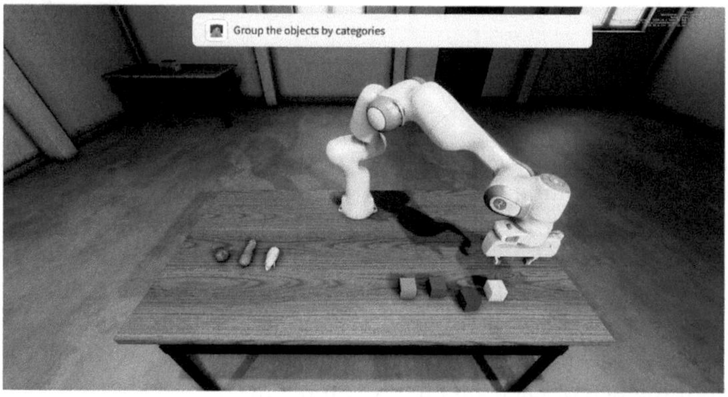

Fig. 7. Scene setup after a sorting task is completed

Various cloud-based multimodal LLMs (GPT-4o, GPT-4o mini, Claude 3.5 Sonnet) were tested as reasoning engines. They were tasked with the interpretation of scene data, planning movement sequences, and verifying task success.

Challenges. Although success has often been observed in these tasks, *Agents* repeatedly faced the same difficulties, particularly in spatial reasoning and self-correction. When stacking (task 2), the *Agent* often tried to place objects "inside" each other rather than on top, failing to account for physical boundaries. A similar issue occurred during swapping objects (task 3) – the *Agent* tried to place the moved object directly in the place of the second object, without considering an intermediate position. Despite explicit instructions to verify the completion using camera images, the *Agent* frequently misjudged its success, assuming that the tasks were completed correctly even when errors were present. These problems were observed in multiple LLMs, suggesting general limitations in spatial reasoning, understanding boundaries, and object interactions.

Results. The *Agent* succeeded in basic manipulation tasks. However, it frequently failed on tasks that require spatial reasoning and action sequencing. Stacking and object replacement errors were common, as the *Agent* lacked an intuitive grasp of the physical constraints. The *Agent* frequently failed to recognize its mistakes due to poor image understanding within the simulation. Most of the LLMs tested were able to complete the assigned tasks with adequate prompt engineering. However, in many cases, the instructions had to be extremely explicit, essentially guiding the LLM step-by-step through each action. Without such detailed instructions, the *Agent* frequently struggled to perform an effective sequence of movements. This highlights a key limitation: while multimodal LLMs can perform complex tasks, their ability to independently reason about spatial interactions remains limited.

3.3 Agriculture: Handling Edge-Cases

Fig. 8. Tractor's image used for enhancing Agent's embodiment

Overview. An autonomous tractor was deployed in O3DE, a ROS 2-enabled simulation environment. The environment was designed for high-fidelity real-time simulation of an orchard with trees. The *Agent* was specifically tasked with handling unexpected situations in an agricultural setting.

The tractor was equipped with a rule-based autonomous system. When that system detected an anomaly, the tractor's control was transferred to the *Agent*. At that point, *Agent* gathered environment understanding through a front camera image and had to determine the most appropriate response to ensure both safety and efficiency. The available *Tools* included replanning the route, driving forward (over the obstacle), using visual and auditory signals, or aborting the task.

Experiments. To evaluate the *Agent*'s performance in agricultural automation, two experimental conditions were tested:

1. Language-only embodiment: a natural language description of the tractor, specifying its size, movement capabilities, and operational constraints;
2. Visual embodiment: an image (Fig. 8) of the tractor, in addition to the description, offering it a direct visual reference of its physical attributes.

A range of multimodal LLMs (GPT-4o, GPT-4o mini, Claude 3.5 Sonnet) was tested as reasoning engines for the agent. The experiments focused on response to anomalies, specifically recognizing, classifying, and responding to obstacles in the environment.

Challenges. The primary issue with the language-only embodiment was misjudging the durability of the tractor. Without a visual reference, the *Agent* was overly cautious, often stopping for small obstacles such as branches, incorrectly assuming they could cause damage.

The visually embodied *Agent* performed significantly better in assessing the tractor's physical capabilities. Both *Agents* occasionally misidentified objects, leading to errors in decision-making.

Results. Providing the *Agent* with a visual reference of the tractor improved its obstacle assessment. With an image of itself, the *Agent* had a better grasp of its dimensions and durability. Unlike the language-only *Agent*, it correctly identified that small branches did not pose a threat. The setup including vision-based embodiment led to an increase in correct hazard classification.

Despite these improvements, both agents struggled with image-based object recognition. Occasionally, classification errors led to incorrect hazard assessments, unnecessary maneuvering, or aborting the mission. While the visual embodiment helped mitigate false positives, the underlying image processing remained a limitation.

4 Conclusions and Future Work

The goal of this work was to develop a scalable, extensible, and flexible system to implement embodied MAS in both simulated and physical environments. To achieve this, the RAI framework was introduced, designed to address common challenges in working with autonomous and semi-autonomous robotic agents. The RAI's architecture supports scalability by allowing the addition of new *Agents* with minimal overhead. It is extensible, enabling users to develop custom *Tools* and functionalities, and flexible, simplifying integration across various deployment scenarios. These capabilities have been demonstrated through successful deployments on multiple robotic platforms, highlighting RAI's potential for embodied agent applications in diverse contexts, as demonstrated in Sect. 3. The framework has also proven valuable for experimenting with embodiment strategies and evaluating LLM capabilities.

The current version of RAI is available at https://github.com/RobotecAI/rai. All of the presented use cases are provided there with deployment instructions (in the examples directory). It should be noted that the framework undergoes constant development. Further work will include expanding the components library (Sect. 2.4) and adding features meant to address limitations of LLMs (e.g. spatio-temporal database, human-in-the loop control, or knowledge streaming).

It will also include the creation of reproducible and quantifiable evaluation mechanisms. Contributions to its further development are welcomed and requested.

References

1. Cetnarowicz, K.: M-agent architecture based method of development of multiagent systems. In: Proceedings of the 8th Join EPS-APS International Conference on Physics Computing, ACC Cyfronet (1996)
2. Coleman, D., Sucan, I.A., Chitta, S., Correll, N.: Reducing the barrier to entry of complex robotic software: a Moveit! Case study. CoRR abs/1404.3785 (2014)
3. Douze, M., et al.: The Faiss library (2024)
4. Duan, K., Suen, C.W.K., Zou, Z.: MARC: A multi-agent robots control framework for enhancing reinforcement learning in construction tasks (2023)
5. Duffy, B., Joue, G.: Intelligent robots: The question of embodiment (2000)
6. Guidi-Polanco, F., Cubillos, C.: An agent-based software framework for robotics and automation systems. In: Crisan, M. (ed.) Convergence and Hybrid Information Technologies, chap. 7. IntechOpen, Rijeka (2010). https://doi.org/10.5772/9652
7. Guzman, L., Morellas, V., Papanikolopoulos, N.: Robotic embodiment of human-like motor skills via reinforcement learning. IEEE Robot. Autom. Lett. **7**(2), 3711–3717 (2022). https://doi.org/10.1109/LRA.2022.3147453
8. Hołda, P., Rachwał, K., Sawicki, J., Ganzha, M., Paprzycki, M.: Agents assembly: domain specific language for agent simulations. In: Dignum, F., Mathieu, P., Corchado, J.M., De La Prieta, F. (eds.) Advances in Practical Applications of Agents, Multi-Agent Systems, and Complex Systems Simulation. The PAAMS Collection, pp. 487–492. Springer International Publishing, Cham (2022)
9. Huang, L., et al.: A survey on hallucination in large language models: principles, taxonomy, challenges, and open questions. ACM Trans. Inf. Syst. **43**(2), 1–55 (2025)
10. Huang, W., Abbeel, P., Pathak, D., Mordatch, I.: Language models as zero-shot planners: extracting actionable knowledge for embodied agents. In: International Conference on Machine Learning, pp. 9118–9147. PMLR (2022)
11. Li, C., et al.: ModelScope-Agent: Building your customizable agent system with open-source large language models. ArXiv abs/2309.00986 (2023)
12. Lim, C.S., Mamat, R., Braunl, T.: Market-based approach for multi-team robot cooperation. In: 2009 4th International Conference on Autonomous Robots and Agents, pp. 62–67. IEEE (2009)
13. Liu, S., et al.: Grounding DINO: Marrying DINO with grounded pre-training for open-set object detection. arXiv preprint arXiv:2303.05499 (2023)
14. Macenski, S., Martin, F., White, R., Ginés Clavero, J.: The marathon 2: a navigation system. In: 2020 IEEE/RSJ International Conference on Intelligent Robots and Systems (IROS) (2020)
15. Macenski, S., Soragna, A., Carroll, M., Ge, Z.: Impact of ROS 2 node composition in robotic systems. IEEE Robotics and Autonomous Letters (RA-L) (2023)
16. Palanca, J.: Smart Python Agent Development Environment. https://github.com/javipalanca/spade. Accessed 10 May 2022
17. Reed, S., et al.: A generalist agent. arXiv preprint arXiv:2205.06175 (2022)
18. Ren, T., et al.: Grounded SAM: Assembling open-world models for diverse visual tasks (2024)

19. Rogers, T.E., Sekmen, A.S., Peng, J.: Attention mechanisms for social engagements of robots with multiple people. In: ROMAN'2006-The 15th IEEE International Symposium on Robot and Human Interactive Communication, pp. 605–610. IEEE (2006)
20. Royce, R., et al.: Enabling novel mission operations and interactions with ROSA: The robot operating system agent (2024)
21. Seredyński, D., Winiarski, T., Zieliński, C.: FABRIC: framework for agent-based robot control systems. In: 2019 12th International Workshop on Robot Motion and Control (RoMoCo), pp. 215–222 (2019). https://doi.org/10.1109/RoMoCo.2019.8787370
22. Wang, G., et al.: Voyager: An open-ended embodied agent with large language models. arXiv preprint arXiv: Arxiv-2305.16291 (2023)
23. Xi, Z., et al.: AgentGym: Evolving large language model-based agents across diverse environments. ArXiv abs/2406.04151 (2024)
24. Xu, Z., Liu, Y., Deng, G., Li, Y., Picek, S.: A comprehensive study of jailbreak attack versus defense for large language models. arXiv:2402.13457 (2024)
25. Yao, S., et al.: ReAct: Synergizing reasoning and acting in language models. arXiv preprint arXiv:2210.03629 (2022)
26. Zhao, H., et al.: Explainability for large language models: a survey. ACM Trans. Intell. Syst. Technol. **15**(2) (2024). https://doi.org/10.1145/3639372
27. Zhu, H.: A role-based approach to robot agent team design. In: 2006 IEEE International Conference on Systems, Man and Cybernetics. vol. 6, pp. 4861–4866. IEEE (2006)

Towards the Generalization of Developing 3D Objects for Extended Reality Training

Mazen Ashraf[1], Nada Nasser[1], and Nada Sharaf[2(✉)]

[1] The German University in Cairo, New Cairo, Egypt
[2] The German International University, Cairo, Egypt
nada.hamed@giu-uni.de

Abstract. The paper provides a comprehensive exploration of the current implementation of 3D model generation and the development of a novel approach to creating 3D models for extended reality (XR) training applications. The work introduces the development of a unique code with a purpose of simplifying the approach while reducing resource usage. The platform interprets engineering drawings, identifies the lines and circles that constitute each shape, and prompts the user for extrusion values. These values are then utilized to extrude the shapes, which are subsequently combined in Blender using a custom Python script.

The paper thoroughly discusses the development process and its steps, the testing process. It also addresses the limitations of the current approach and proposes potential enhancements for future iterations.

Keywords: 3D Object Generation · Automated 3D Generation · Extended Reality

1 Introduction

Extended reality (XR) has revolutionized the way we interact with digital content, particularly in the field of training, visualization, simulations and education [1,4,5,11] This is one of the reasons, virtual and extended reality training are being increasingly applied in different domains [12,13] However, the creation of 3D models for XR training remains a challenging task, often requiring significant time and expertise The paper aims to address this issue by exploring the use of deep learning algorithms for the generation of 3D models and developing a project that is motivated by the need to simplify and streamline the process of creating 3D models for XR training, making it more accessible and efficient This thesis outlines the methodology, implementation, and results of the project, providing a comprehensive overview of the work undertaken.

The rapid advancement of Extended Reality (XR) technologies has revolutionized various fields, including education, construction assistance, and medical training, underscoring the immense potential and importance of this technology This progression has driven extensive research into the application of XR in different forms, such as Virtual Reality (VR), Augmented Reality (AR), and Mixed

A. Nongaillard et al. (Eds.): PAAMS 2025, CCIS 2644, pp. 207–218, 2025.
https://doi.org/10.1007/978-3-032-05925-3_17

Reality (MR) For example, AR technology has been utilized to provide assembly work instructions by highlighting the relevant part or tool currently in use Similarly, VR technology has been implemented to develop safety training simulators for electric overhead crane operations, enabling trainees to identify hazards and accident pathways in a safe and immersive setting Moreover, studies have examined the use of VR to enhance cognitive functions in older adults through games based on real-life tasks like shopping and managing finances, demonstrating that VR-based cognitive training outperforms traditional methods.

Despite the promising opportunities presented by the progression of XR technologies, several challenges must be addressed A significant obstacle is the creation of 3D models for integration within virtual or augmented environments Traditionally, computer-aided design (CAD) software is employed for developing these 3D models However, this process is labor-intensive and requires a high level of expertise, as the models must be crafted with intricate details to accurately represent their real-world counterparts and maintain user immersion.

The aim is to improve the process of creating 3D models for extended reality training This involves identifying and developing the most effective approach for generating 3D models to streamline development, reduce labor intensity, and expedite the creation of extended reality training materials.

2 Related Work

The work presented in [8] designed a framework to enhance shopping on E-commerce websites, by taking several images for the product provided by the manufacturer from various angles, a 3D model is generated through several steps The process begins with feature extraction and matching using ORB and homography for complex images Next, uncalibrated 3D structure and camera pose are estimated using a projective basis and refined via bundle adjustment Epipolar rectification is then performed by computing the fundamental matrix and epilines Finally, texture mapping is applied using OpenCV and OpenGL, followed by model rendering.

Shi et al. [15] survey key three-dimensional generative models, including: the Generative Adversarial Model, with a generator and discriminator working in opposition; the Variational Autoencoder, which enables tractable inference; Normalizing Flows, using invertible transformations for exact likelihoods; Diffusion Models, which denoise data through a Markov process; and Energy-Based Models, which rely on energy functions to model probabilities. They also review common three-dimensional data formats: Voxel Grids (structured volumetric data), Point Clouds (unstructured surface samples), Meshes (non-Euclidean surface representations), and Neural Fields (continuous neural representations of scenes or objects). Seo et al. [14] implemented a framework called 3DFuse which creates a 3D point cloud from text prompt in addition to incorporating 3d awareness into the model This is achieved by conditioning a 2D diffusion model to projected depth maps of generated 3D structures implemented by a point cloud generation module using consistency injection module to optimize the 3D the viewpoints in 3D aware manner.

Several approaches have been proposed for reconstructing three-dimensional models from two-dimensional data Hu et al. [7] treat reconstruction from orthographic drawings as a sequence-to-sequence problem, introducing a Plank Assembly model with a transformer-based architecture to generate three-dimensional computer-aided design models Borrel and Fourches [2] developed RealityConvert, a Python-based tool that integrates PyMol, Blender, OpenBabel, and Molconvert to create biochemical three-dimensional models for use in augmented and virtual reality, with texture mapping handled through Blender Camba and Contero [3] employed Autodesk's Memento (now Recap), which uses photogrammetry to build point clouds from multiple images and generate three-dimensional meshes–highly dependent on image quality Finally, SusheelKumar et al. [17] surveyed various reconstruction algorithms including volumetric and visual hull-based methods, with detailed discussion of voxel coloring techniques and their implementation across single and multi-camera setups.

Recent research explored how people learn about three-dimensional models from two-dimensional data using diverse deep learning approaches. Wang et al. [18] introduced Pixel2Mesh, a method that reconstructs triangular meshes from a single image by deforming a mean shape toward the target geometry using graph-based with two-dimensional convolutional neural networks. Yoo et al. [20] likewise proposed an automated framework that makes and tests three-dimensional CAD models as it uses anti-aliasing, as it groups points, and as it integrates with Autodesk Fusion 360 using two-dimensional images. Moreno-García et al. [10] had focused on the applying of machine vision to these complex engineering drawings. They addressed many of the challenges found in shape detection, text recognition, and feature classification. Sun et al. [16] developed then an algorithm that is for partial three-dimensional reconstruction coming from a single unknown viewpoint through the using of depth-encoded voting, and then they refined it through alignment with texture completion. Wu et al. [19] presented a generative model describing three-dimensional shapes as computer-aided design operation sequences, trained with a transformer-based autoencoder on a large dataset. Yoon et al. [21] created a preprocessing pipeline for augmented reality after they classified real-world scenes via color, generated point clouds, labeled objects by the YOLACT algorithm, as well as produced mesh models. A deep learning framework was developed by Lin et al. [9]. The framework exists for recognizing two-dimensional engineering drawings. Its combination of OpenCV and Yolov7 for the detection of objects plus Tesseract-OCR for the recognition of text supports extracting and classifying structural elements and ultimately automates construction of three-dimensional models.

The work presented in [6] presents a method to convert photographs of 2D engineering drawings into 3D CAD models in SCAD format using OpenCV. Their pipeline detects boundaries, locates features relative to a bounding box, and reconstructs the model through a Jupyter Notebook interface. While effective for simple shapes, the method does not yet handle hidden lines, though future work may integrate neural networks for more complex geometries.

3 Methodology

The goal of this program is to create from its 2D orthogonal engineering views like top, side, as well as front, a 3D object. Image processing along with extrusion are applied to each view in order that individual 3D shapes are created. These shapes are then combined according to their positions, forming the final model. This method ensures accuracy using detailed engineering drawings rather than ambiguous text inputs or unclear images.

This system is divided into two parts. The first focuses on the detection of the shape, how will the extrusion values for each part of shape be acquired and finally how is the extrusion done The second part is about the combination and formation of the shape.

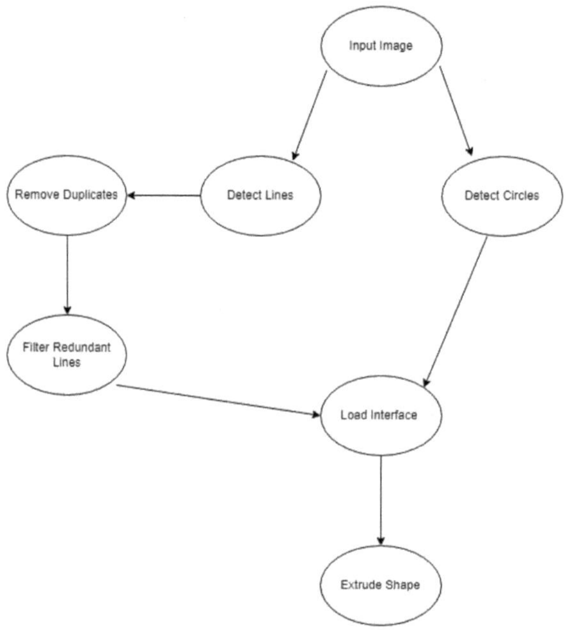

Fig. 1. FlowChart for Detection and Extrusion

As shown in Fig. 1, the first part of the program focuses on employing image processing for detecting the lines defining the 2D shape, with circles handled specially because straight lines do not compose them. Filtered lines remove duplicates and invalid segments for improved accuracy. Then, an interface prompts users for assignment of extrusion values to each line as well as to each circle plus mark circles as either hollow or solid. Once all of the values are entered, the shape is redrawn and then extruded accordingly. This ensures OBJ format export with virtual reality environments compatibility.

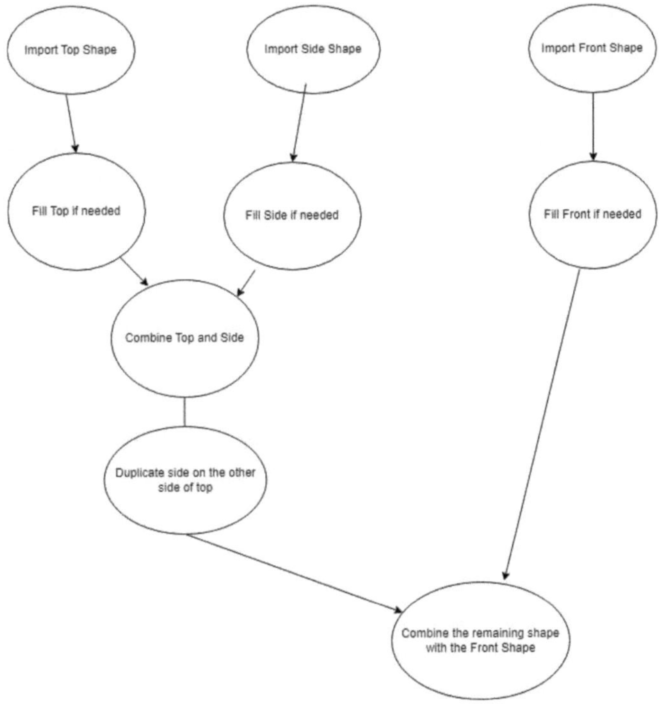

Fig. 2. Flowchart for Combination and Filling

As shown in Fig. 2, the second part focuses on how to load the extruded shapes from each view so as to assemble the final 3D model. Gaps may occur from disconnected lines and circles. Users can choose whether to fill in them. The assembly continues mirroring it to that same opposite side after it places the Side view next to that Top view. Finally, the Front view is positioned to enclose the model as this completes the accurate reconstruction of the 3D object.

The proposed system automates the reconstruction of 3D models from 2D orthographic engineering drawings through a multi-phase pipeline designed for accuracy, customization, and extensibility. The process begins with a setup phase, where users are instructed to place their input drawings–specifically labeled as Top, Side, and Front views–into a designated directory named "Xtrude3D." These drawings must be in standard image formats such as JPG or PNG, and serve as the basis for 3D reconstruction.

In the preprocessing phase, the images are converted to grayscale and denoised using Gaussian blur. Otsu's thresholding is then applied to isolate the shapes from the background. Feature detection is performed to identify straight lines and circular elements using Hough Transforms. Due to the nature of image detection, duplicate and overlapping elements often occur; thus, a filtration step is included to remove redundant or invalid detections. This ensures the extracted geometry represents the true structure of the drawing.

The next stage introduces a user-interactive interface that enables fine control over the model generation process. Each detected line and circle is highlighted in sequence, and the user is prompted to input an extrusion value. For circular features, an additional option allows the user to specify whether the shape should be extruded as a hollow or solid cylinder. Users may also assign a value of zero to exclude specific elements from the final model. This step ensures that the 3D model reflects user-defined structural characteristics while remaining faithful to the original drawing (Fig. 3).

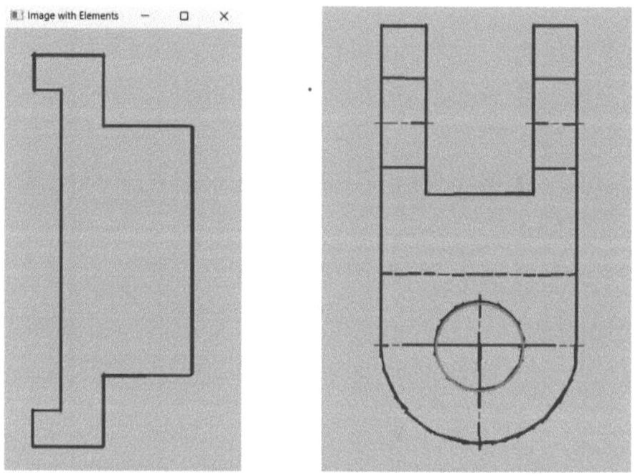

Fig. 3. Feedback for detection example

After all values are collected, the system generates separate 3D shapes for each orthographic view. These shapes are then imported into Blender's scripting environment for automated alignment and combination. The process includes geometric centering, rotation, translation, and mirroring to correctly position each shape based on engineering conventions. A special handling routine is included for cases involving holes or multiple height layers, ensuring that extruded features remain accurately placed within their intended layer.

A key step in the process is obtaining extrusion values for each detected line and circle through user input. An interface is generated that sequentially highlights each element on the drawing and prompts the user to enter a desired extrusion value. Users can input '0' to exclude a shape, and for circles, a checkbox allows them to specify whether the extrusion should be hollow or solid. This ensures flexibility and customization based on the user's design requirements as shown in Fig. 4.

Once the user provides the extrusion values and circle-specific options, the system proceeds to generate the 3D geometry. The extrusion process begins by passing the user inputs–extrusion values and hollow/solid indicators–into a function that constructs the 3D shape and exports it in OBJ format. Each line is extruded according to its assigned value, with zero-valued entries excluded.

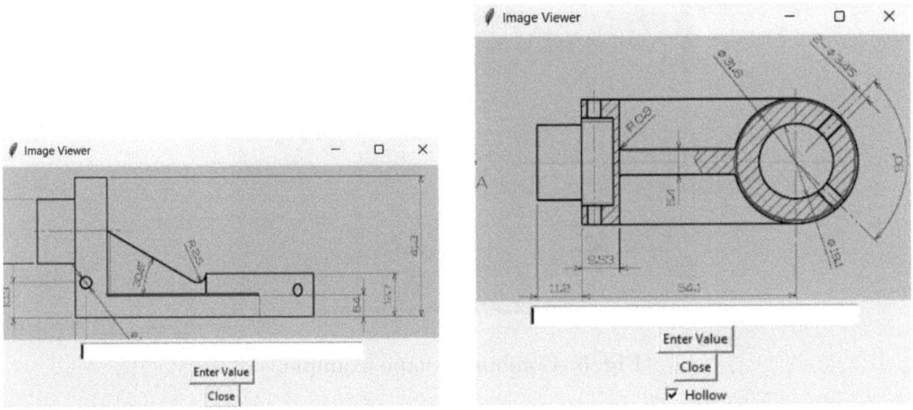

Fig. 4. Interface for entering extrusion values: (Left) line selection, (Right) circle selection with hollow option

Vertices and faces for both the base and the top of each extruded shape are computed and written to the output file. For circular elements, the function distinguishes between hollow and solid extrusions. Hollow cylinders are created using an inner and outer ring of vertices, forming side walls that define the void, while solid cylinders are extruded as filled bodies. A special case is handled if the output file is labeled with the keyword "circle," allowing individual treatment of circular features. This distinction is important when post-processing steps need to isolate certain shapes, especially in complex assemblies.

After the extrusion of individual views (Top, Side, and Front), the system initiates an automated combination routine executed within Blender's scripting environment. This phase begins by importing the three generated OBJ files and aligning them spatially to construct the full 3D model. Each view is reoriented, centered, and positioned based on geometric properties such as bounding box dimensions and vertex locations. The Side view is mirrored to form both lateral faces of the object and is aligned on either side of the Top view. The Top view is then elevated along the Z-axis to match the vertical extent of the Side view. Finally, the Front view is placed in front of the aligned Top and Side shapes, with its vertical position adjusted to ensure all bottom edges align correctly. The resulting model reflects the composite shape derived from the original 2D drawings (Fig. 5).

In cases where the design includes multiple layers of varying heights or holes embedded in lower layers, a modified alignment routine is applied. If a hole is extruded along with the Top shape, it may be incorrectly elevated. To address this, the system uses naming conventions to isolate the circular components during import. After merging the Top shape and the extruded circles into one object, the code separates the mesh into individual parts. The user is prompted to input the number of circles present, which is used to identify and exclude

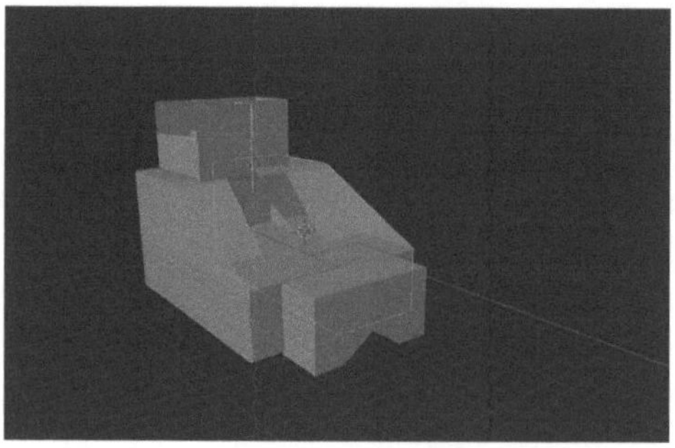

Fig. 5. Combined shape example

them from upward translation. This ensures that holes remain in the correct layer while the rest of the shape is elevated (Fig. 6).

Fig. 6. Combined shape with special case example

This approach enables accurate reconstruction of more complex models, extending the system's applicability beyond basic extrusions and ensuring fidelity to the original design intent. Finally, the system offers an optional reconstruction phase where users can fill residual gaps within any individual view or the fully combined model using automated mesh operations. All generated 3D shapes are exported in the widely supported OBJ format, stored within the original working directory, and can be readily used in computer-aided design tools or virtual and augmented reality environments.

4 Experiment

To evaluate the usability and engagement of the system, 21 participants–ranging from undergraduate to postgraduate students across various disciplines–were recruited. Each participant was provided with two engineering views (Top and Side) and asked to enter extrusion values for detected lines and circles using the interactive interface. They received a brief orientation on the project's purpose, how the interface worked, and how to specify hollow or solid extrusions for circular features. During the session, the system provided visual feedback by highlighting each element in the drawings as users input their values. Participants were also introduced to optional features, such as the Blender-based gap-filling tool, and allowed to observe the resulting extruded shapes before proceeding to the final model combination step. After generating and viewing the complete 3D model, participants completed a short questionnaire capturing demographic information and their experience using the tool, including clarity, ease of interaction, and overall satisfaction with the process.

After completing the testing process, participants signed a consent form and filled out a questionnaire to provide both demographic and feedback data. Basic demographic questions captured age group, gender, and field of study. The second part of the form focused on participants' interaction with the system. Using a 5-point Likert scale, they rated statements related to usability, clarity, and overall experience with the extrusion and model generation process.

4.1 Analyzing Results

A total of 21 participants completed the system testing and questionnaire. Demographic results showed that 85.7% were male, 95.2% were undergraduates, and 71.4% were CS majors (Fig. ??). Feedback from the interaction questionnaire was largely positive. Most participants found the system easy to understand (90.5% chose 4 or 5), with clear instructions (100%) and helpful feedback (90.5%). Some indicated a need for improved automation of extrusion input and more intuitive interface interaction. The average System Usability Scale (SUS) score was 57.4, which corresponds to a B- grade. This suggests that the system is moderately usable but has potential for further refinement.

A second experiment involved generating 3D models from 10 engineering drawings with varying complexity. The models were evaluated based on detection accuracy, redundancy, extrusion precision, and final shape alignment. Shape 2 used all three views, achieved full detection with 36% redundancy, no shape deviations, and reached 90% accuracy after two translation adjustments (Fig. 7).

Several shapes were tried through the experiment. The rest of the section shows the results for some of the shapes.

Shape 3 was extruded from a single top view with 95% detection and a 10% deviation due to missing parts (Fig. 8).

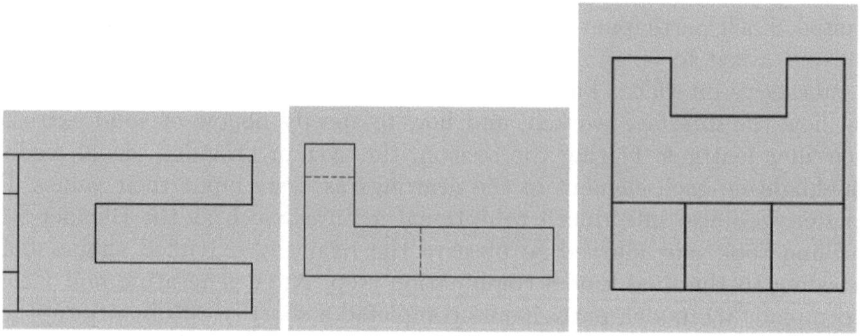

Fig. 7. Shape 2 - All views used

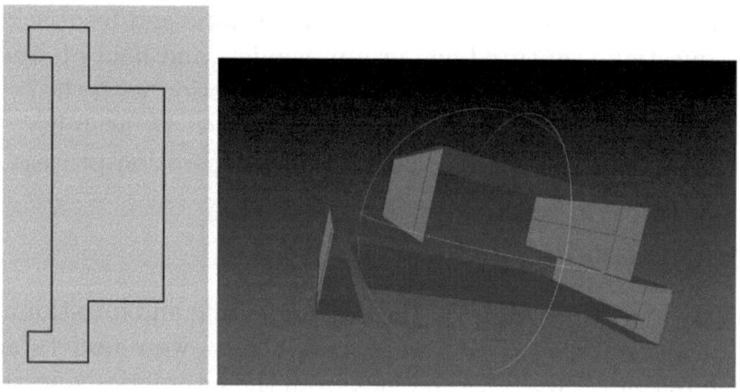

Fig. 8. Shape 3 - Single-view extrusion

5 Conclusions and Future Work

In conclusion, the work exhibited very positive results with simple shapes, moderately positive results with moderately complex shapes due to detection inaccuracies, and neutral results with highly complex shapes affected by the presence of dimension lines.

This study introduced an approach that is based upon lightweight image processing for the purpose of converting 2D engineering drawings into 3D models suitable for XR training. The system effectively detected lines and circles as users guided extrusion, and it automatically combined orthogonal views. Usability testing has confirmed its potential for success. This was especially accurate in poor or learning areas. However, several limitations were identified. The limitations included the reliance on Blender for model assembly, manual input of extrusion values, and the need to separate drawings into distinct views. The next step is improving detection accuracy.

References

1. Abdelhamed, H., El-Faransawy, N., Sharaf, N.: In-place collaboration in extended reality data visualization. In: 2022 26th International Conference Information Visualisation (IV), pp. 215–220. IEEE (2022)
2. Borrel, A., Fourches, D.: Realityconvert: a tool for preparing 3D models of biochemical structures for augmented and virtual reality. Bioinformatics **33**(23), 3816–3818 (2017)
3. Camba, J.D., Contero, M.: From reality to augmented reality: Rapid strategies for developing marker-based AR content using image capturing and authoring tools. In: 2015 IEEE Frontiers in Education Conference (FIE), pp. 1–6. IEEE (2015)
4. Elshahawy, M., Magdy, S., Sharaf, N.: Artour: an augmented reality collaborative experience for enhancing tourism. Inf. Technol. Tourism **25**(4), 549–563 (2023)
5. Farouk, P., Faransawy, N., Sharaf, N.: Using hololens for remote collaboration in extended data visualization. In: 2022 26th International Conference Information Visualisation (IV), pp. 209–214. IEEE (2022)
6. Harish, A.B., Prasad, A.R.: Photo2cad: automated 3D solid reconstruction from 2D drawings using opencv. arXiv:2101.04248 (2023). arXiv:2101.04248
7. Hu, W., Zheng, J., Zhang, Z., Yuan, X., Yin, J., Zhou, Z.: Plankassembly: robust 3D reconstruction from three orthographic views with learnt shape programs. arXiv:2308.05744 (2023). arXiv:2308.05744
8. Khedwala, M., Momin, F., Pachhapure, U., Shaikh, S.: Analysis of auto generation of 3D model using multiple 2D graphics to manifest through augmented reality. In: 2018 International Conference on Smart City and Emerging Technology (ICSCET), Mumbai, pp. 1–5. IEEE (2018)
9. Lin, Yi-Hsin., Ting, Yu-Hung., Huang, Yi-Cyun., Cheng, Kai-Lun., Jong, Wen-Ren.: Integration of deep learning for automatic recognition of 2D engineering drawings. Machines **11**(8), 802 (2023)
10. Moreno-García, C.F., Elyan, E., Jayne, C.: New trends on digitisation of complex engineering drawings. Neural Comput. Appl. **31**(6), 1695–1712 (2019)
11. Nasser, N., Makled, E., Sharaf, N., Abdennadher, S.: Social interaction in virtual shopping. In: 2021 IEEE International Symposium on Multimedia (ISM), pp. 204–205. IEEE (2021)
12. Nasser, N., Sharaf, N., Abdennadher, S.: Transforming organizational training: a study of extended reality applications in industry 4.0. In: González-Briones, A., et al. (eds.) Highlights in Practical Applications of Agents, Multi-Agent Systems, and Digital Twins: The PAAMS Collection. PAAMS 2024. Communications in Computer and Information Science, vol. 2149, pp. 385–393. Springer, Cham (2024)
13. Radwan, Y.M., Amr, K., Nasser, N., Sharaf, N.: From simulation to application: the transformative role of augmented reality in industry 4.0 training. In: González-Briones, A., et al. (eds.) Highlights in Practical Applications of Agents, Multi-Agent Systems, and Digital Twins: The PAAMS Collection - International Workshops of PAAMS 2024. Communications in Computer and Information Science, vol. 2149, pp. 378–384. Springer, Cham (2024)
14. Seo, J., et al.: Let 2D diffusion model know 3D-consistency for robust text-to-3D generation. arXiv:2303.07937 (2024). arXiv:2303.07937
15. Shi, Z., Peng, S., Xu, Y., Geiger, A., Liao, Y., Shen, Y.: Deep generative models on 3D representations: a survey. arXiv:2210.15663 (2023). arXiv:2210.15663

16. Sun, M., Kumar, S.S., Bradski, G., Savarese, S.: Toward automatic 3D generic object modeling from one single image. In: 2011 International Conference on 3D Imaging, Modeling, Processing, Visualization and Transmission, pp. 9–16, Hangzhou, TBD, China. IEEE (2011)
17. SusheelKumar, K., Semwal, V.B., Prasad, S., Tripathi, R.C.: Generating 3D model using 2D images of an object. Int. J. Eng. Sci. Technol. **3**(1) (2011)
18. Wang, N., Zhang, Y., Li, Z., Fu, Y., Liu, W., Jiang, Y.-G.: Pixel2Mesh: generating 3D mesh models from single RGB images. Lecture Notes in Computer Science, vol. 11215, pp. 55–71. Springer, Cham (2018)
19. Wu, R., Xiao, C., Zheng, C.: Deepcad: a deep generative network for computer-aided design models. In: 2021 IEEE/CVF International Conference on Computer Vision (ICCV), pp. 6752–6762, Montreal, QC, Canada. IEEE (2021)
20. Yoo, S., Lee, S., Kim, S., Hwang, K.H., Park, J.H., Kang, N.: Integrating deep learning into CAD/CAE system: generative design and evaluation of 3D conceptual wheel. Struct. Multidisc. Optim. **64**(4), 2725–2747 (2021)
21. Yoon, Y.-S., et al.: Real space 3D mesh transformation preprocessing system for AR services. In: 2020 International Conference on Information and Communication Technology Convergence (ICTC), pp. 1478–1483, Jeju, Korea (South). IEEE (2020)

Author Index

A. Nongaillard et al. (Eds.): PAAMS 2025, CCIS 2644, pp. 219–220, 2025.
https://doi.org/10.1007/978-3-032-05925-3

S

T

X

MIX
Papier aus verantwortungsvollen Quellen
Paper from responsible sources
FSC® C105338

If you have any concerns about our products,
you can contact us on
ProductSafety@springernature.com

In case Publisher is established outside the EU,
the EU authorized representative is:
Springer Nature Customer Service Center GmbH
Europaplatz 3, 69115 Heidelberg, Germany

Printed by Libri Plureos GmbH
in Hamburg, Germany